32 VisiCalc® Worksheets

32 VisiCalc® Worksheets

By T. G. Lewis

TAB **TAB BOOKS Inc.**

BLUE RIDGE SUMMIT. PA. 17214

FIRST EDITION
FIRST PRINTING

Hardcover edition published in 1983 by TAB BOOKS Inc.

Printed in the United States of America

The publisher and author have made every effort to assure that the computer programs and programming information in this publication are accurate and complete. However, this publication is prepared for general readership, and neither the publisher nor the author have any knowledge about or ability to control any third party's use of the programs and programming information. There is no warranty or representation by either the publisher or the author that the programs or programming information in this book will enable the reader or user to achieve any particular result.

Library of Congress Cataloging in Publication Data

Lewis, T. G. (Theodore Gyle), 1941-
    32 VisiCalc worksheets.

    Includes index.
    1. VisiCalc (Computer program) I. Title.
II. Title: Thirty-two VisiCalc worksheets.
HF5548.4.V57L48   1983   001.64'25   83-4925
ISBN 0-8306-1637-3

Preface

The purpose of this collection of worksheets is twofold: first, to provide you with a number of VisiCalc worksheets that can be immediately applied to a variety of situations, and second, to add to your knowledge of the VisiCalc program. I hope that the first goal is met by the diverse and novel worksheets presented in the remainder of this book. The second goal is met, I believe, by careful study of the methods I have used to create the eclectic worksheets. Of course, only you can decide if these worksheets meet these goals.

This book does not attempt to teach you how to use the VisiCalc program, nor does it provide a reference for its use. The reader should refer to one of several books currently available for self-instruction in using VisiCalc. It is possible, though, to gain additional insights into the application of VisiCalc software through this collection. Indeed, the examples here make an excellent supplement to most self-instructional books on the VisiCalc program.

I chose everyday applications of the VisiCalc program from my personal life, from suggestions made by friends, and in many instances, from the daily routine of several businesspeople I know. In this way I hoped to achieve a "realistic" collection of applications rather than a collection of only academic interest. In addition, I have carefully selected examples that form the basis for more challenging applications. I believe many of these examples can be extended and modified to make them even more useful to your daily life.

How To Use This Book

These 32 VisiCalc worksheets (plus two bonus worksheets) illustrate the wide range of applications of the VisiCalc software. The VisiCalc program is a powerful and flexible tool that can be applied to problems and situations as diverse as a game of tic-tac-toe or a financial model of the national economy. This book won't teach you how to use VisiCalc, but it does provide you with a number of "real life" applications that you will find useful right now. The worksheets in this book will trigger your imagination and you will soon be designing your own VisiCalc worksheets.

Each worksheet in this book is designed to work with the VisiCalc program. To use these worksheets, you need to load your VisiCalc program disk first. When the VisiCalc program is loaded, you can load any one of the VisiCalc worksheets in one of two ways. You can type in the formulas listed in the book for each worksheet and create your own VisiCalc worksheet diskette, or you can purchase the diskette containing all of the worksheets directly from the publisher (see the back of the book).

The VisiCalc worksheets included in this book were chosen from the following five areas of application:

Games and Novelties
Business Applications
Household Applications
Statistical Analysis
What-if Models

Each area is a chapter which contains a collection of worksheets, their formulas and examples of their use.

All worksheets in this book are presented in the following format:

Purpose: A brief explanation of the purpose and application of the worksheet is given at the beginning of each section. In some cases the feature of the VisiCalc program that the worksheet uses is noted as well.

Worksheet: The worksheet itself is explained in simple terms. The worksheet is pictured as it appears on the screen of a personal computer. You will learn how to use the worksheet here.

Comments: This section explains subtle details or additional information that might be of use to you when using the worksheet. It also serves to give you more ideas or to suggest changes in the worksheet.

Formulas: The worksheet can be constructed manually, or, if you purchase the worksheet diskette, the worksheet can be constructed by using the /SL command. In either case, this section describes how the worksheet was made. It includes the formulas as they are stored in each cell.

The listing of the formulas gives you an idea of the thought that went into each worksheet. It also reveals how the worksheet can be extended or modified to better serve your needs.

If you decide to enter the worksheet into your VisiCalc program manually, then you will want to become familiar with the DIF standard. The Data Interchange Format (DIF) is used to transfer worksheet data from/to VisiCalc according to convention. Notice that the information is printed in reverse order from the way you normally read a worksheet. Thus, you should read these printed DIF listings from bottom to top (instead of top to bottom) when you enter the worksheet manually.

Example Output: Many of the worksheets are illustrated with a sample output sheet. These show what happens if you do one thing or another. They are especially useful in the last chapter on "What-if Models."

Worksheet Listing: Worksheet listings are given in various forms. The intention is to make it easy for you to reconstruct these worksheets in your own personal computer. All necessary information for constructing a worksheet is included. Of course, you can purchase a diskette containing all of these worksheets from the publisher.

You are encouraged to add to, extend, modify, or remove part or all of the information contained in these worksheets to make them suitable for your own applications.

Contents

32 VisiCalc® Worksheets

Chapter 1
Games and Novelties

This collection of worksheets begins with five simple but amusing games and novelties. The first worksheet deals with the strange and intriguing world of random numbers. RANDOM demonstrates how a VisiCalc worksheet can be turned into a gambling casino.

The second worksheet shows how to implement the familiar game of tic-tac-toe in VisiCalc. TICTAC is for two players; one marks the squares with a "1," and the other marks the squares with a "2." In this way the number processing power of the VisiCalc program can be used to compute a winner.

The third worksheet shows how the VisiCalc sheet can be used as a questionnaire. HEALTH is a personal health questionnaire that lets you find out how well you are taking care of yourself. This questionnaire is scored automatically for you by the VisiCalc software. It tells you how you cope with food, drugs, and exercise. Good luck with this one.

BOWLING is a good example of how the VisiCalc program can be used to keep scores for you. It computes the total bowling score for a single player, including strikes, spares, and open frames. If you have always had trouble remembering how to add up a bowler's total number of pins, then this worksheet is for you.

Finally, this introductory chapter includes the fascinating mathematical recreation called LIFE. The game of LIFE simulates the birth, death, and life of individual two-dimensional "bits" that live in rectangular VisiCalc squares. Imagine yourself as one of these bits. You can survive for another "year" only if you have just the right number of neighbors. The power of VisiCalc is strained just to keep up with the microcosmic world of LIFE.

Games and Novelties were selected as an introduction to this collection because the VisiCalc program can be used for fun as well as for more serious applications. First the fun, and then in the remaining chapters the serious (and more useful) worksheets!

1.1. RANDOM: A Random Number Generator

Purpose

Random numbers have many uses in computing. In particular, they are used to simulate real-world events on a computer. One of the problems of computing random numbers, however, is the fact that computers do not behave randomly. In fact, computers behave very predictably (thank heavens). So, how can we generate random numbers on a machine that does not act randomly? The answer is that we cannot. Instead, we can give the appearance of randomness in what the computer programmers call *pseudo-random number generators*. A psuedo-random number generator, or random number generator for short, is a program that computes a series of numbers that appear to be random, but are not. The idea is to artificially induce randomness by scrambling a collection of numbers.

The purpose of the random number worksheet shown in Figure 1.1(a) is to fake randomness. The numbers produced by this worksheet can be used as part of another worksheet. For example, they can be used to simulate the number of people waiting in line to attend a public event, the toss of a coin, the draw of a shuffled deck of cards, the likelihood of a catastrophe, and so on.

The example shown here is recreated by entering the formulas shown in Figure 1.1(b). The details of its use, and comments on how to recreate the worksheet are discussed, below.

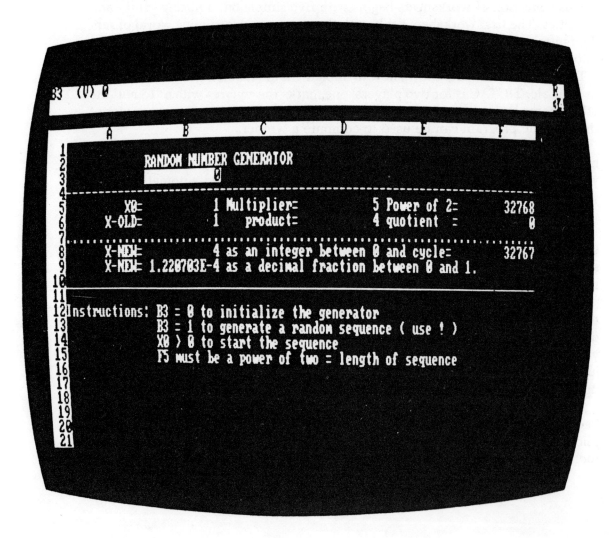

Take a closer look at the worksheet in Figure 1.1(a). This worksheet im- **Worksheet** plements a formula that computes a new random number each time the recalculation (!) operation is performed. The new random number is stored in the worksheet as X-NEW. Both integer and decimal fraction versions of X-NEW are displayed.

```
            RANDOM NUMBER GENERATOR
                    0
--------------------------------------------------------------------
       X0=           1 Multiplier=      5 Power of 2=        32768
    X-OLD=           1    product=      4 quotient  =            0
....................................................................
    X-NEW=           4 as an integer between 0 and cycle=      32767
    X-NEW= 1.220703E-4 as a decimal fraction between 0 and 1.
--------------------------------------------------------------------

Instructions: B3 = 0 to initialize the generator
              B3 = 1 to generate a random sequence ( use ! )
              X0 > 0 to start the sequence
              F5 must be a power of two = length of sequence
```

Figure 1.1(a). Worksheet for a random number generator

The formula for computing X-NEW is given below and implemented in the VisiCalc program as shown in Figure 1.1(b).

$$\text{X-NEW} = (5 * \text{X-OLD} - 1) \text{ modulo } 32768$$

The *modulo* operation means to divide by 32768 and then take the remainder as the value for X-NEW.

The first time this formula is applied, the value of X-OLD must be supplied in advance. This initial value is called X0, and as you can see in the worksheet, it is 1. However, any number between 1 and 32768 can be used. Try several initial values and see what happens.

The "trigger" value in cell B3 is used to tell the VisiCalc program whether to use the initial value X0 or the previous value X-OLD to compute the new value X-NEW. If you set B3 to zero, the value stored as X0 will be used in the formula. If you set B3 to 1 the value stored in X-OLD will be used in the formula.

To use the random number generator, set cell B3 to zero, put some starting value in B5, and press the recalculation operator (!). This will cause the sequence to be "reset." Now, change B3 to 1 and press ! once again. Each time you press ! another random number will be computed and displayed as X-NEW.

```
>E15:" of sequence
>D15:"two = length
>C15:" a power of t
>B15:"  F5 must be
>D14:"quence
>C14:"start the se
>B14:"  X0 > 0 to
>E13:"ce ( use ! )
>D13:"andom sequence
>C13:"generate a r
>B13:"  B3 = 1 to
>D12:"he generator
```

```
>C12:"initialize t
>B12:":  B3 = 0 to
>A12:"Instructions
>F10:/-_
>E10:/-_
>D10:/-_
>C10:/-_
>B10:/-_
>A10:/-_
>F9:"  1.
>E9:"etween 0 and
>D9:"1 fraction b
>C9:" as a decima
>B9:+B8/F5
>A9:/FR"X-NEW=
>F8:(F5)-1
>E8:" and cycle=
>D8:"er between 0
>C8:" as an integ
>B8:/FG+D6-(F6*F5)
>A8:/FR"  X-NEW=
>F7:/FR/-.
>E7:/FR/-.
>D7:/FR/-.
>C7:/FR/-.
>B7:/FR/-.
>A7:/FR/-.
>F6:@INT(D6/F5)
>E6:" quotient  =
>D6:/FG@IF((@INT(B6*D5-1)>0),@INT(B6*D5-1),F5+@INT(B6*D5-1))
>C6:/FR" product=
>B6:@IF(B3=0,B5,B8)
>A6:/FR"X-OLD=
>F5:/FI32768
>E5:/FR"Power of 2=
>D5:/FI5
>C5:/FR"Multiplier=
>B5:1
>A5:/FR"XO=
>F4:/--
>E4:/--
>D4:/--
>C4:/--
>B4:/--
>A4:/--
>B3:0
>C2:"R GENERATOR
>B2:"RANDOM NUMBE
/W1
/GOR
/GRA
/GC12
/X>A1:>A1:
```

Figure 1.1(b). Formulas for random number generator

The most obvious use for this worksheet is in playing games. You can use a varia- **Comments**
tion on this worksheet to simulate the tossing of a pair of dice. The dice can be
assigned numbers corresponding to the numbers generated. For example, the
dice could be assigned 1 if the random number falls between 0 and 0.1667, 2 if
the random number falls between 0.1668 and 0.3333, and so forth. To simulate
the toss of a die, generate a random number. To simulate the toss of two dice,
generate two random numbers.

You can incorporate this worksheet in a simulation by storing it in a disk file,
then retrieve it from the file while in another worksheet. The columns and rows
may not fit your other worksheet, however, so use the /MOVE command of the
VisiCalc program to move the random number worksheet to the desired block.

The random number worksheet is recreated by entering the values, formulas, **Formulas**
and labels shown in Figure 1.1(b). (Note: these worksheets are also available on
diskette for your convenience.) The formulas compute the value of X-NEW in an
indirect fashion because of two limitations of the VisiCalc program:

1. There is no "@MODULO" function in the VisiCalc software so we must
simulate this operation using a combination of @INT functions.

2. The largest integer possible on most microcomputers is 32767, so we must be
careful to not overflow the capacity of the microcomputer while doing these integer calculations.

Suppose we domonstrate how the calculations work on a smaller random
number generator. Here is a generator that scrambles the integers between 0
and 7.

$$X\text{-NEW} = (5 * X\text{-OLD} - 1) \text{ modulo } 8$$

Now, let X0 = 1 and the initial value is used to get the first number.

$$X\text{-NEW} = (5 * 1 - 1) \text{ modulo } 8$$
$$X\text{-NEW} = (4) \text{ modulo } 8$$
$$X\text{-NEW} = 4$$

The first value was easy to get because we did not have to worry about the
calculations exceeding 8, nor did we worry about the modulo operation. The next
number produced by pressing the recalculation operator runs into this problem,
however.

$$X\text{-NEW} = (5 * 4 - 1) \text{ modulo } 8$$
$$X\text{-NEW} = (19) \text{ modulo } 8$$

The remainder after division by 8 is 3, because 2*8 + 3 equals 19.

Suppose further that we generate the remaining numbers in this sequence as
follows, until a zero is encountered:

$$X - \text{NEW} = 3, 6, 5, 0$$

Now notice what happens.

$$X\text{-NEW} = (5 * 0 - 1) \text{ modulo } 8$$
$$X\text{-NEW} = (-1) \text{ modulo } 8$$

The formula in cell D6 takes this into account by testing for the possibility of a
negative product. If the product is less than zero, then the modulo operation is
obtained by adding 32768 to the negative number. In the small example used

above, this corresponds to adding 8 to the negative number. Therefore, the remaining sequence of random numbers is as shown, below.

$$X - NEW = 7, 2, 1, 4, 3, 6, 5, 0, 7 \ldots$$

Notice that this sequence repeats after 8 numbers have been generated. Indeed, the sequence is not truly random, but instead, simply a scrambled sequence of numbers from 0 to 7. This is why the random number generator is really only a pseudo-random number generator.

If you build this random number worksheet you might consider turning off the automatic recalculation feature of VisiCalc. That is, use the /GLOBAL R M command to inhibit automatic recalculation. The manual recalculation operation ! will be necessary anyway to cause the next number in the sequence to be computed.

Notice also that the order of calculation is /GLOBAL O R. In other words, the formulas are evaluated in row-major order. First, row 1 is calculated, followed by rows 2, 3, etc. The calculations must be done in this order to avoid ERRORs in the worksheet.

1.2. TICTAC: Tic-tac-toe Player

Purpose

Tic-tac-toe is one of the oldest and most often used games to demonstrate the versatility of computers. Perhaps this is due to its simplicity. However, Tic-tac-toe is not an easy game to program into a computer. In fact, it is not altogether easy to implement using VisiCalc software as we see in Figure 1.2(a).

Worksheet

Figure 1.2(a) shows one way to implement the game as a VisiCalc worksheet. The rows and columns of the VisiCalc sheet can be used to mark off the Tic-tac-toe grid as shown. The 9 boxes of Tic-tac-toe are assigned a value depending on which player selects a box. Thus Player One uses a value of 1, and Player Two uses a value of 2. If neither player selects a box, then no value appears. To erase a value, use the VisiCalc /BLANK command.

Players take turns placing their values in a box. The "score" for each row, column, and diagonal line is computed by the VisiCalc program and displayed as shown. The row and column sums (scores) must total a certain amount in order to win. For example, the first player has won in Figure 1.2(a) because the sum of the diagonal line is 7. Therefore, the win is recorded as a 1 marker value in the "win" column.

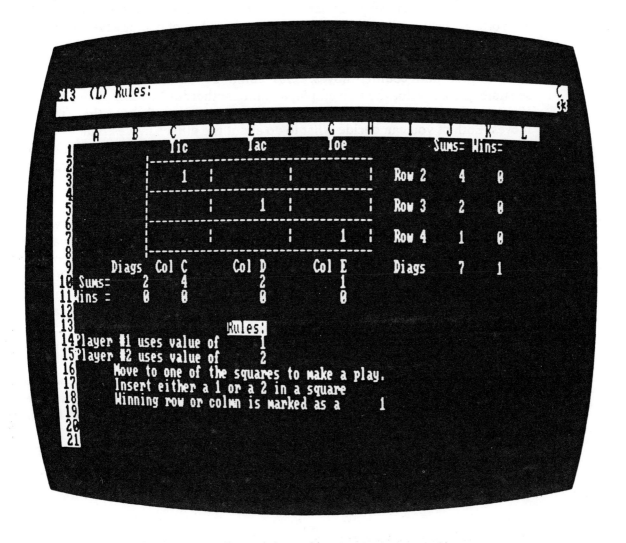

	Tic	Tac	Toe		Sums=	Wins=

	1				Row 2	4	0

		1			Row 3	2	0

			1		Row 4	1	0

Diags	Col C	Col D	Col E		Diags	7	1
Sums=	2	4	2	1			
Wins =	0	0	0	0			

```
                          Rules:
Player #1 uses value of        1
Player #2 uses value of        2
     Move to one of the squares to make a play.
     Insert either a 1 or a 2 in a square.
     Winning row or column is marked as a 1.
```

Figure 1.2(a). A Tic-tac-toe worksheet

Comments   The VisiCalc worksheet given here is good for two human players to use to play each other. The worksheet simply replaces paper. This, of course saves trees, but it is not especially clever. An advanced version of this game would be smart enough to play a human. That is, you could devise formulas to allow VisiCalc to make moves and counter-moves. This could be done by maintaining two separate grids: one for the human player, and another for VisiCalc. This way the VisiCalc player can "observe" your moves and you can observe the VisiCalc moves. Both of you can decide what to do about the other's moves. The VisiCalc strategy would be implemented as a collection of (lengthy) formulas with lots of @IF, @AND, and @OR functions in them. This is a good project for the advanced VisiCalc thinker.

Formulas   The formulas of Figure 1.2(b) can be used to reconstruct the Tic-tac-toe work-sheet. The method used to score a row or column is revealed in the formulas for cells J3, J5, J7, and B10 through G10. Here is the basis for this method of scoring. Each box on the Tic-tac-toe board is given a weight. The boxes are weighted by powers of 2; thus the left-most boxes are assigned a value of 4, the middle boxes a value of 2, and finally the right-most boxes are assigned a value of 1. This causes the score to be unique for every possible pattern a player can enter. Only certain scores are possible for winning patterns. These scores are 7 for Player One and 14 for Player Two.

The formulas in cells K3, K5, K7, K9, and B11 through G11 test the scores to see if one of the players has a winning pattern. The @OR function tests each win-ning value (7 or 14) and if either of these are present then a 1 is computed under the "win" heading.

The worksheet shown in Figure 1.2(a) shows a win for Player One. This is com-puted as follows:

$$J9:(4*C3)+(2*E5)+G7$$
$$J9:(4*1)+(2*1)+1$$
$$J9:(4)+(2)+1$$
$$J9: 7$$

```
>H18:1                              >J7:(4*C7)+(2*E7)+G7
>G18:" as a                         >I7:/FR"Row 4
>F18:"marked                        >H7:"    !
>E18:"mn is                         >G7:1
>D18:"or colum                      >F7:"    !
>C18:"g row or                      >D7:"    !
>B18:"Winning                       >B7:/FR"!
>G17:"square.                       >H6:"----
>F17:" in a                         >G6:"------
>E17:"or a 2                        >F6:"------
>D17:"r a 1                         >E6:"------
>C17:" either                       >D6:"------
>B17:"Insert                        >C6:"------
>H16:" play.                        >B6:/FR"!
>G16:"make a                        >K5:@IF(@OR(J5=7,J5=14),1,0)
>F16:"es to m                       >J5:(4*C5)+(2*E5)+G5
>E16:" square                       >I5:/FR"Row 3
>D16:"of the                        >H5:"    !
>C16:"o one of                      >F5:"    !
>B16:"Move to                       >E5:1
>E15:2                              >D5:"    !
>D15:"ue of                         >B5:/FR"!
>C15:"es val                        >H4:"----
>B15:" #2 uses                      >G4:"------
>A15:"Player                        >F4:"------
>E14:1                              >E4:"------
>D14:"ue of                         >D4:"------
>C14:"es valu                       >C4:"------
>B14:" #1 use                       >B4:/FR"!
>A14:"Player                        >K3:@IF(@OR(J3=7,J3=14),1,0)
>E13:"Rules:                        >J3:(4*C3)+(2*E3)+G3
>G11:@IF(@OR(G10=7,G10=14),1,0)     >I3:/FR"Row 2
>E11:@IF(@OR(E10=7,E10=14),1,0)     >H3:"    !
>C11:@IF(@OR(C10=7,C10=14),1,0)     >F3:"    !
>B11:@IF(@OR(B10=7,B10=14),1,0)     >D3:"    !
>A11:/FR"Wins =                     >C3:1
>G10:(4*G3)+(2*G5)+G7               >B3:/FR"!
>E10:(4*E3)+(2*E5)+E7               >H2:"----
>C10:(4*C3)+(2*C5)+C7               >G2:"------
>B10:(4*G3)+(2*E5)+C7               >F2:"------
>A10:/FR"Sums=                      >E2:"------
>K9:@IF(@OR(J9=7,J9=14),1,0)        >D2:"------
>J9:(4*C3)+(2*E5)+G7                >C2:"------
>I9:/FR"Diags                       >B2:/FR"!
>G9:/FR" Col E                      >K1:/FR"Wins=
>E9:/FR"Col D                       >J1:/FR"Sums=
>C9:/FR"Col C                       >I1:/FR
>B9:"Diags                          >G1:/FR"Toe
>H8:"----                           >E1:/FR"Tac
>G8:"------                         >C1:/FR"Tic
>F8:"------                         /W1
>E8:"------                         /GOC
>D8:"------                         /GRA
>C8:"------                         /GC6
>B8:/FR"!                           /X>A1:>A1:
>K7:@IF(@OR(J7=7,J7=14),1,0)
```

Figure 1.2(b). Formulas for Tic-tac-toe

The score is tested each time a new value is entered into a box. For example, to test the value stored in cell J9, the formula in cell K9 is computed.

K9:@IF(@OR(J9 = 7,J9 = 4),1,0)
K9:@IF(@OR(7 = 7,7 = 14),1,0)
K9:@IF(TRUE,1,0)
K9:1

Therefore, a "win" is recorded for Player One along the diagonal.

If you elect to enter the formulas by hand, it is probably best to set /GLOBAL R M (manual recalculation) during the entry process, and then reset the global calculation back to automatic during the use of the worksheet. You can play the game with either row-major or column-major order in force.

The formulas for rows and columns are somewhat similar, so you can also use the /REPLICATE command in a very limited way. This will save some typing. Also, consider using the /- command to repeat labels used to build the Tic-tac-toe board. For example, the dotted lines "-------" can be entered using /--, instead.

1.3. HEALTH: A Questionnaire For Good Health

If you like to take personality quizzes or answer questionnaires about yourself but hate to tally the scores, then VisiCalc questionnaires are for you.   **Purpose**

The purpose of the questionnaire worksheet discussed here is to show you how the VisiCalc program can be used to tally scores automatically for questionnaires. Those of you who are adventurous can also use it to find out how good you are to yourself. The HEALTH questionnaire shown in Figure 1.3(a) consists of 56 questions that you must answer by entering a "1" value in either the "yes" or "no" column.

After you have entered your answers in the desired places, the VisiCalc program computes your score in each of four areas. Your food, drug, exercise, and care scores are given at the bottom of the worksheet along with ratings. In the example of Figure 1.3(a), the scores of 8, 13, 8, and 11 are better than average. How about your scores?   **Worksheet**

The worksheet can be used a second time (or more) by blanking both columns. Use the /BLANK command in one of the cells and then /REPLICATE it into an entire column. Do the same thing for the other column. This is a quick way to "erase" the marks left there by someone else.

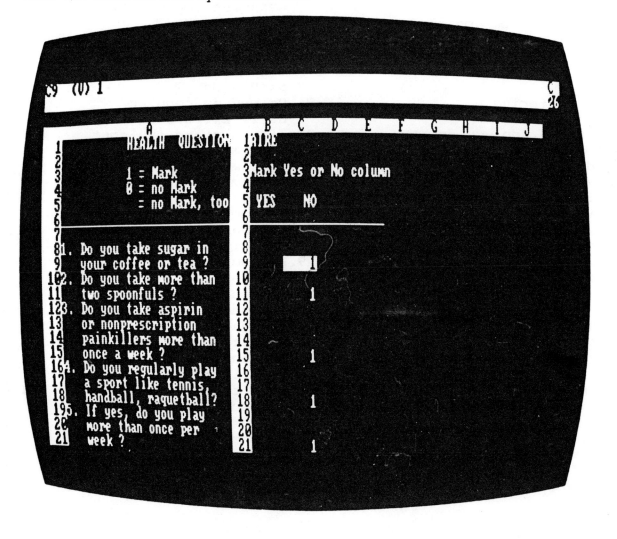

```
                    HEALTH   QUESTIONAIRE

   1 = Mark            Mark Yes or No column
   0 = no Mark
     = no Mark, too    YES    NO                           YES    NO
   -----------------------------------------------------------------------

1.  Do you take sugar in           19.Do you tend to skip
    your coffee or tea ?      1        meals because you are
2.  Do you take more than              too busy ?              1
    two spoonfuls ?          1     20.Has anyone said that
3.  Do you take aspirin                you drink too much ?            1
    or nonprescription            21.Do you feel that you
    painkillers more than              could, with a little
    once a week ?            1         practice, take up a
4.  Do you regularly play              strenuous sport such
    a sport like tennis,               as long distance run-
    handball, raquetball?    1         ning ?                         1
5.  If yes, do you play           22.Do you frequently
    more than once per week ? 1        feel stuffed after
6.  If you smoke, do you               eating out at a rest-
    have a morning cough?    1         aurant ?                1
7.  Do you use marijuana?     1    23.Do you tend to have a
8.  Do you eat rapidly ?      1        weakness for sweet,
9.  Do you walk or jog at              sticky foods ?                 1
    least 1 mile, daily ?  1      24.Do you smoke ?                   1
10.Do you drink at least          25.Do you regularly
    3 pints of fluid,                  smoke more than a
    daily ?               1            pack a day ?                   1
11.When suffering a               26.Do you do regular
    minor cold or                      daily exercises ?              1
    infection, do you see         27.If you stand in front
    a doctor rather than               of a mirror without
    "ride it out" ?          1         clothes on, do you
12.Do you frequently get               notice areas of
    indigestion after                  excess fat ?            1
    eating ?                 1     28.Do you find it a real
13.Do you ride a bicycle               strain to carry heavy
    whenever you can ?     1           parcels upstairs ?             1
14.Do you frequently              29.Do you drink alcohol
    nibble snacks in                   regularly ?                    1
    between meals ?          1     30.Do you ever drink
15.Do you have to                      enough to give you
    squeeze into your                  unpleasant side
    clothes ?                1         effects ?                      1
16.Do you have to use             31.Do you tend to keep
    sleeping pills to                  very late hours, even
    sleep ?                  1         when tired ?                   1
17.Does your diet                 32.Do you have false
    regularly include                  teeth other than
    salads & fresh fruit?  1           crowns, etc ?                  1
18.Do you get regular             33.Do you eat fresh
    doctor and dentist                 fruit (or juice) at
    checkups ?             1            least once a day ?      1
```

```
                 YES    NO                          YES   NO
---------------------------------------------------------------------
34.Do you regularly use          46.Do you receive pre-
   prescribed tranquil-             scription medicines
   izers or anti-                   on a regular basis
   depressants ?          1         from your doctor ?              1
35.Do people tend to say         47.Do spread butter
   how well you look ?    1          liberally on toast ?    1
36.Do you swim regularly         48.Would you honestly
   (in the summer) ?      1          describe yourself as
37.Do you avoid fatty                physically lazy ?       1
   foods such as French          49.Do you brush your
   Fries ?              1             teeth at least twice
38.If you are a smoker,              a day ?                 1
   do you feel uncomfort-         50.Do you walk or jog
   able when you cannot              over 2 miles, daily?    1
   light-up ?           1         51.Do you regularly take
39.If you regularly take             alcohol at lunchtime?         1
   exercise, have you          52.Do you tend to eat out
   done so for the past             more often than home?         1
   two years ?          1         53.Are you short of
40.Do you allow fashions             breath after climbing
   to interfere with                a flight of stairs ?          1
   your physical comfort ? 1      54.Has anyone said to you
41.Do you regularly eat              that you smoke too
   more than 2 cooked               much ?                        1
   meals in the day ?    1         55.Do you find cocktail
42.Do you plan your meals            savories (chips)
   so as to eat a                   impossible to resist?         1
   balanced diet ?      1          56.On the whole, would
43.Is your weight within             you say that your
   ten pounds of that               lifestyle leads you to
   recommended for your             mistreat your body ?          1
   build ?              1         -----------------------------------
44.Do you weigh more than            YOUR FOOD SCORE    =    8
   20 pounds over the               YOUR DRUG SCORE    =    13
   recommended average ?  1         YOUR EXERCISE SCORE = 8
45.Do you tend to take a             YOUR CARE SCORE    =    11
   car when you could as        (0-5 = BELOW AVERAGE)
   easily walk ?        1        (6-9 = AVERAGE )
                                 (10-14 = EXCEPTIONAL)
```

Figure 1.3(a). Personal health questionnaire

You might want to set the /GLOBAL R M switch while you enter the 1s into the **Comments** questionnaire. This will cause the worksheet to wait for you to complete the questionnaire before a score is computed. Then, use ! to recalculate the scores after all entries have been made. This also adds to the suspense.

Clearly, this kind of worksheet can be used for nearly any questionnaire. In fact, we will use this approach again later in the book. Don't hesitate to adapt this worksheet to your own questionnaires.

Formulas

Figure 1.3(b) shows what is inside the worksheet.

Nearly the entire contents of the worksheet are made up of questions. The only calculations that the VisiCalc program makes are shown in cells B173, B174, B175, and B176. These formulas simply total the 1s for each area of good health measured by the questionnaire. As you can see, the questionnaire consists of 14 questions in each area; but they are scrambled up so you won't know which area you are responding to with each question.

If you are using the diskette containing this worksheet, then you will notice that the questionnaire comes up on your screen in split-screen format. The screen will be split vertically so that the questions appear in the left and the responses in the right half of the screen.

```
>A179:"   (10-14 = EXCEPTIONAL)
>A178:"   (6-9 = AVERAGE )
>A177:"   (0-5 = BELOW AVERAGE)
>B176:+C23+C25+C38+C46+B55+C58+C84+C99+C102+C127+B134+C137+B152+C171
>A176:"    YOUR CARE SCORE   =
>B175:+B18+B21+B27+B40+B66+B79+C87+C89+B110+B113+B124+C140+C149+B154+C161
>A175:"    YOUR EXERCISE SCORE   =
>B174:+C15+C24+C35+C49+C60+C74+C77+C93+C96+C108+C121+C144+C156+C164
>A174:"    YOUR DRUG SCORE   =
>B173:+C9+C11+B30+C43+B55+C70+C73+B106+B117+C130+C146+C158+C167
>A173:"    YOUR FOOD SCORE   =
>C172:/--
>B172:/--
>A172:/--
>C171:1
>A171:"    mistreat your body ?
>A170:"    lifestyle leads you to
>A169:"    you say that your
>A168:"56.On the whole, would
>C167:1
>A167:"    impossible to resist?
>A166:"    savories (chips)
>A165:"55.Do you find cocktail
>C164:1
>A164:"    much ?
>A163:"    that you smoke too
>A162:"54.Has anyone said to you
>C161:1
>A161:"    a flight of stairs ?
>A160:"    breath after climbing
>A159:"53.Are you short of
>C158:1
>A158:"    more often than home?
>A157:"52.Do you tend to eat out
>C156:1
>A156:"    alcohol at lunchtime?
>A155:"51.Do you regularly take
>B154:1
>A154:"    over 2 miles, daily?
>A153:"50.Do you walk or jog
>B152:1
>A152:"    a day ?
>A151:"    teeth at least twice
>A150:"49.Do you brush your
>B149:1
>A149:"    physically lazy ?
```

>A148:"   describe yourself as
>A147:"48.Would you honestly
>B146:1
>A146:"   liberally on toast ?
>A145:"47.Do spread butter
>C144:1
>A144:"   from your doctor ?
>A143:"   on a regular basis
>A142:"   scription medicines
>A141:"46.Do you receive pre-
>C140:1
>A140:"   easily walk ?
>A139:"   car when you could as
>A138:"45.Do you tend to take a
>C137:1
>A137:"   recommended average ?
>A136:"   20 pounds over the
>A135:"44.Do you weigh more than
>B134:1
>A134:"   build ?
>A133:"   recommended for your
>A132:"   ten pounds of that
>A131:"43.Is your weight within
>B130:1
>A130:"   balanced diet ?
>A129:"   so as to eat a
>A128:"42.Do you plan your meals
>C127:1
>A127:"   meals in the day ?
>A126:"   more than 2 cooked
>A125:"41.Do you regularly eat
>C124:1
>A124:"   your physical comfort ?
>A123:"   to interfere with
>A122:"40.Do you allow fashions
>B121:1
>A121:"   two years ?
>A120:"   done so for the past
>A119:"   exercise, have you
>A118:"39.If you regularly take
>C117:1
>A117:"   light-up ?
>A116:"   able when you cannot
>A115:"   do you feel uncomfort
>A114:"38.If you are a smoker,
>B113:1
>A113:"   Fries ?
>A112:"   foods such as French
>A111:"37.Do you avoid fatty
>C110:1
>A110:"   (in the summer) ?
>A109:"36.Do you swim regularly
>C108:1
>A108:"   how well you look ?
>A107:"35.Do people tend to say
>C106:1
>A106:"   depressants ?
>A105:"   izers or anti-
>A104:"   prescribed tranquil-
>A103:"34.Do you regularly use
>B102:1

>A102:"   least once a day ?
>A101:"   fruit (or juice) at
>A100:"33.Do you eat fresh
>C99:1
>A99:"   crowns, etc ?
>A98:"   teeth other than
>A97:"32.Do you have false
>C96:1
>A96:"   when tired ?
>A95:"   very late hours, even
>A94:"31.Do you tend to keep
>C93:1
>A93:"   effects ?
>A92:"   unpleasant side
>A91:"   enough to give you
>A90:"30.Do you ever drink
>C89:1
>A89:"   regularly ?
>A88:"29.Do you drink alcohol
>C87:1
>A87:"   parcels upstairs ?
>A86:"   strain to carry heavy
>A85:"28.Do you find it a real
>B84:1
>A84:"   excess fat ?
>A83:"   notice areas of
>A82:"   clothes on, do you
>A81:"   of a mirror without
>A80:"27.If you stand in front
>C79:1
>A79:"   daily exercises ?
>A78:"26.Do you do regular
>C77:1
>A77:"   pack a day ?
>A76:"   smoke more than a
>A75:"25.Do you regularly
>C74:1
>A74:"24.Do you smoke ?
>C73:1
>A73:"   sticky foods ?
>A72:"   weakness for sweet,
>A71:"23.Do you tend to have a
>B70:1
>A70:"   aurant ?
>A69:"   eating out at a rest-
>A68:"   feel stuffed after
>A67:"22.Do you frequently
>C66:1
>A66:"   ning ?
>A65:"   as long distance run-
>A64:"   strenuous sport such
>A63:"   practice, take up a
>A62:"   could, with a little
>A61:"21.Do you feel that you
>C60:1
>A60:"   you drink too much ?
>A59:"20.Has anyone said that
>B58:1
>A58:"   too busy ?
>A57:"   meals because you are
>A56: '19.Do you tend to skip

```
>B55:1                              >A23:"    have a morning cough?
>A55:"     checkups ?              >A22:"6. If you smoke, do you
>A54:"     doctor and dentist      >C21:1
>A53:"18.Do you get regular        >A21:"     week ?
>B52:1                              >A20:"     more than once per
>A52:"     salads & fresh fruit?   >A19:"5. If yes, do you play
>A51:"     regularly include       >C18:1
>A50:"17.Does your diet            >A18:"     handball, raquetball?
>C49:1                             >A17:"     a sport like tennis,
>A49:"     sleep ?                 >A16:"4. Do you regularly play
>A48:"     sleeping pills to       >C15:1
>A47:"16.Do you have to use        >A15:"     once a week ?
>C46:1                             >A14:"     painkillers more than
>A46:"     clothes ?               >A13:"     or nonprescription
>A45:"     squeeze into your       >A12:"3. Do you take aspirin
>A44:"15.Do you have to            >C11:1
>C43:1                             >A11:"     two spoonfuls ?
>A43:"     between meals ?         >A10:"2. Do you take more than
>A42:"     nibble snacks in        >C9:1
>A41:"14.Do you frequently         >A9:"    your coffee or tea ?
>B40:1                             >A8:"1. Do you take sugar in
>A40:"     whenever you can ?      >E6:/-_
>A39:"13.Do you ride a bicycle     >D6:/-_
>C38:1                             >C6:/-_
>A38:"     eating ?                >B6:/-_
>A37:"     indigestion after      >A6:/-_
>A36:"12.Do you frequently get     >C5:/FR" NO
>C35:1                             >B5:" YES
>A35:"     "ride it out" ?        >A5:"           = no Mark, too
>A34:"     a doctor rather than   >A4:"         0 = no Mark
>A33:"     infection, do you see  >F3:"n
>A32:"     minor cold or          >E3:"colum
>A31:"11.When suffering a         >D3:"r No
>B30:1                             >C3:"Yes o
>A30:"     daily ?                 >B3:"Mark
>A29:"     3 pints of fluid,      >A3:"           1 = Mark
>A28:"10.Do you drink at least    >B1:"AIRE
>B27:1                             >A1:"         HEALTH   QUESTION
>A27:"     least 1 mile, daily ?  /W1
>A26:"9. Do you walk or jog at    /GOC
>C25:1                            /GRA
>A25:"8. Do you eat rapidly ?     /XV29
>C24:1                            /GC26
>A24:"7. Do you use marijuana?    /X>A1:>A1:;/GC5
>C23:1                            /X>B1:>B1:/WS
```

Figure 1.3(b). Formulas and labels for HEALTH questions

1.4. BOWLING: A Bowling Score Keeper

VisiCalc worksheets are perfect for keeping totals and scores for games like the one illustrated in this section. A bowling score keeper, golf score keeper, card game score keeper, etc., all require record keeping and summation. The purpose of the worksheet in Figure 1.4(a), then, is to illustrate how you can keep track of your bowling score, and in general, how to build worksheets for other games.

Purpose

Figure 1.4(a) shows one way to lay out a bowling score sheet. Notice that frame #3 is missing. This was done intentionally, just to see if you can insert frame #3 yourself.

Worksheet

Each frame is numbered in column A, and then each frame is divided into three areas: a place to record the number of pins knocked down on the first roll, a place to record the number of pins knocked down on the second roll, and a place to record the total score for the frame. In addition, this version of the bowling score sheet contains two columns not found on an ordinary score sheet. The "strike" and "spare" columns compute (automatically) whether or not you rolled a strike or spare. This added information is used to tally the total number of each one at the end of the game.

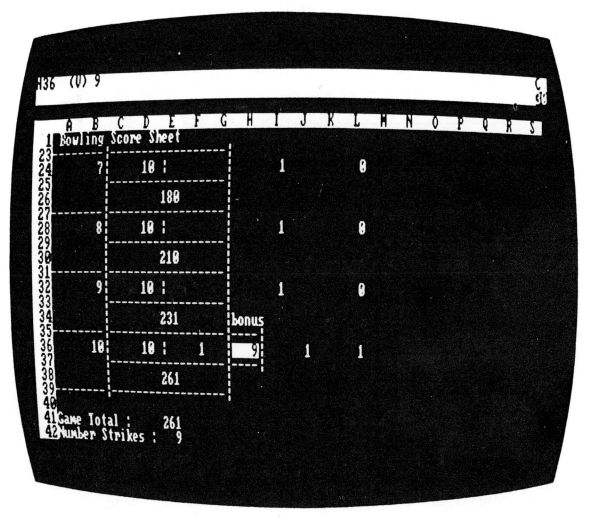

```
 Bowling Score Sheet

--------:-----------------------: Strike        Spare
frame  1:      10  :            :      1            0
        :-----------------------:
        :            30         :
--------:-----------------------:
       2:      10  :            :      1            0
        :-----------------------:
        :            60         :
--------:-----------------------:
       4:      10  :            :      1            0
        :-----------------------:
        :            90         :
--------:-----------------------:
       5:      10  :            :      1            0
        :-----------------------:
        :           120         :
--------:-----------------------:
       6:      10  :            :      1            0
        :-----------------------:
        :           150         :
--------:-----------------------:
       7:      10  :            :      1            0
        :-----------------------:
        :           180         :
--------:-----------------------:
       8:      10  :            :      1            0
        :-----------------------:
        :           210         :
--------:-----------------------:
       9:      10  :            :      1            0
        :-----------------------:
        :           231         :bonus
--------:-----------------:-----:
      10:      10  :    1  :  9 :      1            1
        :-----------------:-----:
        :           261         :
--------:-----------------------:

Game Total  :        261
Number Strikes :        9
Number Spares  :        2
```

Figure 1.4(a). Bowling score worksheet

To use the score sheet, you must first /BLANK out all first and second roll areas in each frame. These areas can then be filled in with the number of pins knocked down. As you enter the number of pins, the sums are computed and stored in the appropriate frame. Notice that strikes and spares cannot be fully added into the score until the results of the next frame or frames are known. Therefore, the calculations may produce partial results until the next frame or two are completed.

The game total, number of strikes, and number of spares are computed and stored at the end of the score sheet; see Figure 1.4(a). In the example, 9 strikes and 2 spares were recorded.

After you have used this example once or twice you should improve it by inserting the third frame which is missing from the score sheet given here. Use the /INSERT command, and /REPLICATE the box around frame #2 to get frame #3. Then /REPLICATE the formulas from frame #2 into frame #3. When you use /REPLICATE to copy the formulas, be sure to adjust the formulas by selecting the RELATIVE option.

Comments

The bowling score keeper works best with a hand-held computer. Thus it is not the most portable score keeper you can obtain. This example demonstrates another dimension of the VisiCalc program, however, and it should give you some ideas for other games.

The formulas for computing the last frame (the one with the extra credit if you get a strike or spare) are a bit tricky. You might want to improve them or change them as you see fit. In the meantime, good luck with your game.

Formulas

Don't let the size of Figure 1.4(b) discourage you. Most of the worksheet contains the broken-line boxes for each score sheet frame. The formulas, however, are of most importance if you want to reconstruct the worksheet.

There are basically three groups of formulas. One group computes the score for each frame, naturally, and the other two groups are for tabulating the number of strikes and spares. Look at the two entries at L16 and I16, for example.

> L16:@IF(@AND((+D16+F16)=10,+D16<10),1,0)
> I16:@IF(+D16=10,1,0)

The formula at I16 computes a 1 if the value of cell D16 is 10 (strike). Otherwise, a 0 is recorded. Hence cell I16 counts the number of strikes.

The formula at L16 computes the number of spares by recording a 1 if no strike was recorded in cell D16 (this is indicated by the test D16<10), and the total of D16+F16 equals 10. The VisiCalc @AND function returns TRUE only if both arguments are true. Thus, the frame must total to 10 pins but must not contain a strike.

Now, the total recorded in any frame is simply the total from the previous frame plus the number of pins knocked down in the current frame. Well, almost, anyway. The trouble with bowling scores is that the total for a strike or spare frame depends on the next frame. Thus, the VisiCalc formula for keeping score must look ahead to the next frame in the event that a strike or spare occurs. For example, look at the formula in cell E14:

> E14:+E10+D12+F12+@IF(+I12=1,+D16+@IF(+D16=10,D20,F16),0)
> +@IF(L12=1,D1 6,0)

The first three terms are for summing the current frame and the previous frame values. The @IF-mess, however, does the job of totaling the strike and spare "extras." Recall from the previous example that I12=1 means that a strike was recorded, and L12=1 means that a spare was recorded. These "extra points" are added in as soon as the next one or two rolls are added into the score sheet.

You will also note in Figure 1.4(b) that the order of calculation is set to /GLOBAL O C so that column-major order is used. This is necessary because of the way we have organized the score sheet.

```
>L45:/-_
>K45:/-_
>J45:/-_
>I45:/-_
>H45:/-_
>G45:/-_
>F45:/-_
>E45:/-_
>D45:/-_
>C45:/-_
>B45:/-_
>A45:/-_
>E43:@SUM(L4...L36)+@IF((+F36+H36)=10,1,0)
>D43:"s  :
>C43:"pares
>B43:"er Str
>A43:"Number
>E42:@SUM(I4...I32,J36)+@IF(H36=10,1,0)
>D42:"es :
>C42:"trike
>B42:"er Str
>A42:"Number
>E41:+E38
>C41:"al :
>B41:" Tota
>A41:"Game
>G39:/FR"---¦
>F39:/--
>E39:/--
>D39:/--
>C39:"¦---
>B39:/--
>A39:/--
>G38:/FR"¦
>E38:+E34+D36+F36+@IF(+D36=10,+F36+H36,+F36)+@IF(F36=10,+F36+H36,+H36)
>C38:"¦
>I37:"¦
>H37:"----
>G37:"---¦
>F37:/--
>E37:/--
>D37:/--
>C37:"¦---
>L36:@IF(@AND((+D36+F36)=10,+D36<10),1,0)+@IF((+F36+H36)=10,1,0)
>J36:@IF(+D36=10,1,0)+@IF(F36=10,1,0)+@IF(H36=10,1,0)
>I36:"¦
>H36:9
>G36:/FR"¦
>F36:1
>E36:"  ¦
>D36:10
>C36:"¦
>B36:10
>I35:"¦
>H35:"----
>G35:/FR"---¦
>F35:/--
>E35:/--
>D35:/--
>C35:"¦---
>B35:/--
>A35:/--
```

```
>I34:"s
>H34:"bonus
>G34:/FR"!
>E34:+E30+D32+F32+∂IF(+I32=1,+D36+F36,0)+∂IF(L32=1,D36,0)
>C34:"!
>G33:"---!
>F33:/--
>E33:/--
>D33:/--
>C33:"!---
>L32:∂IF(∂AND((+D32+F32)=10,+D32<10),1,0)
>I32:∂IF(+D32=10,1,0)
>G32:/FR"!
>E32:"  !
>D32:10
>C32:"!
>B32:9
>G31:/FR"---!
>F31:/--
>E31:/--
>D31:/--
>C31:"!---
>B31:/--
>A31:/--
>G30:/FR"!
>E30:+E26+D28+F28+∂IF(+I28=1,+D32+∂IF(+D32=10,D36,F32),0)+∂IF(L28=1,D32,0)
>C30:"!
>G29:/FR"---!
>F29:/--
>E29:/--
>D29:/--
>C29:"!---
>L28:∂IF(∂AND((+D28+F28)=10,+D28<10),1,0)
>I28:∂IF(+D28=10,1,0)
>G28:/FR"!
>E28:"  !
>D28:10
>C28:"!
>B28:8
>I27:/FR
>G27:/FR"---!
>F27:/--
>E27:/--
>D27:/--
>C27:"!---
>B27:/--
>A27:/--
>G26:/FR"!
>E26:+E22+D24+F24+∂IF(+I24=1,+D28+∂IF(+D28=10,D32,F28),0)+∂IF(L24=1,D28,0)
>C26:"!
>G25:/FR"---!
>F25:/--
>E25:/--
>D25:/--
>C25:"!---
>L24:∂IF(∂AND((+D24+F24)=10,+D24<10),1,0)
>I24:∂IF(+D24=10,1,0)
>G24:/FR"!
>E24:"  !
>D24:10
>C24:"!
>B24:7
>G23:/FR"---!
```

```
>F23:/--
>E23:/--
>D23:/--
>C23:"|---
>B23:/--
>A23:/--
>G22:/FR"|
>E22:+E18+D20+F20+@IF(+I20=1,+D24+@IF(+D24=10,D28,F24),0)+@IF(L20=1,D24,0)
>C22:"|
>G21:/FR"---|
>F21:/--
>E21:/--
>D21:/--
>C21:"|---
>L20:@IF(@AND((+D20+F20)=10,+D20<10),1,0)
>I20:@IF(+D20=10,1,0)
>G20:/FR"|
>E20:"  |
>D20:10
>C20:"|
>B20:6
>G19:/FR"---|
>F19:/--
>E19:/--
>D19:/--
>C19:"|---
>B19:/--
>A19:/--
>G18:/FR"|
>E18:+E14+D16+F16+@IF(+I16=1,+D20+@IF(+D20=10,D24,F20),0)+@IF(L16=1,D20,0)
>C18:"|
>G17:/FR"---|
>F17:/--
>E17:/--
>D17:/--
>C17:"|---
>L16:@IF(@AND((+D16+F16)=10,+D16<10),1,0)
>I16:@IF(+D16=10,1,0)
>G16:/FR"|
>E16:"  |
>D16:10
>C16:"|
>B16:5
>G15:/FR"---|
>F15:/--
>E15:/--
>D15:/--
>C15:"|---
>B15:/--
>A15:/--
>G14:/FR"|
>E14:+E10+D12+F12+@IF(+I12=1,+D16+@IF(+D16=10,D20,F16),0)+@IF(L12=1,D16,0)
>C14:"|
>G13:/FR"---|
>F13:/--
>E13:/--
>D13:/--
>C13:"|---
>L12:@IF(@AND((+D12+F12)=10,+D12<10),1,0)
>I12:@IF(+D12=10,1,0)
>G12:/FR"|
>E12:"  |
>D12:10
```

```
>C12:"!
>B12:4
>G11:/FR"---!
>F11:/--
>E11:/--
>D11:/--
>C11:"!---
>B11:/--
>A11:/--
>G10:/FR"!
>E10:+E6+D8+F8+@IF(+I8=1,+D12+@IF(+D12=10,D16,F12),0)+@IF(L8=1,D12,0)
>C10:"!
>G9:/FR"---!
>F9:/--
>E9:/--
>D9:/--
>C9:"!---
>L8:@IF(@AND((+D8+F8)=10,+D8<10),1,0)
>I8:@IF(+D8=10,1,0)
>G8:/FR"!
>E8:"  !
>D8:10
>C8:"!
>B8:2
>K7:/FR
>J7:/FR
>I7:/FR
>H7:/FR
>G7:/FR"---!
>F7:/--
>E7:/--
>D7:/--
>C7:"!---
>B7:/--
>A7:/--
>G6:/FR"!
>E6:+D4+F4+@IF(+I4=1,+D8+@IF(+D8=10,D12,F8),0)+@IF(L4=1,D8,0)
>C6:"!
>G5:/FR"---!
>F5:/--
>E5:/--
>D5:/--
>C5:"!----
>L4:@IF(@AND((+D4+F4)=10,+D4<10),1,0)
>I4:@IF(+D4=10,1,0)
>G4:/FR"!
>E4:"  !
>D4:10
>C4:"!
>B4:"e   1
>A4:"frame
>L3:"are
>K3:"  Spare
>I3:"ike
>H3:"  Strike
>G3:/FR"---!
>F3:/--
>E3:/--
>D3:/--
>C3:"!---
>B3:/--
>A3:/--
>E1:"heet
```

```
>D1:"re S
>C1:" Scor
>B1:"ling
>A1:/FR"Bow
/W1
/GOC
/GRA
/GFI
/GC4
/X>A1:>A1:/TH
/X>A1:>A1:
```

Figure 1.4(b). Formulas for bowling score keeper

1.5. LIFE: The Mathematical Game of Life

The Game of Life is a popular game played by computer programmers for the past two decades. The game involves a lot of computation with a very unpredictable outcome. The idea is to simulate a population of dots or bits that "live" in a rectangular grid as shown in Figure 1.5(a).

The rectangular grid contains cells. Each cell is much like a VisiCalc cell except that it can hold only a bit with a value of zero or one. A cell containing a 1 bit holds a "living" individual, and a cell containing a 0 bit is said to be empty. The purpose of the game, then, is to find out what happens to the living population. Does it grow or die out?

Each generation of the rectangular population is computed by recalculating the contents of each cell. A 1 or 0 is placed in a cell depending on the number of neighbors in the adjacent cells. Thus a cell gives "birth" to a new 1 bit if there are exactly 3 neighbors. A 1 bit can die from overcrowding if there are too many neighbors. The Game of Life simulates real populations.

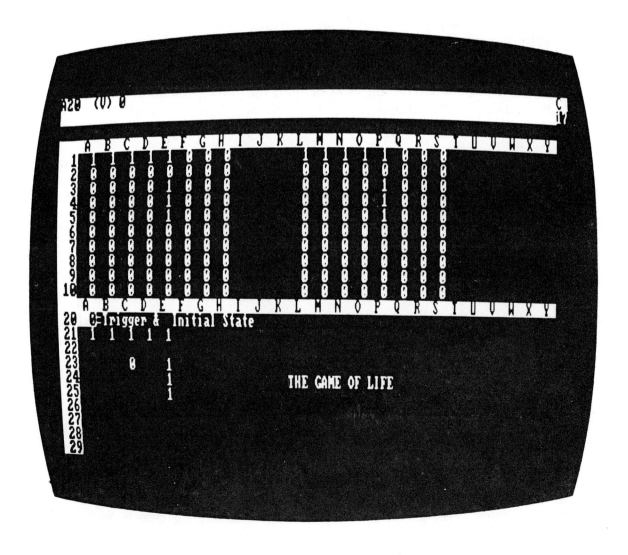

In the worksheets shown in Figures 1.5(a) to 1.5(c) the rules for deciding what is placed in a cell are as follows:

IF cell = 1 and sum = 2 OR sum = 3 THEN 1
IF cell = 0 AND sum = 3 THEN 1

The sum above is computed by adding the contents of all 8 adjacent cells (north, northeast, east, southeast, south, etc.). So, if a given cell contains a 1 in the current generation, it will continue to hold a 1 into the next generation if the number of neighbors totals 2 or 3. Alternately, if a certain cell holds a 0 in the current generation, then it will give "birth" to a new 1 in the next generation if it has exactly 3 neighbors.

LIFE has intrigued mathematicians for years because of its similarity to real populations, and because it defied analysis. In fact, at one time *Scientific American* magazine awarded cash prizes to mathematicians for proving that certain starting populations would live forever, or eventually die out after a finite number of generations. But then computers came along and took all the fun out of LIFE. It became possible to analyze a starting population like the one if Figure 1.5(a) or Figure 1.5(c) by actually computing thousands of generations. Indeed, this is what the VisiCalc worksheet given here does.

Worksheet   In Figure 1.5(a) you will notice that there are two full rectangles and one partially defined rectangle below the others. The lower rectangle is called the starting state, because this is where you specify the initial values or initial population. You will also notice the "trigger" value. This is set to zero when you want to initialize the upper two rectangles by copying the initial population into the upper two rectangles. The trigger is set to one when you want to compute the next generation in the left rectangle and the second next generation in the right rectangle.

You should disable the automatic recalculation option while entering the initial population. Use /GLOBAL R M to do this. The calculations are quite taxing even for a fast computer, so you must use ! to recalculate the next two populations.

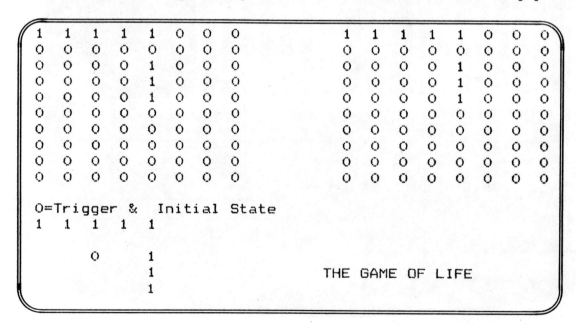

Figure 1.5(a). Initial state of LIFE

```
O 1 1 1 0 0 0 0        O 1 0 1 0 0 0 0
O 1 1 0 1 0 0 0        O 1 0 0 0 0 0 0
O O O O O O O O        O O 1 O O 1 O O
O O O 1 1 1 O O        O O O O 1 O O O
O O O O O O O O        O O O O 1 O O O
O O O O O O O O        O O O O O O O O
O O O O O O O O        O O O O O O O O
O O O O O O O O        O O O O O O O O
O O O O O O O O        O O O O O O O O
O O O O O O O O        O O O O O O O O


1=Trigger &  Initial State
1  1  1  1  1

          O       1
                  1
                  1        THE GAME OF LIFE
                  1
```

Figure 1.5(b). A later generation of LIFE

```
O O O O O O O O        O O O O O O O O
O O O O O O O O        O O O O O O O O
O O O O O O O O        O O O O O O O O
O O O O O O O O        O O O O O O O O
O O O O O O O O        O O O O O O O O
O O O O O O O O        O O O O O O O O
O O O O O O O O        O O O O O O O O
O O O O O O O O        O O O 1 O O O O
O O 1 1 1 O O O        O O O 1 O O O O
O O O O O O O O        O O O 1 O O O O


1=Trigger &  Initial State
          1
          1
          1
          1        THE GAME OF LIFE
1 1 1 1 1 1 1 1
          1
          1
          1
          1
```

Figure 1.5(c). Another example of LIFE

After you have entered a starting population into the initial state rectangle of the VisiCalc worksheet, set the trigger to zero and hit the ! command. The initial state will be loaded into the left and right upper rectangles. Check the two rectangles to see that this has happened.

Now, to get the game to compute the next two generations set the order of calculation to /GLOBAL O C. This causes the left rectangle to be recalculated before the right rectangle. Then the right rectangle is computed using the values stored in the left rectangle.

Notice what happens: the values stored in one upper rectangle are used to compute the values stored in the other rectangle. Each time you press the ! recalculation command, the left rectangle is recalculated using the right rectangle, and then the right rectangle is recalculated using the left rectangle.

The computer will take a long time to recalculate the entire worksheet, so be patient. Watch the upper right-hand corner of the VisiCalc screen and you will see the ! character there while the recalculation is in progress.

Figure 1.5(b)-(c) illustrate some results obtained from two different starting populations. Can you determine the final result just by looking at the starting population? Some populations die out, and others repeat a certain pattern. Patterns that float across the rectangle are called *floaters* or *flyers*. Patterns that flip back and forth between two populations are sometimes called *blinkers*. Also, there are rare *virus* populations that absorb and change another population. Try some experiments with this worksheet and you may be surprised by the shapes you get.

Comments

This worksheet illustrates an interesting limitation of VisiCalc and a way to circumvent it. A VisiCalc worksheet cannot store both numbers and formulas in the same cell. We got around this limitation by maintaining two rectangles. In general, you will have to do this (repeat the cells), in order to store both. You will also have to use an @IF function to "trigger" the initial value of a cell, as we showed here.

Notice also that we used the @AND and @OR functions extensively. Remember that these return either TRUE or FALSE. The arguments of an @AND function must all be true in order for TRUE to be returned. Only one of the arguments of @OR need to be true in order for @OR to return a TRUE.

LIFE is a mathematical game that simulates a "living" population. The rules for this population were set up to simulate a kind of competition versus abundance environment. If competition gets too severe, the bits die out from overcrowding. If the environment is "just right," the population thrives on abundance. But the rules proposed here are somewhat arbitrary. What happens if they change? You can experiment with this game by altering the rules for survival. What happens if new "births" occur when the sum is 2 instead of 3?

Formulas

The formulas of Figure 1.5(d) appear to be complicated and lengthy, but this is not the case. They implement the following rules.

1. Test the trigger at cell A20 and either copy the initial state values or else use the "other" rectangle to recalculate the next generation.

2. Compute the sum of neighboring cells and use this sum to decide if the next generation should be a one or a zero.

The formulas are somehwat complicated by the fact that the border cells do not have as many neighbors as the interior cells. Otherwise, the summation is carried out over 8 neighbors.

You will also notice that the recalculations are based on the values stored in the cell "opposite" of the one being recalculated. This is how the VisiCalc worksheet is able to store a bit and also store a formula for recalculating the value of the bit. We used two adjacent rectangles to fool the VisiCalc program (to get around its limitation, actually). If it were possible to store both a number and a formula in a VisiCalc cell, then this "trick" would not have been necessary.

Do not be dismayed by the large number of formulas in the worksheet. If you are reconstructing the worksheet from Figure 1.5(d), then use the /REPLICATE command extensively. Enter the formula one for an internal cell (border cells must be modified). This formula becomes the model for all other formulas. Use it to /REPLICATE into a complete row, say, then use each row-formula as a model to /REPLICATE into the cells of each column. Thus, you need only enter the first model formula, and then replicate this model into all other internal cells. Use the RELATIVE adjustment option with the /REPLICATE command.

If you purchase the diskette that goes along with the book, then you will simply load the game of LIFE. Use the /SL LIFE command. This worksheet will take quite a long time, so be patient. Keep your eye on the memory size counter in the upper right-hand corner of the screen. It will count down as the worksheet loads.

```
>E25:1
>Q24:"E
>P24:"LIFE
>O24:"OF
>N24:"ME
>M24:" GA
>L24:"THE
>E24:1
>E23:1
>C23:0
>E21:1
>D21:1
>C21:1
>B21:1
>A21:1
>J20:"e
>I20:"tat
>H20:"l S
>G20:"tial
>F20:"Ini
>E20:"&
>D20:"er
>C20:"igger
>B20:"=Tr
>A20:0
>S10:@IF(A20=1,@IF(@OR(@SUM(G9...I9,G10,I10)=3,@AND(H10=1,@SUM(G9...I9,G10,I10)=
2)),1,0),H30)
>R10:@IF(A20=1,@IF(@OR(@SUM(F9...H9,F10,H10)=3,@AND(G10=1,@SUM(F9...H9,F10,H10)=
2)),1,0),G30)
>Q10:@IF(A20=1,@IF(@OR(@SUM(E9...G9,E10,G10)=3,@AND(F10=1,@SUM(E9...G9,E10,G10)=
2)),1,0),F30)
>P10:@IF(A20=1,@IF(@OR(@SUM(D9...F9,D10,F10)=3,@AND(E10=1,@SUM(D9...F9,D10,F10)=
2)),1,0),E30)
>O10:@IF(A20=1,@IF(@OR(@SUM(C9...E9,C10,E10)=3,@AND(D10=1,@SUM(C9...E9,C10,E10)=
2)),1,0),D30)
>N10:@IF(A20=1,@IF(@OR(@SUM(B9...D9,B10,D10)=3,@AND(C10=1,@SUM(B9...D9,B10,D10)=
2)),1,0),C30)
>M10:@IF(A20=1,@IF(@OR(@SUM(A9...C9,A10,C10)=3,@AND(B10=1,@SUM(A9...C9,A10,C10)=
2)),1,0),B30)
>L10:@IF(A20=1,@IF(@OR(@SUM(A9...B9,B10)=3,@AND(A10=1,@SUM(A9...B9,B10)=2)),1,0)
,A30)
>H10:@IF(A20=1,@IF(@OR(@SUM(R9...S9,R10)=3,@AND(S10=1,@SUM(R9...S9,R10)=2)),1,0)
,H30)
>G10:@IF(A20=1,@IF(@OR(@SUM(Q9...S9,Q10,S10)=3,@AND(R10=1,@SUM(Q9...S9,Q10,S10)=
2)),1,0),G30)
>F10:@IF(A20=1,@IF(@OR(@SUM(P9...R9,P10,R10)=3,@AND(Q10=1,@SUM(P9...R9,P10,R10)=
2)),1,0),F30)
>E10:@IF(A20=1,@IF(@OR(@SUM(O9...Q9,O10,Q10)=3,@AND(P10=1,@SUM(O9...Q9,O10,Q10)=
2)),1,0),E30)
```

```
>D10:ƏIF(A20=1,ƏIF(ƏOR(ƏSUM(N9...P9,N10,P10)=3,ƏAND(O10=1,ƏSUM(N9...P9,N10,P10)=
2)),1,0),D30)
>C10:ƏIF(A20=1,ƏIF(ƏOR(ƏSUM(M9...O9,M10,O10)=3,ƏAND(N10=1,ƏSUM(M9...O9,M10,O10)=
2)),1,0),C30)
>B10:ƏIF(A20=1,ƏIF(ƏOR(ƏSUM(L9...N9,L10,N10)=3,ƏAND(M10=1,ƏSUM(L9...N9,L10,N10)=
2)),1,0),B30)
>A10:ƏIF(A20=1,ƏIF(ƏOR(ƏSUM(L9...M9,M10)=3,ƏAND(L10=1,ƏSUM(L9...M9,M10)=2)),1,0)
,A30)
>S9:ƏIF(A20=1,ƏIF(ƏOR(ƏSUM(G8...H8,G9,G10...H10)=3,ƏAND(H9=1,ƏSUM(G8...H8,G9,G10
...H10)=2)),1,0),H29)
>R9:ƏIF(A20=1,ƏIF(ƏOR(ƏSUM(F8...H8,F9,H9,F10...H10)=3,ƏAND(G9=1,ƏSUM(F8...H8,F9,
H9,F10...H10)=2)),1,0),G28)
>Q9:ƏIF(A20=1,ƏIF(ƏOR(ƏSUM(E8...G8,E9,G9,E10...G10)=3,ƏAND(F9=1,ƏSUM(E8...G8,E9,
G9,E10...G10)=2)),1,0),F28)
>P9:ƏIF(A20=1,ƏIF(ƏOR(ƏSUM(D8...F8,D9,F9,D10...F10)=3,ƏAND(E9=1,ƏSUM(D8...F8,D9,
F9,D10...F10)=2)),1,0),E28)
>O9:ƏIF(A20=1,ƏIF(ƏOR(ƏSUM(C8...E8,C9,E9,C10...E10)=3,ƏAND(D9=1,ƏSUM(C8...E8,C9,
E9,C10...E10)=2)),1,0),D28)
>N9:ƏIF(A20=1,ƏIF(ƏOR(ƏSUM(B8...D8,B9,D9,B10...D10)=3,ƏAND(C9=1,ƏSUM(B8...D8,B9,
D9,B10...D10)=2)),1,0),C28)
>M9:ƏIF(A20=1,ƏIF(ƏOR(ƏSUM(A8...C8,A9,C9,A10...C10)=3,ƏAND(B9=1,ƏSUM(A8...C8,A9,
C9,A10...C10)=2)),1,0),B28)
>L9:ƏIF(A20=1,ƏIF(ƏOR(ƏSUM(A10,B9...B10)=3,ƏAND(A9=1,ƏSUM(A10,B9...B10)=2)),1,0)
,A28)
>H9:ƏIF(A20=1,ƏIF(ƏOR(ƏSUM(R8...S8,R9,R10...S10)=3,ƏAND(S9=1,ƏSUM(R8...S8,R9,R10
...S10)=2)),1,0),H29)
>G9:ƏIF(A20=1,ƏIF(ƏOR(ƏSUM(Q8...S8,Q9,S9,Q10...S10)=3,ƏAND(R9=1,ƏSUM(Q8...S8,Q9,
S9,Q10...S10)=2)),1,0),G29)
>F9:ƏIF(A20=1,ƏIF(ƏOR(ƏSUM(P8...R8,P9,R9,P10...R10)=3,ƏAND(Q9=1,ƏSUM(P8...R8,P9,
R9,P10...R10)=2)),1,0),F29)
>E9:ƏIF(A20=1,ƏIF(ƏOR(ƏSUM(O8...Q8,O9,Q9,O10...Q10)=3,ƏAND(P9=1,ƏSUM(O8...Q8,O9,
Q9,O10...Q10)=2)),1,0),E29)
>D9:ƏIF(A20=1,ƏIF(ƏOR(ƏSUM(N8...P8,N9,P9,N10...P10)=3,ƏAND(O9=1,ƏSUM(N8...P8,N9,
P9,N10...P10)=2)),1,0),D29)
>C9:ƏIF(A20=1,ƏIF(ƏOR(ƏSUM(M8...O8,M9,O9,M10...O10)=3,ƏAND(N9=1,ƏSUM(M8...O8,M9,
O9,M10...O10)=2)),1,0),C29)
>B9:ƏIF(A20=1,ƏIF(ƏOR(ƏSUM(L8...N8,L9,N9,L10...N10)=3,ƏAND(M9=1,ƏSUM(L8...N8,L9,
N9,L10...N10)=2)),1,0),B29)
>A9:ƏIF(A20=1,ƏIF(ƏOR(ƏSUM(L10,M9...M10)=3,ƏAND(L9=1,ƏSUM(L10,M9...M10)=2)),1,0)
,A29)
>S8:ƏIF(A20=1,ƏIF(ƏOR(ƏSUM(G7...H7,G8,G9...H9)=3,ƏAND(H8=1,ƏSUM(G7...H7,G8,G9...
H9)=2)),1,0),H28)
>R8:ƏIF(A20=1,ƏIF(ƏOR(ƏSUM(F7...H7,F8,H8,F9...H9)=3,ƏAND(G8=1,ƏSUM(F7...H7,F8,H8
,F9...H9)=2)),1,0),G28)
>Q8:ƏIF(A20=1,ƏIF(ƏOR(ƏSUM(E7...G7,E8,G8,E9...G9)=3,ƏAND(F8=1,ƏSUM(E7...G7,E8,G8
,E9...G9)=2)),1,0),F28)
>P8:ƏIF(A20=1,ƏIF(ƏOR(ƏSUM(D7...F7,D8,F8,D9...F9)=3,ƏAND(E8=1,ƏSUM(D7...F7,D8,F8
,D9...F9)=2)),1,0),E28)
>O8:ƏIF(A20=1,ƏIF(ƏOR(ƏSUM(C7...E7,C8,E8,C9...E9)=3,ƏAND(D8=1,ƏSUM(C7...E7,C8,E8
,C9...E9)=2)),1,0),D28)
>N8:ƏIF(A20=1,ƏIF(ƏOR(ƏSUM(B7...D7,B8,D8,B9...D9)=3,ƏAND(C8=1,ƏSUM(B7...D7,B8,D8
,B9...D9)=2)),1,0),C28)
>M8:ƏIF(A20=1,ƏIF(ƏOR(ƏSUM(A7...C7,A8,C8,A9...C9)=3,ƏAND(B8=1,ƏSUM(A7...C7,A8,C8
,A9...C9)=2)),1,0),B28)
>L8:ƏIF(A20=1,ƏIF(ƏOR(ƏSUM(A9,B8...B9)=3,ƏAND(A8=1,ƏSUM(A9,B8...B9)=2)),1,0),A28
)
>H8:ƏIF(A20=1,ƏIF(ƏOR(ƏSUM(R7...S7,R8,R9...S9)=3,ƏAND(S8=1,ƏSUM(R7...S7,R8,R9...
S9)=2)),1,0),H28)
>G8:ƏIF(A20=1,ƏIF(ƏOR(ƏSUM(Q7...S7,Q8,S8,Q9...S9)=3,ƏAND(R8=1,ƏSUM(Q7...S7,Q8,S8
,Q9...S9)=2)),1,0),G28)
>F8:ƏIF(A20=1,ƏIF(ƏOR(ƏSUM(P7...R7,P8,R8,P9...R9)=3,ƏAND(Q8=1,ƏSUM(P7...R7,P8,R8
,P9...R9)=2)),1,0),F28)
>E8:ƏIF(A20=1,ƏIF(ƏOR(ƏSUM(O7...Q7,O8,Q8,O9...Q9)=3,ƏAND(P8=1,ƏSUM(O7...Q7,O8,Q8
,O9...Q9)=2)),1,0),E28)
>D8:ƏIF(A20=1,ƏIF(ƏOR(ƏSUM(N7...P7,N8,P8,N9...P9)=3,ƏAND(O8=1,ƏSUM(N7...P7,N8,P8
,N9...P9)=2)),1,0),D28)
>C8:ƏIF(A20=1,ƏIF(ƏOR(ƏSUM(M7...O7,M8,O8,M9...O9)=3,ƏAND(N8=1,ƏSUM(M7...O7,M8,O8
,M9...O9)=2)),1,0),C28)
```

```
>B8:ƏIF(A20=1,ƏIF(ƏOR(ƏSUM(L7...N7,L8,N8,L9...N9)=3,ƏAND(M8=1,ƏSUM(L7...N7,L8,N8
,L9...N9)=2)),1,0),B28)
>A8:ƏIF(A20=1,ƏIF(ƏOR(ƏSUM(L9,M8...M9)=3,ƏAND(L8=1,ƏSUM(L9,M8...M9)=2)),1,0),A28
)
>S7:ƏIF(A20=1,ƏIF(ƏOR(ƏSUM(G6...H6,G7,G8...H8)=3,ƏAND(H7=1,ƏSUM(G6...H6,G7,G8...
H8)=2)),1,0),H27)
>R7:ƏIF(A20=1,ƏIF(ƏOR(ƏSUM(F6...H6,F7,H7,F8...H8)=3,ƏAND(G7=1,ƏSUM(F6...H6,F7,H7
,F8...H8)=2)),1,0),G27)
>Q7:ƏIF(A20=1,ƏIF(ƏOR(ƏSUM(E6...G6,E7,G7,E8...G8)=3,ƏAND(F7=1,ƏSUM(E6...G6,E7,G7
,E8...G8)=2)),1,0),F27)
>P7:ƏIF(A20=1,ƏIF(ƏOR(ƏSUM(D6...F6,D7,F7,D8...F8)=3,ƏAND(E7=1,ƏSUM(D6...F6,D7,F7
,D8...F8)=2)),1,0),E27)
>O7:ƏIF(A20=1,ƏIF(ƏOR(ƏSUM(C6...E6,C7,E7,C8...E8)=3,ƏAND(D7=1,ƏSUM(C6...E6,C7,E7
,C8...E8)=2)),1,0),D27)
>N7:ƏIF(A20=1,ƏIF(ƏOR(ƏSUM(B6...D6,B7,D7,B8...D8)=3,ƏAND(C7=1,ƏSUM(B6...D6,B7,D7
,B8...D8)=2)),1,0),C27)
>M7:ƏIF(A20=1,ƏIF(ƏOR(ƏSUM(A6...C6,A7,C7,A8...C8)=3,ƏAND(B7=1,ƏSUM(A6...C6,A7,C7
,A8...C8)=2)),1,0),B27)
>L7:ƏIF(A20=1,ƏIF(ƏOR(ƏSUM(A8,B7...B8)=3,ƏAND(A7=1,ƏSUM(A8,B7...B8)=2)),1,0),A27
)
>H7:ƏIF(A20=1,ƏIF(ƏOR(ƏSUM(R6...S6,R7,R8...S8)=3,ƏAND(S7=1,ƏSUM(R6...S6,R7,R8...
S8)=2)),1,0),H27)
>G7:ƏIF(A20=1,ƏIF(ƏOR(ƏSUM(Q6...S6,Q7,S7,Q8...S8)=3,ƏAND(R7=1,ƏSUM(Q6...S6,Q7,S7
,Q8...S8)=2)),1,0),F27)
>F7:ƏIF(A20=1,ƏIF(ƏOR(ƏSUM(P6...R6,P7,R7,P8...R8)=3,ƏAND(Q7=1,ƏSUM(P6...R6,P7,R7
,P8...R8)=2)),1,0),E27)
>E7:ƏIF(A20=1,ƏIF(ƏOR(ƏSUM(O6...Q6,O7,Q7,O8...Q8)=3,ƏAND(P7=1,ƏSUM(O6...Q6,O7,Q7
,O8...Q8)=2)),1,0),D27)
>D7:ƏIF(A20=1,ƏIF(ƏOR(ƏSUM(N6...P6,N7,P7,N8...P8)=3,ƏAND(O7=1,ƏSUM(N6...P6,N7,P7
,N8...P8)=2)),1,0),D27)
>C7:ƏIF(A20=1,ƏIF(ƏOR(ƏSUM(M6...O6,M7,O7,M8...O8)=3,ƏAND(N7=1,ƏSUM(M6...O6,M7,O7
,M8...O8)=2)),1,0),C27)
>B7:ƏIF(A20=1,ƏIF(ƏOR(ƏSUM(L6...N6,L7,N7,L8...N8)=3,ƏAND(M7=1,ƏSUM(L6...N6,L7,N7
,L8...N8)=2)),1,0),B27)
>A7:ƏIF(A20=1,ƏIF(ƏOR(ƏSUM(L8,M7...M8)=3,ƏAND(L7=1,ƏSUM(L8,M7...M8)=2)),1,0),A27
)
>S6:ƏIF(A20=1,ƏIF(ƏOR(ƏSUM(G5...H5,G6,G7...H7)=3,ƏAND(H6=1,ƏSUM(G5...H5,G6,G7...
H7)=2)),1,0),H26)
>R6:ƏIF(A20=1,ƏIF(ƏOR(ƏSUM(F5...H5,F6,H6,F7...H7)=3,ƏAND(G6=1,ƏSUM(F5...H5,F6,H6
,F7...H7)=2)),1,0),G26)
>Q6:ƏIF(A20=1,ƏIF(ƏOR(ƏSUM(E5...G5,E6,G6,E7...G7)=3,ƏAND(F6=1,ƏSUM(E5...G5,E6,G6
,E7...G7)=2)),1,0),F26)
>P6:ƏIF(A20=1,ƏIF(ƏOR(ƏSUM(D5...F5,D6,F6,D7...F7)=3,ƏAND(E6=1,ƏSUM(D5...F5,D6,F6
,D7...F7)=2)),1,0),E26)
>O6:ƏIF(A20=1,ƏIF(ƏOR(ƏSUM(C5...E5,C6,E6,C7...E7)=3,ƏAND(D6=1,ƏSUM(C5...E5,C6,E6
,C7...E7)=2)),1,0),D26)
>N6:ƏIF(A20=1,ƏIF(ƏOR(ƏSUM(B5...D5,B6,D6,B7...D7)=3,ƏAND(C6=1,ƏSUM(B5...D5,B6,D6
,B7...D7)=2)),1,0),C26)
>M6:ƏIF(A20=1,ƏIF(ƏOR(ƏSUM(A5...C5,A6,C6,A7.   C7)=3,ƏAND(B6=1,ƏSUM(A5...C5,A6,C6
,A7...C7)=2)),1,0),B26)
>L6:ƏIF(A20=1,ƏIF(ƏOR(ƏSUM(A7,B6...B7)=3,ƏAND(A6=1,ƏSUM(A7,B6...B7)=2)),1,0),A26
)
>H6:ƏIF(A20=1,ƏIF(ƏOR(ƏSUM(R5...S5,R6,R7...S7)=3,ƏAND(S6=1,ƏSUM(R5...S5,R6,R7...
S7)=2)),1,0),H26)
>G6:ƏIF(A20=1,ƏIF(ƏOR(ƏSUM(Q5...S5,Q6,S6,Q7...S7)=3,ƏAND(R6=1,ƏSUM(Q5...S5,Q6,S6
,Q7...S7)=2)),1,0),G26)
>F6:ƏIF(A20=1,ƏIF(ƏOR(ƏSUM(P5...R5,P6,R6,P7...R7)=3,ƏAND(Q6=1,ƏSUM(P5...R5,P6,R6
,P7...R7)=2)),1,0),F26)
>E6:ƏIF(A20=1,ƏIF(ƏOR(ƏSUM(O5...Q5,O6,Q6,O7...Q7)=3,ƏAND(P6=1,ƏSUM(O5...Q5,O6,Q6
,O7...Q7)=2)),1,0),E26)
>D6:ƏIF(A20=1,ƏIF(ƏOR(ƏSUM(N5...P5,N6,P6,N7...P7)=3,ƏAND(O6=1,ƏSUM(N5...P5,N6,P6
,N7...P7)=2)),1,0),D26)
>C6:ƏIF(A20=1,ƏIF(ƏOR(ƏSUM(M5...O5,M6,O6,M7...O7)=3,ƏAND(N6=1,ƏSUM(M5...O5,M6,O6
,M7...O7)=2)),1,0),C26)
>B6:ƏIF(A20=1,ƏIF(ƏOR(ƏSUM(L5...N5,L6,N6,L7...N7)=3,ƏAND(M6=1,ƏSUM(L5...N5,L6,N6
,L7...N7)=2)),1,0),B26)
>A6:ƏIF(A20=1,ƏIF(ƏOR(ƏSUM(L7,M6...M7)=3,ƏAND(L6=1,ƏSUM(L7,M6...M7)=2)),1,0),A26
)
```

```
>S5:@IF(A20=1,@IF(@OR(@SUM(G4...H4,G5,G6...H6)=3,@AND(H5=1,@SUM(G4...H4,G5,G6...
H6)=2)),1,0),H25)
>R5:@IF(A20=1,@IF(@OR(@SUM(F4...H4,F5,H5,F6...H6)=3,@AND(G5=1,@SUM(F4...H4,F5,H5
,F6...H6)=2)),1,0),G25)
>Q5:@IF(A20=1,@IF(@OR(@SUM(E4...G4,E5,G5,E6...G6)=3,@AND(F5=1,@SUM(E4...G4,E5,G5
,E6...G6)=2)),1,0),F25)
>P5:@IF(A20=1,@IF(@OR(@SUM(D4...F4,D5,F5,D6...F6)=3,@AND(E5=1,@SUM(D4...F4,D5,F5
,D6...F6)=2)),1,0),E25)
>O5:@IF(A20=1,@IF(@OR(@SUM(C4...E4,C5,E5,C6...E6)=3,@AND(D5=1,@SUM(C4...E4,C5,E5
,C6...E6)=2)),1,0),D25)
>N5:@IF(A20=1,@IF(@OR(@SUM(B4...D4,B5,D5,B6...D6)=3,@AND(C5=1,@SUM(B4...D4,B5,D5
,B6...D6)=2)),1,0),C25)
>M5:@IF(A20=1,@IF(@OR(@SUM(A4...C4,A5,C5,A6...C6)=3,@AND(B5=1,@SUM(A4...C4,A5,C5
,A6...C6)=2)),1,0),B25)
>L5:@IF(A20=1,@IF(@OR(@SUM(A6,B5...B6)=3,@AND(A5=1,@SUM(A6,B5...B6)=2)),1,0),A25
)
>H5:@IF(A20=1,@IF(@OR(@SUM(R4...S4,R5,R6...S6)=3,@AND(S5=1,@SUM(R4...S4,R5,R6...
S6)=2)),1,0),H25)
>G5:@IF(A20=1,@IF(@OR(@SUM(Q4...S4,Q5,S5,Q6...S6)=3,@AND(R5=1,@SUM(Q4...S4,Q5,S5
,Q6...S6)=2)),1,0),G25)
>F5:@IF(A20=1,@IF(@OR(@SUM(P4...R4,P5,R5,P6...R6)=3,@AND(Q5=1,@SUM(P4...R4,P5,R5
,P6...R6)=2)),1,0),F25)
>E5:@IF(A20=1,@IF(@OR(@SUM(O4...Q4,O5,Q5,O6...Q6)=3,@AND(P5=1,@SUM(O4...Q4,O5,Q5
,O6...Q6)=2)),1,0),E25)
>D5:@IF(A20=1,@IF(@OR(@SUM(N4...P4,N5,P5,N6...P6)=3,@AND(O5=1,@SUM(N4...P4,N5,P5
,N6...P6)=2)),1,0),D25)
>C5:@IF(A20=1,@IF(@OR(@SUM(M4...O4,M5,O5,M6...O6)=3,@AND(N5=1,@SUM(M4...O4,M5,O5
,M6...O6)=2)),1,0),C25)
>B5:@IF(A20=1,@IF(@OR(@SUM(L4...N4,L5,N5,L6...N6)=3,@AND(M5=1,@SUM(L4...N4,L5,N5
,L6...N6)=2)),1,0),B25)
>A5:@IF(A20=1,@IF(@OR(@SUM(L6,M5...M6)=3,@AND(L5=1,@SUM(L6,M5...M6)=2)),1,0),A25
)
>S4:@IF(A20=1,@IF(@OR(@SUM(G3...H3,G4,G5...H5)=3,@AND(H4=1,@SUM(G3...H3,G4,G5...
H5)=2)),1,0),H24)
>R4:@IF(A20=1,@IF(@OR(@SUM(F3...H3,F4,H4,F5...H5)=3,@AND(G4=1,@SUM(F3...H3,F4,H4
,F5...H5)=2)),1,0),G24)
>Q4:@IF(A20=1,@IF(@OR(@SUM(E3...G3,E4,G4,E5...G5)=3,@AND(F4=1,@SUM(E3...G3,E4,G4
,E5...G5)=2)),1,0),F24)
>P4:@IF(A20=1,@IF(@OR(@SUM(D3...F3,D4,F4,D5...F5)=3,@AND(E4=1,@SUM(D3...F3,D4,F4
,D5...F5)=2)),1,0),E24)
>O4:@IF(A20=1,@IF(@OR(@SUM(C3...E3,C4,E4,C5...E5)=3,@AND(D4=1,@SUM(C3...E3,C4,E4
,C5...E5)=2)),1,0),D24)
>N4:@IF(A20=1,@IF(@OR(@SUM(B3...D3,B4,D4,B5...D5)=3,@AND(C4=1,@SUM(B3...D3,B4,D4
,B5...D5)=2)),1,0),C24)
>M4:@IF(A20=1,@IF(@OR(@SUM(A3...C3,A4,C4,A5...C5)=3,@AND(B4=1,@SUM(A3...C3,A4,C4
,A5...C5)=2)),1,0),B24)
>L4:@IF(A20=1,@IF(@OR(@SUM(A5,B4...B5)=3,@AND(A4=1,@SUM(A5,B4...B5)=2)),1,0),A24
)
>H4:@IF(A20=1,@IF(@OR(@SUM(R3...S3,R4,R5...S5)=3,@AND(S4=1,@SUM(R3...S3,R4,R5...
S5)=2)),1,0),H24)
>G4:@IF(A20=1,@IF(@OR(@SUM(Q3...S3,Q4,S4,Q5...S5)=3,@AND(R4=1,@SUM(Q3...S3,Q4,S4
,Q5...S5)=2)),1,0),G24)
>F4:@IF(A20=1,@IF(@OR(@SUM(P3...R3,P4,R4,P5...R5)=3,@AND(Q4=1,@SUM(P3...R3,P4,R4
,P5...R5)=2)),1,0),F24)
>E4:@IF(A20=1,@IF(@OR(@SUM(O3...Q3,O4,Q4,O5...Q5)=3,@AND(P4=1,@SUM(O3...Q3,O4,Q4
,O5...Q5)=2)),1,0),E24)
>D4:@IF(A20=1,@IF(@OR(@SUM(N3...P3,N4,P4,N5...P5)=3,@AND(O4=1,@SUM(N3...P3,N4,P4
,N5...P5)=2)),1,0),D24)
>C4:@IF(A20=1,@IF(@OR(@SUM(M3...O3,M4,O4,M5...O5)=3,@AND(N4=1,@SUM(M3...O3,M4,O4
,M5...O5)=2)),1,0),C24)
>B4:@IF(A20=1,@IF(@OR(@SUM(L3...N3,L4,N4,L5...N5)=3,@AND(M4=1,@SUM(L3...N3,L4,N4
,L5...N5)=2)),1,0),B24)
>A4:@IF(A20=1,@IF(@OR(@SUM(L5,M4...M5)=3,@AND(L4=1,@SUM(L5,M4...M5)=2)),1,0),A24
)
>S3:@IF(A20=1,@IF(@OR(@SUM(G2...H2,G3,G4...H4)=3,@AND(H3=1,@SUM(G2...H2,G3,G4...
H4)=2)),1,0),H23)
>R3:@IF(A20=1,@IF(@OR(@SUM(F2...H2,F3,H3,F4...H4)=3,@AND(G3=1,@SUM(F2...H2,F3,H3
,F4...H4)=2)),1,0),G23)
```

```
>Q3:∂IF(A20=1,∂IF(∂OR(∂SUM(E2...G2,E3,G3,E4...G4)=3,∂AND(F3=1,∂SUM(E2...G2,E3,G3
,E4...G4)=2)),1,0),F23)
>P3:∂IF(A20=1,∂IF(∂OR(∂SUM(D2...F2,D3,F3,D4...F4)=3,∂AND(E3=1,∂SUM(D2...F2,D3,F3
,D4...F4)=2)),1,0),E23)
>O3:∂IF(A20=1,∂IF(∂OR(∂SUM(C2...E2,C3,E3,C4...E4)=3,∂AND(D3=1,∂SUM(C2...E2,C3,E3
,C4...E4)=2)),1,0),D23)
>N3:∂IF(A20=1,∂IF(∂OR(∂SUM(B2...D2,B3,D3,B4...D4)=3,∂AND(C3=1,∂SUM(B2...D2,B3,D3
,B4...D4)=2)),1,0),C23)
>M3:∂IF(A20=1,∂IF(∂OR(∂SUM(A2...C2,A3,C3,A4...C4)=3,∂AND(B3=1,∂SUM(A2...C2,A3,C3
,A4...C4)=2)),1,0),B23)
>L3:∂IF(A20=1,∂IF(∂OR(∂SUM(A4,B3...B4)=3,∂AND(A3=1,∂SUM(A4,B3...B4)=2)),1,0),A23
)
>H3:∂IF(A20=1,∂IF(∂OR(∂SUM(R2...S2,R3,R4...S4)=3,∂AND(S3=1,∂SUM(R2...S2,R3,R4...
S4)=2)),1,0),H23)
>G3:∂IF(A20=1,∂IF(∂OR(∂SUM(Q2...S2,Q3,S3,Q4...S4)=3,∂AND(R3=1,∂SUM(Q2...S2,Q3,S3
,Q4...S4)=2)),1,0),G23)
>F3:∂IF(A20=1,∂IF(∂OR(∂SUM(P2...R2,P3,R3,P4...R4)=3,∂AND(Q3=1,∂SUM(P2...R2,P3,R3
,P4...R4)=2)),1,0),F23)
>E3:∂IF(A20=1,∂IF(∂OR(∂SUM(O2...Q2,O3,Q3,O4...Q4)=3,∂AND(P3=1,∂SUM(O2...Q2,O3,Q3
,O4...Q4)=2)),1,0),E23)
>D3:∂IF(A20=1,∂IF(∂OR(∂SUM(N2...P2,N3,P3,N4...P4)=3,∂AND(O3=1,∂SUM(N2...P2,N3,P3
,N4...P4)=2)),1,0),D23)
>C3:∂IF(A20=1,∂IF(∂OR(∂SUM(M2...O2,M3,O3,M4...O4)=3,∂AND(N3=1,∂SUM(M2...O2,M3,O3
,M4...O4)=2)),1,0),C23)
>B3:∂IF(A20=1,∂IF(∂OR(∂SUM(L2...N2,L3,N3,L4...N4)=3,∂AND(M3=1,∂SUM(L2...N2,L3,N3
,L4...N4)=2)),1,0),B23)
>A3:∂IF(A20=1,∂IF(∂OR(∂SUM(L4,M3...M4)=3,∂AND(L3=1,∂SUM(L4,M3...M4)=2)),1,0),A23
)
>S2:∂IF(A20=1,∂IF(∂OR(∂SUM(G1...H1,G2,G3...H3)=3,∂AND(H2=1,∂SUM(G1...H1,G2,G3...
H3)=2)),1,0),H22)
>R2:∂IF(A20=1,∂IF(∂OR(∂SUM(F1...H1,F2,H2,F3...H3)=3,∂AND(G2=1,∂SUM(F1...H1,F2,H2
,F3...H3)=2)),1,0),G22)
>Q2:∂IF(A20=1,∂IF(∂OR(∂SUM(E1...G1,E2,G2,E3...G3)=3,∂AND(F2=1,∂SUM(E1...G1,E2,G2
,E3...G3)=2)),1,0),F22)
>P2:∂IF(A20=1,∂IF(∂OR(∂SUM(D1...F1,D2,F2,D3...F3)=3,∂AND(E2=1,∂SUM(D1...F1,D2,F2
,D3...F3)=2)),1,0),E22)
>O2:∂IF(A20=1,∂IF(∂OR(∂SUM(C1...E1,C2,E2,C3...E3)=3,∂AND(D2=1,∂SUM(C1...E1,C2,E2
,C3...E3)=2)),1,0),D22)
>N2:∂IF(A20=1,∂IF(∂OR(∂SUM(B1...D1,B2,D2,B3...D3)=3,∂AND(C2=1,∂SUM(B1...D1,B2,D2
,B3...D3)=2)),1,0),C22)
>M2:∂IF(A20=1,∂IF(∂OR(∂SUM(A1...C1,A2,C2,A3...C3)=3,∂AND(B2=1,∂SUM(A1...C1,A2,C2
,A3...C3)=2)),1,0),B22)
>L2:∂IF(A20=1,∂IF(∂OR(∂SUM(A3,B2...B3)=3,∂AND(A2=1,∂SUM(A3,B2...B3)=2)),1,0),A22
)
>H2:∂IF(A20=1,∂IF(∂OR(∂SUM(R1...S1,R2,R3...S3)=3,∂AND(S2=1,∂SUM(R1...S1,R2,R3...
S3)=2)),1,0),H22)
>G2:∂IF(A20=1,∂IF(∂OR(∂SUM(Q1...S1,Q2,S2,Q3...S3)=3,∂AND(R2=1,∂SUM(Q1...S1,Q2,S2
,Q3...S3)=2)),1,0),G22)
>F2:∂IF(A20=1,∂IF(∂OR(∂SUM(P1...R1,P2,R2,P3...R3)=3,∂AND(Q2=1,∂SUM(P1...R1,P2,R2
,P3...R3)=2)),1,0),F22)
>E2:∂IF(A20=1,∂IF(∂OR(∂SUM(O1...Q1,O2,Q2,O3...Q3)=3,∂AND(P2=1,∂SUM(O1...Q1,O2,Q2
,O3...Q3)=2)),1,0),E22)
>D2:∂IF(A20=1,∂IF(∂OR(∂SUM(N1...P1,N2,P2,N3...P3)=3,∂AND(O2=1,∂SUM(N1...P1,N2,P2
,N3...P3)=2)),1,0),D22)
>C2:∂IF(A20=1,∂IF(∂OR(∂SUM(M1...O1,M2,O2,M3...O3)=3,∂AND(N2=1,∂SUM(M1...O1,M2,O2
,M3...O3)=2)),1,0),C22)
>B2:∂IF(A20=1,∂IF(∂OR(∂SUM(L1...N1,L2,N2,L3...N3)=3,∂AND(M2=1,∂SUM(L1...N1,L2,N2
,L3...N3)=2)),1,0),B22)
>A2:∂IF(A20=1,∂IF(∂OR(∂SUM(L3,M2...M3)=3,∂AND(L2=1,∂SUM(L3,M2...M3)=2)),1,0),A22
)
>S1:∂IF(A20=1,∂IF(∂OR(∂SUM(G1,G2...H2)=3,∂AND(H1=1,∂SUM(G1,G2...H2)=2)),1,0),H21
)
>R1:∂IF(A20=1,∂IF(∂OR(∂SUM(F1,H1,F2...H2)=3,∂AND(G1=1,∂SUM(F1,H1,F2...H2)=2)),1,
0),G21)
>Q1:∂IF(A20=1,∂IF(∂OR(∂SUM(E1,G1,E2...G2)=3,∂AND(F1=1,∂SUM(E1,G1,E2...G2)=2)),1,
0),F21)
>P1:∂IF(A20=1,∂IF(∂OR(∂SUM(D1,F1,D2...F2)=3,∂AND(E1=1,∂SUM(D1,F1,D2...F2)=2)),1,
0),E21)
```

```
>O1:@IF(A20=1,@IF(@OR(@SUM(C1,E1,C2...E2)=3,@AND(D1=1,@SUM(C1,E1,C2...E2)=2)),1,
0),D21)
>N1:@IF(A20=1,@IF(@OR(@SUM(B1,D1,B2...D2)=3,@AND(C1=1,@SUM(B1,D1,B2...D2)=2)),1,
0),C21)
>M1:@IF(A20=1,@IF(@OR(@SUM(A1,C1,A2...C2)=3,@AND(B1=1,@SUM(A1,C1,A2...C2)=2)),1,
0),B21)
>L1:@IF(A20=1,@IF(@OR(@SUM(A2,B1...B2)=3,@AND(A1=1,@SUM(A2,B1...B2)=2)),1,0),A21
)
>H1:@IF(A20=1,@IF(@OR(@SUM(R1,R2...S2)=3,@AND(S1=1,@SUM(R1,R2...S2)=2)),1,0),H21
)
>G1:@IF(A20=1,@IF(@OR(@SUM(Q1,S1,Q2...S2)=3,@AND(R1=1,@SUM(Q1,S1,Q2...S2)=2)),1,
0),G21)
>F1:@IF(A20=1,@IF(@OR(@SUM(P1,R1,P2...R2)=3,@AND(Q1=1,@SUM(P1,R1,P2...R2)=2)),1,
0),F21)
>E1:@IF(A20=1,@IF(@OR(@SUM(O1,Q1,O2...Q2)=3,@AND(P1=1,@SUM(O1,Q1,O2...Q2)=2)),1,
0),E21)
>D1:@IF(A20=1,@IF(@OR(@SUM(N1,P1,N2...P2)=3,@AND(O1=1,@SUM(N1,P1,N2...P2)=2)),1,
0),D21)
>C1:@IF(A20=1,@IF(@OR(@SUM(M1,O1,M2...O2)=3,@AND(N1=1,@SUM(M1,O1,M2...O2)=2)),1,
0),C21)
>B1:@IF(A20=1,@IF(@OR(@SUM(L1,N1,L2...N2)=3,@AND(M1=1,@SUM(L1,N1,L2...N2)=2)),1,
0),B21)
>A1:@IF(A20=1,@IF(@OR(@SUM(L2,M1...M2)=3,@AND(L1=1,@SUM(L2,M1...M2)=2)),1,0),A21
)
/W1
/GOC
/GRA
/XH10
/GC3
/X>A1:>E2:;/GC3
/X>A20:>A20:;
```

Figure 1.5(d). Formulas for the game of LIFE

Chapter 2
Business Applications

In this chapter we get down to the serious business of using the techniques displayed in the previous chapter in designing business application worksheets. After all, it was business needs that prompted its inventors to create the VisiCalc program. A balance sheet, general ledger, and numerous journals all closely resemble VisiCalc worksheets.

We will use real estate property management as our example of a small business enterprise. However, the worksheets are equally applicable to other small businesses, so do not be put off by the seleciton of a real estate example.

The first worksheet illustrates one of the most obvious and common applications of computers to business. DEPREC is a depreciation schedule for use in computing the amount of depreciation on assets. This is a handy worksheet for anyone who wants to save on income taxes.

PAYROLL is an individual employee payroll worksheet that helps you keep track of your paychecks. It computes time and overtime payments (and totals) for a 13-week quarter. Again, this is helpful to know when you must supply the IRS with those bothersome quarterly tax returns for your employees.

TENANTS and RENTS are used to record and manage income from rentals such as an apartment house. TENANTS keeps tabs on the monthly rent and deposits made by individual tenants. RENTS helps you keep track of a full year's worth of income from the entire complex. You will need this information in order to complete your income tax return.

QSTATE and YSTATE could be any quarterly and yearly statements, but in this collection we apply them to the property management business. Total income, expenses, and deductions are reported here. The bottom line from the YSTATE worksheet will tell you how much money you made.

The balance sheet in BALANCE takes current assets, fixed assets, and liabilities into account when coming up with your total net worth. This can be used to apply for a loan for a new house, or to convince your partners that you can afford to fund the oil well out west.

The worksheet in AR uses some of the tricks developed in the previous chapter to build a nifty accounts receivable system. This will allow you to trigger an initial set of inputs, then enter a set of payments, and finally, update the balance to a new outstanding balance. The AR worksheet should be studied closely because it shows how to use the VisiCalc program most cleverly.

BUILDER and SIDING are two business worksheets that can be used in cost estimating. A home-building cost worksheet is given in BUILDER and a home siding estimator worksheet is given in SIDING. SIDING is an extra or "bonus" worksheet, because it brings the total number of worksheets up to 33, instead of 32.

2.1. DEPREC: Depreciation Schedule

The Federal government tries to encourage businesses to buy equipment, buildings, etc., in order to stimulate the economy. At the same time the government wants businesses to maintain modern equipment and factories, so it gives incentives to do this in the form of tax credits. One of the best tax incentives comes from depreciation of equipment, or what the IRS calls "depreciable assets."

Purpose

A computer is a depreciable asset when used by a business. Thus, if you are trying to decide whether to buy a computer or simply buy computer time from some other business, you will be interested in the advantage of ownership. If you buy a computer, then you can deduct the amount of yearly depreciation from your taxes. The purpose of this worksheet, then, is to show you how much can be deducted from your taxes by depreciating a computer.

Certain high-technology purchases, like computers, qualify for accelerated depreciation. This means you can depreciate a greater portion of the purchase price in early years than in later years. For example, because of obsolescence computers are thought to depreciate faster than, say, furniture. Therefore, a 200% yearly rate of depreciation might be in order for sophisticated computer equipment.

Figure 2.1(a) shows the results of a 200%, or double-declining rate of depreciation for a computer that initially costs $10,000.

	A	B	C	D	E	F
1		DEPRECIATION TABLE				
2						
3	Description	:	Computer			
4	Original Cost	$	10000.00	Dollars		
5	Salvage Value	$	2000.00	Dollars		
6	Length of Term	:	7	Years		
7	Rate of Deprciation		200.00	Per cent		
8						
9						
10		Schedule of Remaining Value				
11						
12	Year	Current	Amount of	Value		
13		Value	Depreciation	Remaining		
14						
15	1	10000.00	2857.14	7142.86		
16	2	7142.86	2040.82	5102.04		
17	3	5102.04	1457.73	3644.31		
18	4	3644.31	1041.23	2603.08		
19	5	2603.08	603.08	2000.00		
20	6	2000.00	0.00	2000.00		
21	7	2000.00	0.00	2000.00		

```
/===============================================================\
|                   DEPRECIATION   TABLE                        |
| ============================================================= |
| Description       :          Computer                         |
| Original    Cost  $          10000.00        Dollars          |
| Salvage Value     $           2000.00        Dollars          |
| Length of    Term :                 7        Years            |
| Rate of Deprciation          200.00          Per cent         |
|                                                               |
| -------------------------------------------------------------- |
|                                                               |
|            Schedule of Remaining Value                        |
| -------------------------------------------------------------- |
|                                                               |
| Year           Current      Amount of          Value          |
|                Value        Depreciation     Remaining        |
| ............................................................. |
|           1    10000.00       2857.14         7142.86         |
|           2     7142.86       2040.82         5102.04         |
|           3     5102.04       1457.73         3644.31         |
|           4     3644.31       1041.23         2603.08         |
|           5     2603.08        603.08         2000.00         |
|           6     2000.00          0.00         2000.00         |
|           7     2000.00          0.00         2000.00         |
| -------------------------------------------------------------- |
| Average Amount of Depreciation       $        1142.86         |
|                                                               |
\===============================================================/
```

Figure 2.1(a). Depreciation table worksheet

Worksheet   The worksheet in Figure 2.1(a) is used by entering the name (computer), cost ($10000), salvage value ($2000), length of time to depreciate (7 years), and the rate of depreciation (200%) into the top portion of the worksheet.

The original cost is how much you paid for the equipment (or fair market value if it was a trade). The salvage value is the estimated value at the end of the depreciation period. Thus, in Figure 2.1(a), we have guessed that the computer will be worth $2,000 at the end of 7 years. The rate of depreciation is also entered. Here it is assumed that the computer will qualify for double-declining depreciation. If so, then the remaining value at the end of each year will be depreciated at twice the rate of "straight-line" depreciation.

After the inputs are properly made, look at the table below which gives the schedule. The amount of depreciation is what you can claim as a deduction on your income tax return. The value remaining column tells how much value remains to be depreciated in subsequent years. Notice that this value never goes below the salvage value.

Finally, the average amount of depreciation is computed and shown at the bottom of the schedule. This is just for your information and might be used to estimate the savings made possible by purchasing a computer rather than renting time from a computer service company.

Comments   The depreciation schedule worksheet can be used for most depreciation schedules that depend on the rate of depreciation. For example, straight-line depreciation is obtained by setting the rate to 100%. Other rates of 150% or 125% might be used also.

Figure 2.1(b) shows what formulas to use to reconstruct the worksheet in **Formulas**
Figure 2.1(a). These formulas were entered by constructing a model formula for
computing the first year's depreciation first. Then the model first-year formula
was /REPLICATEd into the remaining cells in the same column. The RELATIVE
option was used in every cell name except C5, C6, and C7.

The @IF function is used in these formulas to check the remaining value to see
if it is greater than the salvage value. Remember, the remaining value must be as
large, or larger than the salvage value.

The amount of depreciation is equal to the amount that would be deducted by a
straight-line calculation times the rate of depreciation. The straight-line calculation is obtained by taking the difference between the current value and the
salvage value, divided by the number of years, C6. For example, in cell C16, this
is obtained by the following:

$$+C7*B16/(100*C6)$$
$$200*B16/(100*7)$$

But if the current value drops below the salvage value, the amount of depreciation in cell C16, for example, is zero.

$$-C5+B16$$
$$-2000+2000$$

```
>D24:/-_
>C24:/-_
>B24:/-_
>A24:/-_
>D23:@AVERAGE(C15...C21)
>C23:"iation    $
>B23:"nt of Depreciation
>A23:"Average Amount
>D22:/--
>C22:/--
>B22:/--
>A22:/--
>D21:@IF((-C21+B21)>C5,-C21+B21,C5)
>C21:@IF((+B21-(C7*B21/(100*C6))>C5),+C7*B21/(100*C6),-C5+B21)
>B21:+D20
>A21:/FI7
>D20:@IF((-C20+B20)>C5,-C20+B20,C5)
>C20:@IF((+B20-(C7*B20/(100*C6))>C5),+C7*B20/(100*C6),-C5+B20)
>B20:+D19
>A20:/FI6
>D19:@IF((-C19+B19)>C5,-C19+B19,C5)
>C19:@IF((+B19-(C7*B19/(100*C6))>C5),+C7*B19/(100*C6),-C5+B19)
>B19:+D18
>A19:/FI5
>D18:@IF((-C18+B18)>C5,-C18+B18,C5)
>C18:@IF((+B18-(C7*B18/(100*C6))>C5),+C7*B18/(100*C6),-C5+B18)
>B18:+D17
>A18:/FI4
>D17:@IF((-C17+B17)>C5,-C17+B17,C5)
>C17:@IF((+B17-(C7*B17/(100*C6))>C5),+C7*B17/(100*C6),-C5+B17)
>B17:+D16
```

```
>A17:/FI3
>D16:@IF((-C16+B16)>C5,-C16+B16,C5)
>C16:@IF((+B16-(C7*B16/(100*C6)))>C5),+C7*B16/(100*C6),-C5+B16)
>B16:+D15
>A16:/FI2
>D15:@IF((-C15+B15)>C5,-C15+B15,C5)
>C15:@IF((+B15-(C7*B15/(100*C6)))>C5),+C7*B15/(100*C6),-C5+B15)
>B15:+C4
>A15:/FI1
>D14:/-.
>C14:/-.
>B14:/-.
>A14:/-.
>D13:/FR"Remaining
>C13:"Depreciation
>B13:"Value
>D12:/FR"Value
>C12:"Amount of
>B12:"Current
>A12:" Year
>D11:/--
>C11:/--
>B11:/--
>A11:/--
>D10:"lue
>C10:"Remaining Va
>B10:"Schedule of
>D8:/-_
>C8:/-_
>B8:/-_
>A8:/-_
>D7:/FR"Per cent
>C7:200
>B7:"ciation
>A7:"Rate of Depre
>D6:/FR"Years
>C6:/FI7
>B6:" Term :
>A6:"Length of
>D5:/FR"Dollars
>C5:/F$2000
>B5:"e        $
>A5:"Salvage Value
>D4:/FR"Dollars
>C4:/F$10000
>B4:"Cost   $
>A4:"Original
>C3:/FR"Computer
>B3:"         :
>A3:"Description
>D2:/-=
>C2:/-=
>B2:/-=
>A2:/-=
```

```
>C1:"   TABLE
>B1:"DEPRECIATION
/W1
/GOR
/GRA
/GF$
/GC12
/X>A1:>A1:
```

Figure 2.1(b). Formulas for depreciation table worksheet

2.2. PAYROLL: Employee Payroll

Purpose   Every business must pay its employees, and as a result it must report these payments to the tax man. This places a burden on the small business, because a record of payment must be kept for the quarterly reporting period. The purpose of this worksheet is to help you keep this information in an orderly and timely fashion.

Figure 2.2(a) shows a worksheet for a single employee. It contains the amount paid to this employee for each of 13 weeks during the quarter. This information is needed to compute the amount of taxes, retirement, insurance, etc., paid by you on behalf of the employee.

Worksheet   This worksheet is so simple to use it hardly needs explanation. The hours worked (both regular and overtime) are entered for each week in the quarter. The hourly rate of pay is also adjustable, as shown in the example of Figure 2.2(a). The formulas in this worksheet compute the total earnings per week as well as the total paid for the quarter.

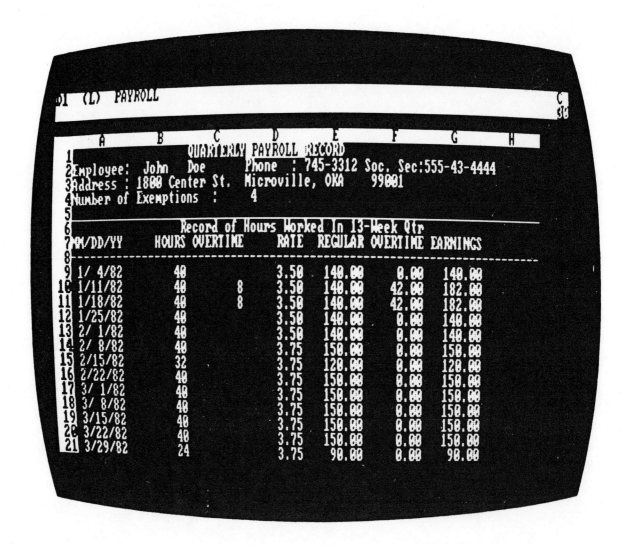

```
                    QUARTERLY  PAYROLL  RECORD
 Employee:  John    Doe         Phone  : 745-3312  Soc. Sec:555-43-4444
 Address : 1800 Center St.  Microville, OKA      99001
 Number of Exemptions  :     4

 -------------------------------------------------------------------------
                 Record of Hours Worked In 13-Week Qtr
 MM/DD/YY    HOURS OVERTIME        RATE   REGULAR OVERTIME EARNINGS
 -------------------------------------------------------------------------
   1/ 4/82     40                  3.50    140.00    0.00    140.00
   1/11/82     40       8          3.50    140.00   42.00    182.00
   1/18/82     40       8          3.50    140.00   42.00    182.00
   1/25/82     40                  3.50    140.00    0.00    140.00
   2/ 1/82     40                  3.50    140.00    0.00    140.00
   2/ 8/82     40                  3.75    150.00    0.00    150.00
   2/15/82     32                  3.75    120.00    0.00    120.00
   2/22/82     40                  3.75    150.00    0.00    150.00
   3/ 1/82     40                  3.75    150.00    0.00    150.00
   3/ 8/82     40                  3.75    150.00    0.00    150.00
   3/15/82     40                  3.75    150.00    0.00    150.00
   3/22/82     40                  3.75    150.00    0.00    150.00
   3/29/82     24                  3.75     90.00    0.00     90.00
 -------------------------------------------------------------------------
 Qtr Total    496      16         47.50   1810.00   84.00   1894.00

 -------------------------------------------------------------------------
```

Figure 2.2(a). Quarterly payroll worksheet

This example shows you how to build a very simple payroll worksheet. But a better worksheet could be constructed by including such things as FICA, savings deductions, tax withholding, insurance, etc. These additions to the basic table could be appended to the right of the columns shown in Figure 2.2(a). In addition, you will want to add the tax rate percentages, and other parameters to the heading of the table.

Keep in mind that the totals obtained from this worksheet can be combined with other worksheets (discussed later) in order to make a complete system of business worksheets.

Comments

Figure 2.2(b) contains the formulas necessary to reconstruct the worksheet shown in Figure 2.2(a). The @SUM functions in cells B45 to G45 compute the totals that you can see at the bottom of the worksheet. The other @SUM functions compute the total amount paid each week.

You should be careful when entering the dates in column A of the worksheet. These dates begin with a number, so VisiCalc will think that the entry is a number instead of a label unless you prefix the entry with a quotation mark.

Formulas

```
 >H46:/--_                      >C46:/--_
 >G46:/--_                      >B46:/--_
 >F46:/--_                      >A46:/--_
 >E46:/--_                      >G45:/F$@SUM(G31...G43)
 >D46:/--_                      >F45:/F$@SUM(F31...F43)
```

>E45: /F$@SUM(E31...E43)
>D45: /F$@SUM(D31...D43)
>C45: /F$@SUM(C31...C43)
>B45: /F$@SUM(B31...B43)
>A45: "TOTALS $
>H44: /--
>G44: /--
>F44: /--
>E44: /--
>D44: /--
>C44: /--
>B44: /--
>A44: /--
>H43: 1930
>G43: /F$-F43+G21
>F43: /F$@SUM(B43...E43)
>E43: /F$50
>D43: /F$24
>C43: /F$+C29*G21/100
>B43: /F$+B29*G21/100
>A43: " 3/29/82
>H42: 1790
>G42: /F$-F42+G20
>F42: /F$@SUM(B42...E42)
>E42: /F$50
>D42: /F$24
>C42: /F$+C29*G20/100
>B42: /F$+B29*G20/100
>A42: " 3/22/82
>H41: 1789
>G41: /F$-F41+G19
>F41: /F$@SUM(B41...E41)
>E41: /F$50
>D41: /F$24
>C41: /F$+C29*G19/100
>B41: /F$+B29*G19/100
>A41: " 3/15/82
>H40: 1675
>G40: /F$-F40+G18
>F40: /F$@SUM(B40...E40)
>E40: /F$50
>D40: /F$24
>C40: /F$+C29*G18/100
>B40: /F$+B29*G18/100
>A40: " 3/ 8/82
>H39: 1650
>G39: /F$-F39+G17
>F39: /F$@SUM(B39...E39)
>E39: /F$50
>D39: /F$24
>C39: /F$+C29*G17/100
>B39: /F$+B29*G17/100
>A39: " 3/ 1/82
>H38: 1587
>G38: /F$-F38+G16
>F38: /F$@SUM(B38...E38)

>E38: /F$50
>D38: /F$24
>C38: /F$+C29*G16/100
>B38: /F$+B29*G16/100
>A38: " 2/22/82
>H37: 1499
>G37: /F$-F37+G15
>F37: /F$@SUM(B37...E37)
>E37: /F$50
>D37: /F$24
>C37: /F$+C29*G15/100
>B37: /F$+B29*G15/100
>A37: " 2/15/82
>H36: 1465
>G36: /F$-F36+G14
>F36: /F$@SUM(B36...E36)
>E36: /F$50
>D36: /F$24
>C36: /F$+C29*G14/100
>B36: /F$+B29*G14/100
>A36: " 2/ 8/82
>H35: 1234
>G35: /F$-F35+G13
>F35: /F$@SUM(B35...E35)
>E35: /F$50
>D35: /F$24
>C35: /F$+C29*G13/100
>B35: /F$+B29*G13/100
>A35: " 2/ 1/82
>H34: 1030
>G34: /F$-F34+G12
>F34: /F$@SUM(B34...E34)
>E34: /F$50
>D34: /F$24
>C34: /F$+C29*G12/100
>B34: /F$+B29*G12/100
>A34: " 1/25/82
>H33: 985
>G33: /F$-F33+G11
>F33: /F$@SUM(B33...E33)
>E33: /F$50
>D33: /F$24
>C33: /F$+C29*G11/100
>B33: /F$+B29*G11/100
>A33: " 1/18/82
>H32: 501
>G32: /F$-F32+G10
>F32: /F$@SUM(B32...E32)
>E32: /F$50
>D32: /F$24
>C32: /F$+C29*G10/100
>B32: /F$+B29*G10/100
>A32: " 1/11/82
>H31: 311
>G31: /F$-F31+G9
>F31: /F$@SUM(B31...E31)

```
>E31:/F$50                    >H22:/--
>D31:/F$24                    >G22:/--
>C31:/F$+C29*G9/100           >F22:/--
>B31:/F$+B29*G9/100           >E22:/--
>A31:"  1/ 4/82               >D22:/--
>H30:/--                      >C22:/--
>G30:/--                      >B22:/--
>F30:/--                      >A22:/--
>E30:/--                      >G21:/F$+E21+F21
>D30:/--                      >F21:/F$+C21*D21*1.5
>C30:/--                      >E21:/F$+B21*D21
>B30:/--                      >D21:/F$3.75
>A30:/--                      >B21:24
>H29:"Number                  >A21:"  3/29/82
>G29:"Paid                    >G20:/F$+E20+F20
>F29:"Deducted                >F20:/F$+C20*D20*1.5
>E29:"Bonds                   >E20:/F$+B20*D20
>D29:" Insure                 >D20:/F$3.75
>C29:/FG7.85                  >B20:40
>B29:/F$3.5                   >A20:"  3/22/82
>A29:"MM/DD/YY                >G19:/F$+E19+F19
>H28:"Check                   >F19:/F$+C19*D19*1.5
>G28:"Net Amt                 >E19:/F$+B19*D19
>F28:"Total                   >D19:/F$3.75
>E28:"Savings                 >B19:40
>D28:" Medical                >A19:"  3/15/82
>C28:/FR" FICA                >G18:/F$+E18+F18
>B28:"State Ins               >F18:/F$+C18*D18*1.5
>H27:/--                      >E18:/F$+B18*D18
>G27:/--                      >D18:/F$3.75
>F27:/--                      >B18:40
>E27:/--                      >A18:"  3/ 8/82
>D27:/--                      >G17:/F$+E17+F17
>C27:/--                      >F17:/F$+C17*D17*1.5
>B27:/--                      >E17:/F$+B17*D17
>A27:/--                      >D17:/F$3.75
>F26:"eek Qtr                 >B17:40
>E26:"s In 13-W               >A17:"  3/ 1/82
>D26:"Deductions              >G16:/F$+E16+F16
>C26:"ecord of                >F16:/F$+C16*D16*1.5
>B26:/FR"R                    >E16:/F$+B16*D16
>H24:/-_                      >D16:/F$3.75
>G24:/-_                      >B16:40
>F24:/-_                      >A16:"  2/22/82
>E24:/-_                      >G15:/F$+E15+F15
>D24:/-_                      >F15:/F$+C15*D15*1.5
>C24:/-_                      >E15:/F$+B15*D15
>B24:/-_                      >D15:/F$3.75
>A24:/-_                      >B15:32
>G23:/F$@SUM(G9...G21)        >A15:"  2/15/82
>F23:/F$@SUM(F9...F21)        >G14:/F$+E14+F14
>E23:/F$@SUM(E9...E21)        >F14:/F$+C14*D14*1.5
>D23:/F$@SUM(D9...D21)        >E14:/F$+B14*D14
>C23:@SUM(C9...C21)           >D14:/F$3.75
>B23:@SUM(B9...B21)           >B14:40
>A23:"Qtr Total               >A14:"  2/ 8/82
```

```
>G13:/F$+E13+F13              >C7:/FR"OVERTIME
>F13:/F$+C13*D13*1.5          >B7:/FR"HOURS
>E13:/F$+B13*D13              >A7:"MM/DD/YY !
>D13:/F$3.5                   >F6:"-Week Qtr
>B13:40                       >E6:"ked In 13-Week
>A13:"  2/ 1/82               >D6:"Hours Worked
>G12:/F$+E12+F12              >C6:"ecord of
>F12:/F$+C12*D12*1.5          >B6:/FR"R
>E12:/F$+B12*D12              >H5:/-_
>D12:/F$3.5                   >G5:/-_
>B12:40                       >F5:/-_
>A12:"  1/25/82               >E5:/-_
>G11:/F$+E11+F11              >D5:/-_
>F11:/F$+C11*D11*1.5          >C5:/-_
>E11:/F$+B11*D11              >B5:/-_
>D11:/F$3.5                   >A5:/-_
>C11:8                        >D4:/FL4
>B11:40                       >C4:"ns  :
>A11:"  1/18/82               >B4:" Exemptio
>G10:/F$+E10+F10              >A4:"Number of
>F10:/F$+C10*D10*1.5          >F3:" 99001
>E10:/F$+B10*D10              >E3:"e, OKA
>D10:/F$3.5                   >D3:"Microville
>C10:8                        >C3:"ter St.
>B10:40                       >B3:" 1800 Cent
>A10:"  1/11/82               >A3:"Address :
>G9:/F$+E9+F9                 >H2:"44
>F9:/F$+C9*D9*1.5             >G2:"555-43-44
>E9:/F$+B9*D9                 >F2:"Soc. Sec:
>D9:/F$3.5                    >E2:"745-3312
>B9:40                        >D2:"Phone  :
>A9:"  1/ 4/82                >C2:/FL"Doe
>H8:/--                       >B2:"   John
>G8:/--                       >A2:"Employee:
>F8:/--                       >E1:"RECORD
>E8:/--                       >D1:" PAYROLL
>D8:/--                       >C1:"QUARTERLY
>C8:/--                       /W1
>B8:/--                       /GOC
>A8:/--                       /GRA
>G7:/FR"EARNINGS              /GFI
>F7:/FR"OVERTIME              /GC9
>E7:/FR"REGULAR               /X>A1:>A1:
>D7:/FR"RATE
```

Figure 2.2(b). Formulas for quarterly payroll worksheet

2.3. TENANTS: Tenant's Record For Rentals

Suppose you are an owner or manager of an apartment complex. The tenants in this apartment probably pay different rents, different deposits, and each has a different due date for his rent. So you need a record keeping system that keeps track of all the tenants and their status. The purpose of this worksheet is to help you manage your tenants.

Purpose

Figure 2.3(a) shows what the tenant record worksheet might look like for a 7-unit apartment house. Of course, the idea is the same for a 100-unit apartment, only the worksheet would be longer.

Worksheet

Names and telephone numbers are entered as labels into the first two columns (use " to enter labels). The amount of rent is entered next as a /F$ formatted number. The due date is also entered as a label and right-justified using the /FR format.

If you require first and last month's rent, then this amount is entered as an "advance" payment of the last month's rent. The amount of the cleaning deposit is also kept in the last column of the table.

	A	B	C	D	E	F	G	H
1				TENANT	RECORD			
2								
3	Rental Unit Name	:Greenacre	Plaza			Managers Name :	Smythe	
4	Rental Address	:2251 Whitefence Dr				Phone #	722-3329	
5								
6	Unit # :	Name of Tenant	:Phone #	:$ Rent :	Due	:$ Advance	:$ Deposit	
7								
8	1	Robert Strong	735-8392	350.00	10-th	350.00	175.00	
9	2	Unoccupied						
10	3	Carrie Scott	821-5501	325.00	1-st	0.00	300.00	
11	11	Mr & Mrs Jones	none	475.00	15-th	400.00	400.00	
12	12	Larry Smythe	754-3274	375.00	5-th	300.00	150.00	
13	13	Harold Lawson	735-1856	195.00	1-st	150.00	250.00	
14	20	Jan & Tom Rosen	735-4983	250.00	10-th	250.00	100.00	
15								
16			Totals $	1970.00		1450.00	1375.00	

```
                         TENANT    RECORD
==========================================================================
Rental Unit Name :Greenacre    Plaza        Managers Name :    Smythe
Rental Address    :2251 Whitefence Dr        Phone #         722-3329

--------------------------------------------------------------------------
 Unit # |   Name of Tenant |Phone # |$ Rent  |   Due   |$ Advance|$Deposit
--------------------------------------------------------------------------
         1   Robert Strong  735-8392  350.00   10-th    350.00    175.00
         2   Unoccupied
         3   Carrie Scott   821-5501  325.00   1-st       0.00    300.00
        11 Mr & Mrs  Jones    none    475.00   15-th    400.00    400.00
        12    Larry Smythe   754-3274  375.00   5-th     300.00    150.00
        13    Harold Lawson  735-1856  195.00   1-st     150.00    250.00
        20Jan & Tom Rosen    735-4983  250.00   10-th    250.00    100.00
--------------------------------------------------------------------------
                          Totals $   1970.00            1450.00   1375.00
```

Figure 2.3(a). Tenant record worksheet

Comments   You will probably want to use this worksheet in conjunction with the other worksheets discussed here. In particular, the next worksheet is used to record the actual rent that is collected for each month of the year.

Formulas   Figure 2.3(b) contains the necessary information to reconstruct the worksheet of Figure 2.3(a). There is nothing unusual or tricky about this worksheet, but notice the @SUMs in cells E16 through H16. These compute the totals displayed at the bottom of the worksheet.

The other entries are formatted to either properly align the labels that they contain or else display numerical values as "dollar and cents."

```
>H16:/F$@SUM(H8...H14)        >E13:/F$195
>G16:/F$@SUM(G8...G14)        >D13:"735-1856
>E16:/F$@SUM(E8...E14)        >C13:" Lawson
>D16:"Totals $               >B13:/FR"Harold
>H15:/--                      >A13:13
>G15:/--                      >H12:/F$150
>F15:/--                      >G12:/F$300
>E15:/--                      >F12:/FR"5-th
>D15:/--                      >E12:/F$375
>C15:/--                      >D12:"754-3274
>B15:/--                      >C12:" Smythe
>A15:/--                      >B12:/FR"Larry
>H14:/F$100                   >A12:12
>G14:/F$250                   >H11:/F$400
>F14:/FR"10-th                >G11:/F$400
>E14:/F$250                   >F11:/FR"15-th
>D14:"735-4983                >E11:/F$475
>C14:" Rosen                  >D11:"    none
>B14:"Jan & Tom               >C11:/FR"Jones
>A14:20                       >B11:/FR"Mr & Mrs
>H13:/F$250                   >A11:11
>G13:/F$150                   >H10:/F$300
>F13:/FR"1-st                 >G10:/F$0
```

```
>F10:/FR"1-st                    >F5:"_____
>E10:/F$325                      >E5:"_____
>D10:"821-5501                   >D5:"_____
>C10:" Scott                     >C5:"_____
>B10:/FR"Carrie                  >B5:"_____
>A10:3                           >A5:"_____
>C9:"pied                        >H4:/FL"3329
>B9:/FR"Unoccu                   >G4:/FR" 722-
>A9:2                            >F4:"Phone #
>H8:/F$175                       >D4:"efence Dr.
>G8:/F$350                       >C4:"2251 Whitefen
>F8:/FR"10-th                    >B4:"dress    :
>E8:/F$350                       >A4:"Rental Add
>D8:"735-8392                    >H3:"Smythe
>C8:" Strong                     >G3:"Name :
>B8:/FR"Robert                   >F3:"Managers
>A8:1                            >D3:/FR"Plaza
>H7:/--                          >C3:"Greenacres
>G7:/--                          >B3:"it Name :
>F7:/--                          >A3:"Rental Unit
>E7:/--                          >H2:/-=
>D7:/--                          >G2:/-=
>C7:/--                          >F2:/-=
>B7:/--                          >E2:/-=
>A7:/--                          >D2:/-=
>H6:"!$Deposit                   >C2:/-=
>G6:"$ Advance!                  >B2:/-=
>F6:/FR"Due   !                  >A2:/-=
>E6:/FR"$ Rent   !               >E1:"RECORD
>D6:/FR"Phone # !                >D1:"TENANT
>C6:" Tenant !                   /W1
>B6:/FR"Name of                  /GOC
>A6:/FR"Unit # !                 /GRA
>H5:"_____                   /GC9
>G5:"_____                   /X>A1:>A1:
```

Figure 2.3(b). Formulas for tenant record worksheet

2.4. RENTS: Monthly Rental Income Record

Purpose   Now that you have a record of the rents and when they are due, you need to tally them for each month. Also, the monthly rents should be summed for the entire year so you will be able to figure out the income totals for the year on each apartment house.

The purpose of the worksheet in Figure 2.4(a) is to record and total the rental income for a single complex. This worksheet contains the same number of units as the previous one, plus it keeps track of the amount actually received from each renter.

Worksheet   The worksheet in Figure 2.4(a) is used by entering the date in the row labeled "period 19." The rental name and address is also entered for a certain property. Then the amount of rent actually collected each month of the year is entered for each unit. Notice, for example, that unit #2 was vacant for most of the year. Also notice the change in rents throughout the year.

The sample worksheet in Figure 2.4(a) shows the amount collected for only 8 months. The final months have not been collected, yet. However, the unit totals and grand totals are always calculated, as shown in the bottom row of the worksheet.

```
24  (/-)

        A        B       C        D        E        F        G        H
3 Period 19 80      To  :81 Rental Name  :   Greenacre    Plaza
4                          Rental Address :   2251 Whitfence Rd.
5
6 Month    :              Unit No.                                Month
7 Rented   :       1       2      11       12       13      20:   Totals
8 ----------------------------------------------------------------------
10 FEBRUARY:  300.00  275.00  450.00   325.00   150.00  210.00  1710.00
11 MARCH   :  325.00          467.50   350.00   175.00  230.00  1547.50
12 APRIL   :  325.00          467.50   350.00   175.00  230.00  1547.50
13 MAY     :  325.00          467.50   350.00   175.00  230.00  1547.50
14 JUNE    :  325.00          467.50   350.00   175.00  230.00  1547.50
15 JULY    :  350.00          475.00   375.00   195.00  250.00  1645.00
16 AUGUST  :  350.00          475.00   375.00   195.00  250.00  1645.00
17 SEPTEMBER:                                                       0.00
18 OCTOBER :                                                        0.00
19 NOVEMBER:                                                        0.00
20 DECEMBER:                                                        0.00
21 ----------------------------------------------------------------------
22 Unit    :                                Cross Check Total= 12900.00
23 Totals  : 2600.00  550.00 3720.00  2800.00  1390.00 1840.00 12900.00
24
```

```
        Monthly  Rental   Record
===========================================================================
Period 19 80      To   :81 Rental  Name  :    Greenacre    Plaza
                          Rental  Address :  2251 Whitfence Rd.

--------------------------------------------------------------------------
Month   :                  Unit No.                        :    Month
Rented  :      1       2       11      12      13      20:   Totals
--------------------------------------------------------------------------

JANUARY :   300.00  275.00  450.00  325.00  150.00  210.00  1710.00
FEBRUARY:   300.00  275.00  450.00  325.00  150.00  210.00  1710.00
MARCH   :   325.00          467.50  350.00  175.00  230.00  1547.50
APRIL   :   325.00          467.50  350.00  175.00  230.00  1547.50
MAY     :   325.00          467.50  350.00  175.00  230.00  1547.50
JUNE    :   325.00          467.50  350.00  175.00  230.00  1547.50
JULY    :   350.00          475.00  375.00  195.00  250.00  1645.00
AUGUST  :   350.00          475.00  375.00  195.00  250.00  1645.00
SEPTEMBER                                                      0.00
OCTOBER :                                                      0.00
NOVEMBER:                                                      0.00
DECEMBER:                                                      0.00
--------------------------------------------------------------------------
Unit    :                                 Cross Check Total= 12900.00
Totals  :  2600.00  550.00 3720.00 2800.00 1390.00 1840.00 12900.00
--------------------------------------------------------------------------
```

Figure 2.4(a). Monthly rental record worksheet

This worksheet contains the grand total income derived from the property. **Comments**
Therefore, it also contains information needed in other forms, like the income
statements discussed next.

Figure 2.4(b) shows what you need to reconstruct the worksheet. The cross **Formulas**
check total in cell H22 must match with the total in cell H23. This is a check on
the calculations just to make sure nothing has been left out by accident.

```
>H24:/FR/-_                          >A22:"Unit       :
>G24:/-_                             >H21:/--
>F24:/-_                             >G21:/--
>E24:/-_                             >F21:/--
>D24:/-_                             >E21:/--
>C24:/-_                             >D21:/--
>B24:/-_                             >C21:/--
>A24:/-_                             >B21:/--
>H23:/F$@SUM(B23...G23)              >A21:/--
>G23:/F$@SUM(G9...G20)               >H20:/F$@SUM(B20...G20)
>F23:/F$@SUM(F9...F20)               >G20:/F$
>E23:/F$@SUM(E9...E20)               >F20:/F$
>D23:/F$@SUM(D9...D20)               >E20:/F$
>C23:/F$@SUM(C9...C20)               >D20:/F$
>B23:/F$@SUM(B9...B20)               >C20:/F$
>A23:"Totals  :                      >B20:/F$
>H22:/F$@SUM(H9...H20)               >A20:"DECEMBER:
>G22:"ck Total=                      >H19:/F$@SUM(B19...G19)
>F22:"Cross Che                      >G19:/F$
```

```
>F19:/F$
>E19:/F$
>D19:/F$
>C19:/F$
>B19:/F$
>A19:"NOVEMBER!
>H18:/F$@SUM(B18...G18)
>G18:/F$
>F18:/F$
>E18:/F$
>D18:/F$
>C18:/F$
>B18:/F$
>A18:"OCTOBER !
>H17:/F$@SUM(B17...G17)
>G17:/F$
>F17:/F$
>E17:/F$
>D17:/F$
>C17:/F$
>B17:/F$
>A17:"SEPTEMBER
>H16:/F$@SUM(B16...G16)
>G16:/F$250
>F16:/F$195
>E16:/F$375
>D16:/F$475
>C16:/F$
>B16:/F$350
>A16:"AUGUST   !
>H15:/F$@SUM(B15...G15)
>G15:/F$250
>F15:/F$195
>E15:/F$375
>D15:/F$475
>C15:/F$
>B15:/F$350
>A15:"JULY     !
>H14:/F$@SUM(B14...G14)
>G14:/F$230
>F14:/F$175
>E14:/F$350
>D14:/F$467.5
>C14:/F$
>B14:/F$325
>A14:"JUNE     !
>H13:/F$@SUM(B13...G13)
>G13:/F$230
>F13:/F$175
>E13:/F$350
>D13:/F$467.5
>C13:/F$
>B13:/F$325
>A13:"MAY      !
>H12:/F$@SUM(B12...G12)

>G12:/F$230
>F12:/F$175
>E12:/F$350
>D12:/F$467.5
>C12:/F$
>B12:/F$325
>A12:"APRIL    !
>H11:/F$@SUM(B11...G11)
>G11:/F$230
>F11:/F$175
>E11:/F$350
>D11:/F$467.5
>C11:/F$
>B11:/F$325
>A11:"MARCH    !
>H10:/F$@SUM(B10...G10)
>G10:/F$210
>F10:/F$150
>E10:/F$325
>D10:/F$450
>C10:/F$275
>B10:/F$300
>A10:"FEBRUARY!
>H9:/F$@SUM(B9...G9)
>G9:/F$210
>F9:/F$150
>E9:/F$325
>D9:/F$450
>C9:/F$275
>B9:/F$300
>A9:"JANUARY !
>H8:/--
>G8:/--
>F8:/--
>E8:/--
>D8:/--
>C8:/--
>B8:/--
>A8:/--
>H7:/FR"Totals
>G7:/FR"20!
>F7:13
>E7:12
>D7:11
>C7:2
>B7:1
>A7:"Rented  !
>H6:/FR"Month
>G6:/FR"!
>D6:"Unit No.
>A6:"Month   !
>H5:"_____
>G5:"_____
>F5:"_____
>E5:"_____
```

```
>D5:"_____          >H2:/-==
>C5:"_____          >G2:/-==
>B5:"_____          >F2:/-==
>A5:"_____          >E2:/-==
>G4:"fence Rd.                 >D2:/-==
>F4:"2251 White                >C2:/-==
>E4:"dress :                   >B2:/-==
>D4:"Rental Addres             >A2:/-==
>G3:/FR"Plaza                  >D1:"Record
>F3:"Greenacre                 >C1:"Rental
>E3:"me   :                    >B1:"Monthly
>D3:"Rental Nam                /W1
>C3:"To   :81                  /GOC
>B3:/FL80                      /GRA
>A3:"Period 19                 /GC9
>J2:/-==                       /X>A1:>A1:
>I2:/-==
```

Figure 2.4(b). Formulas for monthly rental record

2.5. QSTATE: Quarterly Income Statement

Purpose   A quarterly statement of income is needed to track the progress of any business. In the property management business you want to know (before it is too late) how much money is coming in and how much is going out. Thus, a quarterly statement is maintained that takes the totals from the other worksheets and uses them to tell you what the net income is for the quarter.

The purpose of QSTATE and YSTATE is to compute the net income for the business. If this number turns out to be negative as shown in the sample of Figure 2.5(a), then the business is turning a loss.

Worksheet   The worksheet of Figure 2.5(a) takes the total income reported for each month of the quarter and the itemized expenses for each month and computes the totals shown at the bottom of the statement. This is the kind of thing that VisiCalc was designed to do, so it is no surprise that its use in this manner is so simple.

Comments   You might not find this statement adequate for your business. If this is the case, then you will want to change it by adding or deleting certain rows or columns. This is done by using the /DELETE and/or /INSERT commands of

```
            QUARTERLY STATEMENT OF INCOME
Quarter=      1   Jan 81  to      Apr 81
================================================================
      Item           |         Month          |    Qtr
                     |January  February March  |  Totals
----------------------------------------------------------------
    INCOME
Rental Income        $   1710.00  1710.00  1547.50   4967.50
Other Income         $                                  0.00
        Total Income $   1710.00  1710.00  1547.50   4967.50
----------------------------------------------------------------
  EXPENSES
Mortgage Payments    $     14.23    15.05    15.78     45.06
Interest Paid        $   1385.77  1384.95  1384.22   4154.94
Taxes & Licenses     $    345.00   345.00   345.00   1035.00
Insurance            $     20.00    20.00    20.00     60.00
Utilities            $                                  0.00
Accountants Fee      $                       310.00    310.00
Advertising Fee      $                        25.75     25.75
Equipment Repairs    $                                  0.00
Managers Fee         $    150.00   150.00   150.00    450.00
Parts & Materials    $                                  0.00
Repair Labor Fee     $                                  0.00
Sales Taxes Paid     $                                  0.00
Misc. Services       $     25.00    35.00    20.00     80.00
Misc. Supplies       $                                  0.00
Transportation       $     12.00     8.50    10.75     31.25
Employee Payroll  Total $                                0.00
Estimated Depreciation $  175.00   175.00   175.00    525.00
Bad debts            $             250.00              250.00
Contributions & Other $                                 0.00
----------------------------------------------------------------
    Total Expenses   $   2127.00  2383.50  2456.50   6967.00
----------------------------------------------------------------
----------------------------------------------------------------
  Net Income (Qtr) $    -417.00  -673.50  -909.00  -1999.50
----------------------------------------------------------------
```

Figure 2.5(a). Quarterly income statement worksheet

VisiCalc. For example, to add a row in the EXPENSES section of the worksheet, simply position the VisiCalc cursor in the row before which you want to insert the new row. Then press /INSERT and the rows will be moved down to make room for the new row. Be careful to adjust the formulas, if needed, to include your new row or column in the summations, etc.

Formulas

The formulas shown in Figure 2.5(b) compute the obvious. The income items are totaled, the expense items are totaled, and then the net income is computed by subtracting the expenses from the income. This is done for each month, and then for the entire quarter (three months).

```
>G37:/-_                         >G28:@SUM(D28...F28)
>F37:/-_                         >C28:/FR"Total    $
>E37:/-_                         >B28:"Payroll
>D37:/-_                         >A28:"Employee
>C37:/-_                         >G27:@SUM(D27...F27)
>B37:/-_                         >F27:10.75
>A37:/-_                         >E27:8.5
>G36:-G33+G10                    >D27:12
>F36:-F33+F10                    >C27:/FR"$
>E36:-E33+E10                    >B27:"ation
>D36:-D33+D10                    >A27:"Transportation
>C36:"e (Qtr) $                  >G26:@SUM(D26...F26)
>B36:"Net Income                 >C26:/FR"$
>G35:/--                         >B26:"plies
>F35:/--                         >A26:"Misc. Sup
>E35:/--                         >G25:@SUM(D25...F25)
>D35:/--                         >F25:20
>C35:/--                         >E25:35
>B35:/--                         >D25:25
>A35:/--                         >C25:/FR"$
>G34:/-_                         >B25:"vices
>F34:/-_                         >A25:"Misc. Ser
>E34:/-_                         >G24:@SUM(D24...F24)
>D34:/-_                         >C24:/FR"$
>C34:/-_                         >B24:"es Paid
>B34:/-_                         >A24:"Sales Taxes
>A34:/-_                         >G23:@SUM(D23...F23)
>G33:@SUM(G13...G31)             >C23:/FR"$
>F33:@SUM(F13...F31)             >B23:"bor Fee
>E33:@SUM(E13...E31)             >A23:"Repair La
>D33:@SUM(D13...D31)             >G22:@SUM(D22...F22)
>C33:"enses    $                 >C22:/FR"$
>B33:"Total Exp                  >B22:"aterials
>G32:/--                         >A22:"Parts & M
>F32:/--                         >G21:@SUM(D21...F21)
>E32:/--                         >F21:150
>D32:/--                         >E21:150
>C32:/--                         >D21:150
>B32:/--                         >C21:/FR"$
>A32:/--                         >B21:"Fee
>G31:@SUM(D31...F31)             >A21:"Managers
>C31:"her       $                >G20:@SUM(D20...F20)
>B31:"ions & Oth                 >C20:/FR"$
>A31:"Contribution               >B20:" Repairs
>G30:@SUM(D30...F30)             >A20:"Equipment
>E30:250                         >G19:@SUM(D19...F19)
>C30:/FR"$                       >F19:25.75
>A30:"Bad debts                  >C19:/FR"$
>G29:@SUM(D29...F29)             >B19:"ng Fee
>F29:175                         >A19:"Advertising
>E29:175                         >G18:@SUM(D18...F18)
>D29:175                         >F18:310
>C29:/FR"tion    $               >C18:/FR"$
>B29:" Depreciation              >B18:"ts Fee
>A29:"Estimated                  >A18:"Accountant
```

>G17:@SUM(D17...F17)
>C17:/FR"$
>A17:"Utilities
>G16:@SUM(D16...F16)
>F16:20
>E16:20
>D16:20
>C16:/FR"$
>A16:"Insurance
>G15:@SUM(D15...F15)
>F15:345
>E15:345
>D15:345
>C15:/FR"$
>B15:"Licenses
>A15:"Taxes &
>G14:@SUM(D14...F14)
>F14:1384.22
>E14:1384.95
>D14:1385.77
>C14:/FR"$
>B14:"Paid
>A14:"Interest
>G13:@SUM(D13...F13)
>F13:15.78
>E13:15.05
>D13:14.23
>C13:/FR"$
>B13:"Payments
>A13:"Mortgage
>A12:/FR"EXPENSES
>G11:/--
>F11:/--
>E11:/--
>D11:/--
>C11:/--
>B11:/--
>A11:/--
>G10:/F$@SUM(G8...G9)
>F10:@SUM(F8...F9)
>E10:@SUM(E8...E9)
>D10:@SUM(D8...D9)
>C10:"ome $
>B10:"Total Inc
>G9:/F$@SUM(D9...F9)
>C9:/FR"$
>B9:"ome
>A9:"Other Incom

>G8:/F$@SUM(D8...F8)
>F8:/F$1547.5
>E8:/F$1710
>D8:/F$1710
>C8:/FR"$
>B8:"come
>A8:"Rental Inc
>A7:/FR"INCOME
>G6:/-_
>F6:/-_
>E6:/-_
>D6:/-_
>C6:/-_
>B6:/-_
>A6:/-_
>G5:" Totals
>F5:"March   !
>E5:"February
>D5:"January
>C5:/FR"!
>G4:/FR"Qtr
>F4:/FR"!
>E4:"Month
>C4:/FR"!
>B4:"Item
>G3:/-=
>F3:/-=
>E3:/-=
>D3:/-=
>C3:/-=
>B3:/-=
>A3:/-=
>E2:"Apr 81
>D2:" to
>C2:/FR"Jan 81
>B2:/FI1
>A2:"Quarter=
>F1:"ME
>E1:"T OF INCOME
>D1:" STATEMEN
>C1:"QUARTERLY
/W1
/GOC
/GRA
/GF$
/GC9
/X>A1:>A6:/TH
/X>A1:>A1:

Figure 2.5(b). Formulas for quarterly income statement worksheet

2.6. YSTATE: Yearly Income Statement

Purpose   The yearly income statement is used to summarize the quarterly income statement information. This is the statement that you will need at the end of the year to compute your income taxes.

Worksheet   Figure 2.6(a) shows you what is included in the yearly income statement for the real estate property management business we are using as an example. Each quarter has a reported income which is the total of all rents paid by tenants. The expenses are totals taken from the quarterly expense statements as shown in the previous section.

The rental property is a depreciable asset, according to the IRS, so you can include the amount of depreciation, here. Bad debts, like unpaid rents, etc., are also reported in the worksheet.

The net income for the year is computed and shown in the lower-right hand corner of the worksheet.

```
H38  (V) +H37                                                        C
                                                                    31
       A       B       C       D       E       F       G       H
        1              YEAR-END STATEMENT OF INCOME
        2 Year Ending    :  Dec 1981
        3 ===============================================================
        4          Item              :        Quarters          :   Qtr
        5                            :   First   Second   Third  Fourth : Totals
        6
       25 Misc. Services      $     25.00    35.00    20.00    30.00    110.00
       26 Misc. Supplies      $                                          0.00
       27 Transportation      $     12.00     8.50    10.75    14.50     45.75
       28 Employee Payroll  Total  $                                     0.00
       29           Total Expenses $   1952.00  1958.50  2281.50  1985.25  8177.25
       30 ---------------------------------------------------------------
       31 Estimated Depreciation $    175.00   175.00   175.00   175.00    700.00
       32 Bad debts           $              250.00                       250.00
       33 Contributions & Other $                                         0.00
       34 ---------------------------------------------------------------
       35        Total Deductions $    175.00   425.00   175.00   175.00    950.00
       36
       37       Net Income (Qtr) $   2640.50  2259.00  2186.00  2482.25   9567.75
       38       Net Profit(Year) $                                        9567.75
       39
```

```
                  YEAR-END   STATEMENT OF INCOME
Year Ending    :    Dec 1981
=================================================================
      Item           !         Quarters            !    Qtr
                     !      First    Second    Third   Fourth ! Totals
-----------------------------------------------------------------
   INCOME
Rental Income     $   4767.50   4642.50   4642.50   4642.50  18695.00
Other Income      $                                              0.00
      Total Income $   4767.50   4642.50   4642.50   4642.50  18695.00
-----------------------------------------------------------------
 EXPENSES
Mortgage Payments $     14.23     15.05     15.78     16.45     61.51
Interest Paid     $   1385.77   1384.95   1384.22   1383.55   5538.49
Taxes &  Licenses $    345.00    345.00    345.00    345.00   1380.00
Insurance         $     20.00     20.00     20.00     20.00     80.00
Utilities         $                                              0.00
Accountants Fee   $                         310.00             310.00
Advertising Fee   $                          25.75     25.75     51.50
Equipment Repairs $                                              0.00
Managers Fee      $    150.00    150.00    150.00    150.00    600.00
Parts & Materials $                                              0.00
Repair Labor Fee  $                                              0.00
Sales Taxes Paid  $                                              0.00
Misc. Services    $     25.00     35.00     20.00     30.00    110.00
Misc. Supplies    $                                              0.00
Transportation    $     12.00      8.50     10.75     14.50     45.75
Employee Payroll  Total $                                        0.00
      Total Expenses $ 1952.00   1958.50   2281.50   1985.25   8177.25
-----------------------------------------------------------------
Estimated Depreciation $ 175.00   175.00    175.00    175.00    700.00
Bad debts         $               250.00                       250.00
Contributions & Other $                                          0.00
-----------------------------------------------------------------
      Total Deductions $ 175.00    425.00    175.00    175.00    950.00
-----------------------------------------------------------------
      Net Income (Qtr) $ 2640.50   2259.00   2186.00   2482.25   9567.75
      Net Profit(Year) $                                         9567.75
-----------------------------------------------------------------
```

Figure 2.6(a). Yearly income statement worksheet

Comments

You may want to modify this worksheet by inserting or deleting certain rows or columns. As suggested in the previous section, the /INSERT and /DELETE commands can be used to do this. You should be careful that such modifications do not alter the calculations. Also, if you want to include your additions in the calculations, make sure they show up in the sums, etc.

Formulas

Figure 2.6(b) contains the information needed to reconstruct the worksheet. This worksheet is much like the one shown for the quarterly statement. Again, the sums are used to obtain subtotals, then the subtotals are subtracted to come up with a net income.

```
>H39:/-_                          >B31:" Depreciation
>G39:/-_                          >A31:"Estimated
>F39:/-_                          >H30:/--
>E39:/-_                          >G30:/--
>D39:/-_                          >F30:/--
>C39:/-_                          >E30:/--
>B39:/-_                          >D30:/--
>A39:/-_                          >C30:/--
>H38:+H37                         >B30:/--
>C38:"t(Year) $                   >A30:/--
>B38:"Net Profit                  >H29:@SUM(H13...H28)
>H37:-H35-H29+H10                 >G29:@SUM(G13...G28)
>G37:-G35-G29+G10                 >F29:@SUM(F13...F28)
>F37:-F35-F29+F10                 >E29:@SUM(E13...E28)
>E37:-E35-E29+E10                 >D29:@SUM(D13...D28)
>D37:-D35-D29+D10                 >C29:"enses    $
>C37:"e (Qtr) $                   >B29:"Total Exp
>B37:"Net Income                  >H28:@SUM(D28...G28)
>H36:/-_                          >C28:/FR"Total     $
>G36:/-_                          >B28:"Payroll
>F36:/-_                          >A28:"Employee
>E36:/-_                          >H27:@SUM(D27...G27)
>D36:/-_                          >G27:14.5
>C36:/-_                          >F27:10.75
>B36:/-_                          >E27:8.5
>A36:/-_                          >D27:12
>H35:@SUM(H31...H33)              >C27:/FR"$
>G35:@SUM(G31...G33)              >B27:"ation
>F35:@SUM(F31...F33)              >A27:"Transportation
>E35:@SUM(E31...E33)              >H26:@SUM(D26...G26)
>D35:@SUM(D31...D33)              >C26:/FR"$
>C35:"uctions $                   >B26:"plies
>B35:"Total Deduct                >A26:"Misc. Sup
>H34:/--                          >H25:@SUM(D25...G25)
>G34:/--                          >G25:30
>F34:/--                          >F25:20
>E34:/--                          >E25:35
>D34:/--                          >D25:25
>C34:/--                          >C25:/FR"$
>B34:/--                          >B25:"vices
>A34:/--                          >A25:"Misc. Ser
>H33:@SUM(D33...F33)              >H24:@SUM(D24...G24)
>C33:"her       $                 >C24:/FR"$
>B33:"ions & Oth                  >B24:"es Paid
>A33:"Contribution                >A24:"Sales Taxes
>H32:@SUM(D32...F32)              >H23:@SUM(D23...G23)
>E32:250                          >C23:/FR"$
>C32:/FR"$                        >B23:"bor Fee
>A32:"Bad debts                   >A23:"Repair La
>H31:@SUM(D31...G31)              >H22:@SUM(D22...G22)
>G31:175                          >C22:/FR"$
>F31:175                          >B22:"aterials
>E31:175                          >A22:"Parts & M
>D31:175                          >H21:@SUM(D21...G21)
>C31:/FR"tion     $               >G21:150
```

>F21:150
>E21:150
>D21:150
>C21:/FR"$
>B21:"Fee
>A21:"Managers
>H20:@SUM(D20...G20)
>C20:/FR"$
>B20:" Repairs
>A20:"Equipment
>H19:@SUM(D19...G19)
>G19:25.75
>F19:25.75
>C19:/FR"$
>B19:"ng Fee
>A19:"Advertising
>H18:@SUM(D18...G18)
>F18:310
>C18:/FR"$
>B18:"ts Fee
>A18:"Accountant
>H17:@SUM(D17...G17)
>C17:/FR"$
>A17:"Utilities
>H16:@SUM(D16...G16)
>G16:20
>F16:20
>E16:20
>D16:20
>C16:/FR"$
>A16:"Insurance
>H15:@SUM(D15...G15)
>G15:345
>F15:345
>E15:345
>D15:345
>C15:/FR"$
>B15:"Licenses
>A15:"Taxes &
>H14:@SUM(D14...G14)
>G14:1383.55
>F14:1384.22
>E14:1384.95
>D14:1385.77
>C14:/FR"$
>B14:"Paid
>A14:"Interest
>H13:@SUM(D13...G13)
>G13:16.45
>F13:15.78
>E13:15.05
>D13:14.23
>C13:/FR"$
>B13:"Payments
>A13:"Mortgage

>A12:/FR"EXPENSES
>H11:/--
>G11:/--
>F11:/--
>E11:/--
>D11:/--
>C11:/--
>B11:/--
>A11:/--
>H10:/F$@SUM(H8...H9)
>G10:@SUM(G8...G9)
>F10:@SUM(F8...F9)
>E10:@SUM(E8...E9)
>D10:@SUM(D8...D9)
>C10:"ome $
>B10:"Total Inc
>H9:/F$@SUM(D9...G9)
>C9:/FR"$
>B9:"ome
>A9:"Other Incom
>H8:/F$@SUM(D8...G8)
>G8:4642.5
>F8:/F$4642.5
>E8:/F$4642.5
>D8:/F$4767.5
>C8:/FR"$
>B8:"come
>A8:"Rental Inc
>A7:/FR"INCOME
>H6:/-_
>G6:/-_
>F6:/-_
>E6:/-_
>D6:/-_
>C6:/-_
>B6:/-_
>A6:/-_
>H5:" Totals
>G5:/FR"Fourth !
>F5:/FR"Third
>E5:/FR"Second
>D5:/FR"First
>C5:/FR"!
>H4:/FR"Qtr
>G4:/FR"!
>F4:/FR
>E4:"Quarters
>C4:/FR"!
>B4:"Item
>H3:/-=
>G3:/-=
>F3:/-=
>E3:/-=
>D3:/-=
>C3:/-=

```
>B3:/-=                          >C1:"YEAR-END
>A3:/-=                          /W1
>C2:/FR"Dec 1981                 /GOC
>B2:/FI"ng       :               /GRA
>A2:"Year Endin                  /GF$
>F1:"ME                          /GC9
>E1:"T OF INCOME                 /X>A1:>A6:/TH
>D1:" STATEMEN                   /X>A1:>A1:
```

Figure 2.6(b). Formulas for yearly income statement worksheet

2.7. BALANCE: Balance Sheet and Net Worth

If you walk into a bank for a personal loan, if you are thinking of buying something on installment credit, or if your partners want to know how much you are worth, then you need a worksheet for computing your net worth.

The idea of a Balance Sheet is to find out the strengths and weaknesses of a company, or of a person, in terms of assets and liabilities.

Purpose

The worksheet shown in Figure 2.7(a) is made up of two parts: the section for listing your assets, and the section for listing your liabilities. Enter the numerical dollars and cents figures into each row as shown. The formulas of the worksheet will compute the subtotals and then the grand total (net worth).

Worksheet

Again, because the VisiCalc program was designed for this kind of use, this example does not show how to do anything fancy. Instead, it shows how easy it is to implement business applications in VisiCalc software.

You might add to this worksheet by extending the list of assets and the list of liabilities. For example, the list of liabilities might be expanded to include credit card debts, alimony, and school loans. The list of assets could include furniture, collectors items, and royalties.

Comments

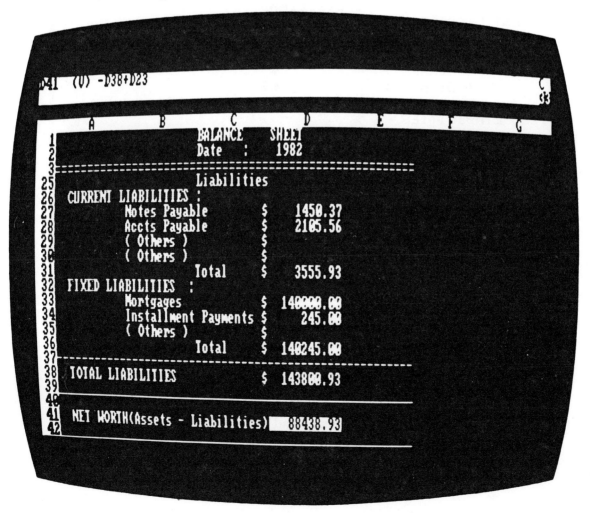

```
                        BALANCE      SHEET
                        Date    :     1982
=========================================================
                        Assets
    CURRENT    ASSETS :
                Cash on Hand        $        35.50
                Cash in Bank        $      1024.76
                Notes Receivables   $       279.60
                Accts Receivables   $      1400.00
                Inventory on hand   $
                        Total       $      2739.86
    FIXED ASSETS    :
                Land                $     25000.00
                Buildings           $    145000.00
                Equipment           $     12500.00
                Furniture           $     19500.00
                        Total       $    202000.00
    OTHER   ASSETS    :
                Boat                $      5500.00
                Cars                $     22000.00
                        Total       $     27500.00
    -----------------------------------------------------
    TOTAL ASSETS                    $    232239.86

                        Liabilities
    CURRENT LIABILITIES :
                Notes Payable       $      1450.37
                Accts Payable       $      2105.56
                ( Others )          $
                ( Others )          $
                        Total       $      3555.93
    FIXED LIABILITIES   :
                Mortgages           $    140000.00
                Installment Payments $      245.00
                ( Others )          $
                        Total       $    140245.00
    -----------------------------------------------------
    TOTAL LIABILITIES               $    143800.93
    -----------------------------------------------------
    NET WORTH(Assets - Liabilities)      88438.93
    -----------------------------------------------------
```

Figure 2.7(a). Balance sheet worksheet

Formulas   Figure 2.7(b) gives the formulas and labels needed to reconstruct the balance sheet. If you add or delete rows or columns in this worksheet be sure to check the formulas again to make sure they correctly compute the net worth.

```
>E42:/-_                          >B23:"ETS
>D42:/-_                          >A23:"   TOTAL ASS
>C42:/-_                          >E22:/--
>B42:/-_                          >D22:/--
>A42:/-_                          >C22:/--
>D41:-D38+D23                     >B22:/--
>C41:"iabilities)                 >A22:/--
>B41:"(Assets - L                 >D21:@SUM(D19...D20)
>A41:"   NET WORTH                >C21:"Total        $
>E39:/-_                          >D20:22000
>D39:/-_                          >C20:/FR"$
>C39:/-_                          >B20:"Cars
>B39:/-_                          >D19:5500
>A39:/-_                          >C19:/FR"$
>D38:@SUM(D31,D36)                >B19:"Boat
>C38:/FR"$                        >B18:"SETS    :
>B38:"BILITIES                    >A18:"   OTHER  AS
>A38:"   TOTAL LIA                >D17:@SUM(D13...D16)
>E37:/--                          >C17:/FR"Total       $
>D37:/--                          >D16:19500
>C37:/--                          >C16:/FR"$
>B37:/--                          >B16:"Furniture
>A37:/--                          >D15:12500
>D36:@SUM(D33...D35)              >C15:/FR"$
>C36:"Total        $              >B15:"Equipment
>C35:/FR"$                        >D14:145000
>B35:"( Others )                  >C14:/FR"$
>D34:245                          >B14:"Buildings
>C34:" Payments $                 >D13:25000
>B34:"Installment                 >C13:/FR"$
>D33:140000                       >B13:"Land
>C33:/FR"$                        >B12:"ETS     :
>B33:"Mortgages                   >A12:"   FIXED ASS
>B32:"BILITIES  :                 >D11:@SUM(D6...D10)
>A32:"   FIXED LIA                >C11:"Total       $
>D31:@SUM(D27...D30)              >C10:"n hand     $
>C31:"Total       $               >B10:"Inventory o
>C30:/FR"$                        >D9:1400
>B30:"( Others )                  >C9:"vables      $
>C29:/FR"$                        >B9:"Accts Receiv
>B29:"( Others )                  >D8:279.6
>D28:2105.56                      >C8:"vables      $
>C28:"le         $                >B8:"Notes Recei
>B28:"Accts Payable               >D7:1024.76
>D27:1450.37                      >C7:"k          $
>C27:"le          $               >B7:"Cash in Ban
>B27:"Notes Payable               >D6:35.5
>C26:":                           >C6:"d          $
>B26:"IABILITIES :                >B6:"Cash on Han
>A26:"   CURRENT LI               >B5:" ASSETS :
>C25:"Liabilities                 >A5:"   CURRENT
>D23:+D11+D17+D21                 >C4:"Assets
>C23:/FR"$                        >E3:/-=
```

```
>D3:/-=                              /W1
>C3:/-=                              /GOC
>B3:/-=                              /GRA
>A3:/-=                              /GF$
>D2:/FL1982                          /GC11
>C2:"Date    :                       /X>A1:>A3:/TH
>D1:"SHEET                           /X>A1:>A1:
>C1:"BALANCE
```

Figure 2.7(b). Formulas for balance sheet

2.8. AR: Accounts Receivable Worksheet

Every successful business must collect bills on a timely basis in order to stay in business. Therefore, every successful business needs a good accounts receivable system. The worksheet given in this section is a simple but effective accounts receivable system.

The idea is to keep a record of all outstanding charges owed the company by its customers. Another list of payments made by the customers is also kept. Then at the end of the month (or whenever bills are due), the charges and payments are "posted" against the accounts. This means the total charges are added to the amount due, and the total payments are subtracted from the amount due. If the payments are insufficient to cover the amount due, then the amount due becomes the amount past due. One of the main uses of an AR system is for identifying the accounts with an amount past due. These overdue accounts should be carefully watched and efforts made to collect the past due amount.

On first inspection you might think that it is rather difficult to build a VisiCalc worksheet that does accounts receivable processing. For example, posting the charges and payments does not seem like something that a worksheet calculator can do. However, if we are clever and use the techniques shown earlier, then a reasonable AR system can indeed be implemented in the VisiCalc program.

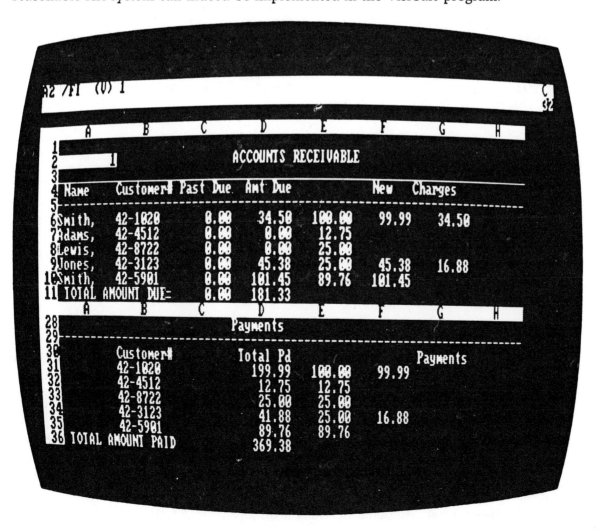

Worksheet   Figure 2.8(a) shows the accounts receivable (AR) worksheet in its "initial" state. Notice that cell A2 is a trigger that tells the formulas in the other cells what to do. When the trigger is set to zero, the worksheet is ready for you to enter charges and payments.

Suppose the charges 100.00, 99.99, and 34.50 are entered for the first account in the row labeled "Smith." Smith is customer #42-1020, and in the lower portion of the worksheet (the screen is split), account #42-1020 appears again. Smith has also made two payments as shown in the lower half of the worksheet. Thus a total of $199.99 has been paid and a total of $234.49 charges made.

The charges and payments for every customer are entered as shown for as long as the trigger is set to zero. Then, as soon as you want to post the charges minus the payments, change the trigger to A2 = 1. This is shown in Figure 2.8(b). The amount due for Smith becomes the total amount from charges minus the total amount paid. Check the top and bottom half of the worksheet.

Now, the amount that is still due becomes the "past due" amount, as shown in Figure 2.8(c). This is obtained by setting the trigger back to zero, and recalculating the entire worksheet.

```
          0                    ACCOUNTS RECEIVABLE

-------------------------------------------------------------------------------
 Name      Customer# Past Due  Amt Due          New     Charges
-------------------------------------------------------------------------------
Smith,     42-1020    0.00      0.00    100.00   99.99    34.50
Adams,     42-4512    0.00      0.00     12.75
Lewis,     42-8722    0.00      0.00     25.00
Jones,     42-3123    0.00      0.00     25.00   45.38    16.88
Smith,     42-5901    0.00      0.00     89.76  101.45
  TOTAL AMOUNT DUE=   0.00      0.00


-------------------------------------------------------------------------------

                          Payments
-------------------------------------------------------------------------------
           Customer#          Total Pd              Payments
           42-1020            199.99    100.00   99.99
           42-4512             12.75     12.75
           42-8722             25.00     25.00
           42-3123             41.88     25.00   16.88
           42-5901             89.76     89.76
 TOTAL AMOUNT PAID            369.38


Instructions : Set A2 to 0: Store Amt Due in Past Due and set Past Due=0
                   A2 to 1: Compute Amt Due from New Charges & Past Due.
                   A2 to 2: Change Charges & Payments without updates.
            Pattern of use: A2=0, enter charges & payments, at first.
                            A2=1, recalculates totals,etc.
                            A2=0, reset Past Due.
                            A2=2, blank & enter New Charges & new Paymen
                            Repeating cycle :1,0,2,1,0,2,1,0,2.
                            Two A2=0 in series causes zeros everywhere.
```

Figure 2.8(a). Accounts receivable worksheet with A2=0

```
         1              ACCOUNTS RECEIVABLE
-------------------------------------------------------------------
 Name     Customer# Past Due  Amt Due          New    Charges
-------------------------------------------------------------------
Smith,   42-1020      0.00     34.50   100.00  99.99   34.50
Adams,   42-4512      0.00      0.00    12.75
Lewis,   42-8722      0.00      0.00    25.00
Jones,   42-3123      0.00     45.38    25.00  45.38   16.88
Smith,   42-5901      0.00    101.45    89.76 101.45
 TOTAL AMOUNT DUE=    0.00    181.33


------------------------------------------------------------------

                      Payments
------------------------------------------------------------------
         Customer#         Total Pd          Payments
         42-1020           199.99   100.00  99.99
         42-4512            12.75    12.75
         42-8722            25.00    25.00
         42-3123            41.88    25.00  16.88
         42-5901            89.76    89.76
TOTAL AMOUNT PAID          369.38
```

Figure 2.8(b). Accounts receivable worksheet with A2=1

At this point in the cycle, the charges and payments must be erased because they have been posted against each account. We do not want to double post the amounts under "new charges" and "payments," so erase these values using the VisiCalc /BLANK command. Suppose we enter next month's charges and payments as shown in Figure 2.8(d).

Figure 2.8(d) shows what happens next. The trigger is set to A2 = 2, and the new charges and new payments from the next period are entered. The amount in the past due column is not altered, because the customer still owes this amount. In addition, now the customer owes the new charges minus the new payments. To get a new amount due you must post the charges and payments again. This is done by setting the trigger to 1 so the amount due becomes the amount charged plus the amount past due minus the payments.

To see how all this is done, look at the formulas in the worksheet.

Comments

You may become confused when using this worksheet because it requires a few tricks to fool the VisiCalc program. Consult the directions at the bottom of the worksheet. These directions suggest that you use the trigger sequence 1,0,2... after you initialize the worksheet. You may also find it more convenient to disable the automatic recalculation option.

Although this collection does not include an accounts payable worksheet you should be able to modify the AR worksheet to do that operation too. The ideas are the same. Likewise, other operations such as inventory tracking can be done with VisiCalc worksheets.

```
       0                ACCOUNTS RECEIVABLE

 ---------------------------------------------------------------------
 Name     Customer# Past Due  Amt Due           New     Charges
 ---------------------------------------------------------------------
 Smith,   42-1020     34.50     0.00   100.00   99.99    34.50
 Adams,   42-4512      0.00     0.00    12.75
 Lewis,   42-8722      0.00     0.00    25.00
 Jones,   42-3123     45.38     0.00    25.00   45.38    16.88
 Smith,   42-5901    101.45     0.00    89.76  101.45
  TOTAL AMOUNT DUE=   181.33     0.00



 ---------------------------------------------------------------------
                         Payments
 ---------------------------------------------------------------------
          Customer#           Total Pd              Payments
          42-1020              199.99   100.00   99.99
          42-4512               12.75    12.75
          42-8722               25.00    25.00
          42-3123               41.88    25.00   16.88
          42-5901               89.76    89.76
  TOTAL AMOUNT PAID            369.38


 Instructions : Set A2 to 0: Store Amt Due in Past Due and set Past Due=0
                   A2 to 1: Compute Amt Due from New Charges & Past Due.
                   A2 to 2: Change Charges & Payments without updates.
             Pattern of use: A2=0, enter charges & payments, at first.
                             A2=1, recalculates totals,etc.
                             A2=0, reset Past Due.
                             A2=2, blank & enter New Charges & new Paymen
                             Repeating cycle :1,0,2,1,0,2,1,0,2.
                             Two A2=0 in series causes zeros everywhere.
```

Figure 2.8(c). Accounts receivable worksheet with A2=0 after being 1

```
       2                ACCOUNTS RECEIVABLE

 ---------------------------------------------------------------------
 Name     Customer# Past Due  Amt Due           New     Charges
 ---------------------------------------------------------------------
 Smith,   42-1020     34.50     0.00
 Adams,   42-4512      0.00     0.00           5.50
 Lewis,   42-8722      0.00     0.00
 Jones,   42-3123     45.38     0.00           4.95    14.00
 Smith,   42-5901    101.45     0.00
  TOTAL AMOUNT DUE=   181.33     0.00
```

```
--------------------------------------------------------------------------------
                            Payments
--------------------------------------------------------------------------------
         Customer#          Total Pd                    Payments
         42-1020             34.50      34.50
         42-4512              0.00
         42-8722              0.00
         42-3123              4.95       4.95
         42-5901              0.00
TOTAL AMOUNT PAID            39.45



Instructions : Set A2 to 0: Store Amt Due in Past Due and set Past Due=0
               A2 to 1: Compute Amt Due from New Charges & Past Due.
               A2 to 2: Change Charges & Payments without updates.
            Pattern of use: A2=0, enter charges & payments, at first.
                            A2=1, recalculates totals,etc.
                            A2=0, reset Past Due.
                            A2=2, blank & enter New Charges & new Paymen
                            Repeating cycle :1,0,2,1,0,2,1,0,2.
                            Two A2=0 in series causes zeros everywhere.
```

Figure 2.8(d). Accounts receivable worksheet with A2=2 after being 0

Formulas

Figure 2.8(e) contains the formulas needed to reconstruct the AR worksheet. even if you are using the storage diskette containing this information, you may be interested in seeing how the trigger is used to post charges and payments.

Look at the formula in cell D10 as an example of how this worksheet fools the VisiCalc program.

> D10:@IF(A2 > 0,@IF(A2 = 1,@SUM(E10...AE10) − D35 + C10,D10),0)

Notice that the formula contains two nested @IF statements. The first one decides whether the trigger (A2) is zero or not. If it is, then zero is stored in cell D10. Otherwise the second @IF function is evaluated.

In the second @IF function the trigger is tested again, and if it is equal to one, the charges and payments are posted. Otherwise, the trigger must be equal to 2, so the value of D10 is used.

Also notice the number of cells that are used to compute the total charges. In @SUM the cells are

E10...AE10

This means you can put 27 charges in a row and they will be included in the updated amount due.

Finally, the formulas can use the previous value of the cell as the result calculated. For example, notice cell C10 uses the value currently stored in cell C10 if the trigger is greater than zero.

> C10:@IF(A2 = 0,D10,C10)

Although a VisiCalc cell cannot store both a formula and a constant, it can store a formula. That formula can use its own computed value in a subsequent recalculation.

```
>H47:"rywhere.
>G47:"zeros ever
>F47:"s causes
>E47:" in serie
>D47:" Two A2=0
>G46:",2,1,0,2.
>F46:"1,0,2,1,0
>E46:"g cycle :
>D46:" Repeatin
>I45:"ts.
>H45:"ew Payment
>G45:"arges & n
>F45:"er New Ch
>E45:"ank & ente
>D45:" A2=2, bl
>F44:"Due.
>E44:"set Past
>D44:" A2=0, re
>G43:"etc.
>F43:"s totals,
>E43:"calculate
>D43:" A2=1, re
>H42:"first.
>G42:"ents, at
>F42:"es & payment
>E42:"ter charges
>D42:" A2=0, en
>C42:"n of use:
>B42:"    Patter
>H41:"pdates.
>G41:"without u
>F41:"Payments
>E41:"harges &
>D41:" Change C
>C41:" A2 to 2:
>H40:"Past Due.
>G40:"harges &
>F40:"rom New C
>E40:"Amt Due f
>D40:" Compute
>C40:" A2 to 1:
>H39:"ast Due=0
>G39:"and set P
>F39:"Past Due
>E39:"t Due in
>D39:" Store Amt
>C39:" A2 to 0:
>B39:"ons : Set
>A39:"Instructi
>D36:@SUM(D31...D35
>B36:"OUNT PAID
>A36:" TOTAL AM
>D35:@SUM(E35...AE35)
>B35:"42-5901
>E34:4.95
```

```
>D34:@SUM(E34...AE34)
>B34:"42-3123
>D33:@SUM(E33...AE33)
>B33:"42-8722
>D32:@SUM(E32...AE32)
>B32:"42-4512
>E31:34.5
>D31:@SUM(E31...AE31)
>B31:"42-1020
>G30:/FR"Payments
>D30:/FR"Total Pd
>B30:"Customer#
>A30:/FR
>H29:/--
>G29:/--
>F29:/--
>E29:/--
>D29:/--
>C29:/--
>B29:/--
>A29:/--
>D28:"Payments
>H26:/-_
>G26:/-_
>F26:/-_
>E26:/-_
>D26:/-_
>C26:/-_
>B26:/-_
>A26:/-_
>D11:@SUM(D6...D10
>C11:@SUM(C6...C10)
>B11:"OUNT DUE=
>A11:" TOTAL AMOU
>D10:@IF(A2>0,@IF(A2=1,@SUM(E10...AE10)-D35+C10,D10),0)
>C10:@IF(A2=0,D10,C10)
>B10:"42-5901
>A10:"Smith,
>F9:14
>E9:4.95
>D9:@IF(A2>0,@IF(A2=1,@SUM(E9...AE9)-D34+C9,D9),0)
>C9:@IF(A2=0,D9,C9)
>B9:"42-3123
>A9:"Jones,
>D8:@IF(A2>0,@IF(A2=1,@SUM(E8...AE8)-D33+C8,D8),0)
>C8:@IF(A2=0,D8,C8)
>B8:"42-8722
>A8:"Lewis,
>E7:5.5
>D7:@IF(A2>0,@IF(A2=1,@SUM(E7...AE7)-D32+C7,D7),0)
>C7:@IF(A2=0,D7,C7)
>B7:"42-4512
>A7:"Adams,
>D6:@IF(A2>0,@IF(A2=1,@SUM(E6...AE6)-D31+C6,D6),0)
>C6:@IF(A2=0,D6,C6)
```

```
>B6:"42-1020
>A6:"Smith,
>H5:/--
>G5:/--
>F5:/--
>E5:/--
>D5:/--
>C5:/--
>B5:/--
>A5:/--
>G4:"Charges
>F4:"    New
>D4:/FR"Amt Due
>C4:/FR"Past Due
>B4:"Customer#
>A4:/FL" Name
>H3:/-_
>G3:/-_
>F3:/-_
>E3:/-_
>D3:/-_
>C3:/-_
>B3:/-_
>A3:/-_
>F2:"E
>E2:"RECEIVABLE
>D2:"ACCOUNTS
>A2:/FI2
/W1
/GOC
/GRA
/XH11
/GF$
/GC9
/X>A1:>A1:;/GF$
/GC9
/X>A41:>H49:;
```

Figure 2.8(e). Formulas for accounts receivable worksheet

2.9. BUILDER: Home Building Cost Estimator

Purpose

So far in this collection we have concentrated on accounting types of worksheets. These are the most obvious examples of VisiCalc worksheets, but they are not the only ones. In this and the next section, we present two cost estimation worksheets. The purpose of the home builder worksheet is to show you how a cost estimation worksheet is implemented in the VisiCalc program, and to give you a worksheet that you might find useful if you ever decide to build a new home.

Worksheet

Figure 2.9(a) shows a typical home construction worksheet. The items that go into building a house are listed down the first column followed by an estimate of the cost. In the right-most column you will enter the amount actually paid out during construction. In Figure 2.9(a) we have shown three separate payments in each row, because this house took three months to build.

The VisiCalc program will recalculate the actual total paid on each item by summing the (three) payments. You may want to disable the automatic recalculation option until all payments have been entered.

The most expensive and least expensive item are listed in the statistics section at the bottom of the cost estimator sheet. The average value is also listed there. See the formulas in Figure 2.9(b) that are used to compute these values.

	Estimate	Actual	Paid #1	Paid #2	Paid #3
C2 (/-)					

BUILDERS COST BREAKDOWN

Job Address :	3221 NW Niere Lane				
Owner	spec				
Builder	R & G General Contractors				

	Estimate	Actual	Paid #1	Paid #2	Paid #3
Accessories & built-ins	1600.00	450.00	450.00		
Brick & Stone work (firepl)	900.00	900.00	400.00	500.00	
Building Permit	415.00	415.00	415.00		
Cabinets & millwork	4850.00	4850.00		2425.00	2425.00
Carpenter Labor - Rough	3700.00	3500.00	2000.00	1500.00	
Carpenter Labor - Finish	2180.00	2840.00		300.00	2540.00
Cleanup (final)	400.00	400.00			400.00
Concrete Foundation	3695.00	3600.00	3600.00		
Doors (interior)	2200.00	2300.00	300.00	1950.00	50.00
Doors (garage)	650.00	600.00		600.00	
Electric wiring	2700.00	2700.00		500.00	2200.00
Excavation & Grading	750.00	800.00	550.00		250.00
Fence		0.00			
Floors (composition)	3460.00	3600.00	500.00	1500.00	1600.00

```
                    BUILDERS    COST    BREAKDOWN
------------------------------------------------------------------------
Job Address :      3221 NW  Miere Lane
Owner       :      spec
Builder     :      R & G General Contractors
------------------------------------------------------------------------
```

	Estimate	Actual	Paid #1	Paid #2	Paid #3
Accessories & built-ins	1600.00	450.00	450.00		
Brick & Stone work (firepl)	900.00	900.00	400.00	500.00	
Building Permit	415.00	415.00	415.00		
Cabinets & millwork	4850.00	4850.00		2425.00	2425.00
Carpenter Labor - Rough	3700.00	3500.00	2000.00	1500.00	
Carpenter Labor - Finish	2180.00	2840.00		300.00	2540.00
Cleanup (final)	400.00	400.00			400.00
Concrete Foundation	3695.00	3600.00	3600.00		
Doors (interior)	2200.00	2300.00	300.00	1950.00	50.00
Doors (garage)	650.00	600.00		600.00	
Electric wiring	2700.00	2700.00		500.00	2200.00
Excavation & Grading	750.00	800.00	550.00		250.00
Fence		0.00			
Floors (composition)	3460.00	3600.00	500.00	1500.00	1600.00
Floors (hardwood)	4560.00	5475.00	1500.00	2975.00	1000.00
Frames (doors, etc.)		0.00			
Glass & Glazing	120.00	120.00		120.00	
Hardware (rough)	500.00	500.00	200.00	300.00	
Hardware (finish)	400.00	400.00		200.00	200.00
Heating & airconditioning	3700.00	3700.00			3700.00
Incinerator		0.00			
Insulation	1600.00	1500.00		700.00	800.00
Insurance (construction)	250.00	250.00	250.00		
Lath & plaster or sheetrock	4310.00	4400.00		4000.00	400.00
Lawn & shrubs (bark dust)	250.00	250.00			250.00
Lawn sprinklers		0.00			
Lighting fixtures	600.00	600.00		600.00	
Linoleum	150.00	120.00			120.00
Lumber (rough)	10690.00	10700.00	9500.00	1200.00	
Lumber (finish)	2180.00	2500.00			2500.00
Ornamental ironwork		0.00			
Painting	2900.00	3150.00		2900.00	250.00
Paving, flatwork, steps	950.00	950.00			950.00
Plumbing	5500.00	5500.00	1000.00	3000.00	1500.00
Roofing material	350.00	350.00		350.00	
Roofing labor	900.00	900.00		900.00	
Sewer or septic	2000.00	2000.00	2000.00		
Shades & blinds	1200.00	1100.00			1100.00
Sheet metal	300.00	300.00		300.00	
Survey & sitework	250.00	250.00	250.00		
Tile work	2000.00	2650.00		2500.00	150.00
Water meter	100.00	100.00		100.00	
Weatherstripping	200.00	200.00			200.00
Windows & screens	5600.00	5600.00		4000.00	1600.00
Miscellaneous		0.00			
Well drilling	2800.00	2500.00	2500.00		
Well pump	2120.00	2120.00	2120.00		
Vacuum system	600.00	600.00		600.00	
SUBTOTAL -------->	$ 84580.00	ERROR	27535.00	34020.00	24185.00
Builders Profit	$ 14300.00	14300.00	4700.00	4700.00	4900.00
Arcitectural	$ 1050.00	1050.00			
Lot or Land	$ 35000.00	35000.00			
TOTAL COST	$ 134	Thousand	930	Dollars	0

```
                    STATISTICS

Most expensive item        $  35000.00  35000.00
Average item cost          $   2998.44   2668.43
Least expensive item       $      0.00      0.00
```

Figure 2.9(a). Builders cost sheet for a home

Comments

You can design your own cost estimator sheet using the same ideas illustrated here. Also, you can add or delete items from this example to make up your own worksheet.

The formulas in cells H60, F60, and D60 were used to adjust the large total cost so it would be easy to read.

There are some other subtle things going on in this worksheet. For example, cell E56 has an impossible task to perform. The value displayed in Figure 2.9(a) shows an ERROR! The value is supposed to compute a cross-footing total for comparison with the SUBTOTAL in cell D56. But to do this the sum of the right-most columns must be known. If column-major order of recalculation is used the same error occurs. If we change the order to row-major we still cannot escape the error. The only thing that can be done in this case is to ask for an entire recalculation using the ! command. If you press ! a second time, the error will go away.

Formulas

Figure 2.9(b) contains all the formulas needed to reconstruct the cost sheet. Notice the @MIN, @MAX, and @AVERAGE functions are used in E67, D67, E66, D66, E65, and D65 to compute the statistics mentioned above.

Most of the cost sheet is made up of the itemized list of cost items. This list is just a sample of the things that might go into a cost sheet.

```
>H68:/-_                          >C65:"m          $
>G68:/-_                          >B65:"nsive item
>F68:/-_                          >A65:"Most expen
>E68:/-_                          >D63:"S
>D68:/-_                          >C63:"STATISTIC
>C68:/-_                          >H61:/-_
>B68:/-_                          >G61:/-_
>A68:/-_                          >F61:/-_
>E67:@MIN(E8...E55,E57...E59      >E61:/-_
>D67:@MIN(D8...D55,D57...D59      >D61:/-_
>C67:"em          $              >C61:/-_
>B67:"ensive ite                 >B61:/-_
>A67:"Least exp                  >A61:/-_
>E66:@AVERAGE(E8...E55,E57...E59  >H60:/FI@INT(@SUM(D56...D59)
>D66:@AVERAGE(D8...D55,D57...D59   -(1000*D60)-F60)
>C66:/FR"$                        >G60:/FR"Dollars
>B66:"tem cost                   >F60:/FI@INT(@SUM(D56...D59)
>A66:"Average it                  -(1000*D60))
>E65:@MAX(E8...E55,E57...E59      >E60:/FR"Thousand
>D65:@MAX(D8...D55,D57...D59      >D60:/FI@INT(@SUM(D56...D59)/1000)
```

>C60:/FR"$
>B60:"T
>A60:"TOTAL COS
>E59:35000
>D59:35000
>C59:"nd $
>B59:"Lot or La
>E58:1050
>D58:1050
>C58:"ral $
>B58:"Arcitectur
>H57:4900
>G57:4700
>F57:4700
>E57:@SUM(F57...H57
>D57:14300
>C57:"Profit $
>B57:"Builders
>H56:@SUM(H8...H55)
>G56:@SUM(G8...G55)
>F56:@SUM(F8...F55)
>E56:@SUM(F56...H56
>D56:@SUM(D8...D55)
>C56:/FR"$
>B56:"-------->
>A56:"SUBTOTAL
>G55:600
>E55:@SUM(F55...H55
>D55:600
>B55:"system
>A55:"   Vacuum
>F54:2120
>E54:@SUM(F54...H54
>D54:2120
>B54:"mp
>A54:"   Well pum
>F53:2500
>E53:@SUM(F53...H53
>D53:2800
>B53:"illing
>A53:"   Well dr
>E52:@SUM(F52...H52
>B52:"eous
>A52:"Miscellaneous
>H51:1600
>G51:4000
>E51:@SUM(F51...H51
>D51:5600
>B51:" screens
>A51:"Windows &
>H50:200
>E50:@SUM(F50...H50
>D50:200
>B50:"ripping
>A50:"Weatherst
>G49:100

>E49:@SUM(F49...H49
>D49:100
>B49:"er
>A49:"Water met
>H48:150
>G48:2500
>E48:@SUM(F48...H48
>D48:2000
>A48:"Tile work
>F47:250
>E47:@SUM(F47...H47
>D47:250
>B47:"sitework
>A47:"Survey &
>G46:300
>E46:@SUM(F46...H46
>D46:300
>B46:"al
>A46:"Sheet met
>H45:1100
>E45:@SUM(F45...H45
>D45:1200
>B45:"blinds
>A45:"Shades &
>F44:2000
>E44:@SUM(F44...H44
>D44:2000
>B44:"septic
>A44:"Sewer or
>G43:900
>E43:@SUM(F43...H43
>D43:900
>B43:"labor
>A43:"Roofing
>G42:350
>E42:@SUM(F42...H42
>D42:350
>B42:"material
>A42:"Roofing
>H41:1500
>G41:3000
>F41:1000
>E41:@SUM(F41...H41
>D41:5500
>A41:"Plumbing
>H40:950
>E40:@SUM(F40...H40
>D40:950
>C40:"steps
>B40:"latwork,
>A40:"Paving, f
>H39:250
>G39:2900
>E39:@SUM(F39...H39
>D39:2900
>A39:"Painting

```
>E38:@SUM(F38...H38           >E27:@SUM(F27...H27
>C38:"k                       >D27:3700
>B38:"1 ironwork              >C27:"tioning
>A38:"Ornamental              >B27:" aircondi
>H37:2500                     >A27:"Heating & Air
>E37:@SUM(F37...H37           >H26:200
>D37:2180                     >G26:200
>B37:"(finish)                >E26:@SUM(F26...H26
>A37:"Lumber                  >D26:400
>G36:1200                     >B26:"(finish)
>F36:9500                     >A26:"Hardware (
>E36:@SUM(F36...H36           >G25:300
>D36:10690                    >F25:200
>B36:"(rough)                 >E25:@SUM(F25...H25
>A36:"Lumber                  >D25:500
>H35:120                      >B25:"(rough)
>E35:@SUM(F35...H35           >A25:"Hardware
>D35:150                      >G24:120
>A35:"Linoleum                >E24:@SUM(F24...H24
>G34:600                      >D24:120
>E34:@SUM(F34...H34           >B24:"lazing
>D34:600                      >A24:"Glass & G
>B34:"fixtures               >E23:@SUM(F23...H23
>A34:"Lighting                >C23:"tc.)
>E33:@SUM(F33...H33           >B23:"(doors, e
>B33:"nklers                  >A23:"Frames
>A33:"Lawn sprink             >H22:1000
>H32:250                      >G22:2975
>E32:@SUM(F32...H32           >F22:1500
>D32:250                      >E22:@SUM(F22...H22
>C32:"k dust)                 >D22:4560
>B32:"rubs (bark              >B22:"ardwood)
>A32:"Lawn & shr              >A22:"Floors (h
>H31:400                      >H21:1600
>G31:4000                     >G21:1500
>E31:@SUM(F31...H31           >F21:500
>D31:4310                     >E21:@SUM(F21...H21
>C31:"sheetrock               >D21:3460
>B31:"aster or                >C21:"ion)
>A31:"Lath & plast            >B21:"(composition
>F30:250                      >A21:"Floors
>E30:@SUM(F30...H30           >E20:@SUM(F20...H20
>D30:250                      >A20:"Fence
>C30:"ction)                  >H19:250
>B30:" (construc               >F19:550
>A30:"Insurance               >E19:@SUM(F19...H19
>H29:800                      >D19:750
>G29:700                      >C19:"ng
>E29:@SUM(F29...H29           >B19:"n & Gradin
>D29:1600                     >A19:"Excavation
>B29:"n                       >H18:2200
>A29:"Insulation              >G18:500
>E28:@SUM(F28...H28           >E18:@SUM(F18...H18
>B28:"or                      >D18:2700
>A28:"Incinerat               >B18:"wiring
>H27:3700                     >A18:"Electric
```

```
>G17:600                          >C9:/FR"(firepl)
>E17:@SUM(F17...H17               >B9:"tone work
>D17:650                          >A9:"Brick & Stone
>B17:"(garage)                    >F8:450
>A17:"Doors                       >E8:@SUM(F8...H8
>H16:50                           >D8:1600
>G16:1950                         >C8:"t-ins
>F16:300                          >B8:"es & built
>E16:@SUM(F16...H16               >A8:"Accessories
>D16:2200                         >H7:/FR"Paid #3
>C16:")                           >G7:/FR"Paid #2
>B16:"(interior                   >F7:/FR"Paid #1
>A16:"Doors                       >E7:/FR"Actual
>F15:3600                         >D7:/FR"Estimate
>E15:@SUM(F15...H15               >H6:/--
>D15:3695                         >G6:/--
>C15:"n                           >F6:/--
>B15:"Foundation                  >E6:/--
>A15:"Concrete                    >D6:/--
>H14:400                          >C6:/--
>E14:@SUM(F14...H14               >B6:/--
>D14:400                          >A6:/--
>B14:"(final)                     >E5:"ractors
>A14:"Cleanup                     >D5:"eral Contract
>H13:2540                         >C5:"R & G Gen
>G13:300                          >B5:"   :
>E13:@SUM(F13...H13               >A5:"Builder
>D13:2180                         >C4:"spec
>C13:"Finish                      >B4:"    :
>B13:" Labor -                    >A4:"Owner
>A13:"Carpenter                   >E3:"e
>G12:1500                         >D3:"Miere Lane
>F12:2000                         >C3:"3221 NW
>E12:@SUM(F12...H12               >B3:"ss :
>D12:3700                         >A3:"Job Addres
>C12:"Rough                       >H2:/-_
>B12:" Labor -                    >G2:/-_
>A12:"Carpenter                   >F2:/-_
>H11:2425                         >E2:/-_
>G11:2425                         >D2:/-_
>E11:@SUM(F11...H11               >C2:/-_
>D11:4850                         >B2:/-_
>C11:"k                           >A2:/-_
>B11:"& millwor                   >E1:"BREAKDOWN
>A11:"Cabinets -                  >D1:"   COST
>F10:415                          >C1:"BUILDERS
>E10:@SUM(F10...H10               /W1
>D10:415                          /GOC
>B10:"Permit                      /GRA
>A10:"Building                    /GF$
>G9:500                           /GC9
>F9:400                           /X>A1:>A6:/TH
>E9:@SUM(F9...H9                  /X>A1:>A1:
>D9:900
```

Figure 2.9(b). Formulas for builders cost sheet

2.10. SIDING: Home Siding Estimator (Bonus)

The final example in this collection of business applications is a bonus worksheet. The worksheet of Figure 2.10(a) illustrates how to use the VisiCalc program to estimate construction jobs like siding, cement work, and roads. Anything
that requires measurements to get an estimate is a candidate for VisiCalc
calculation.

Purpose

Figure 2.10(a) computes the total area of a rectangular house so that siding can
be ordered. The SUBTOTALs for the walls and gables are computed first. Then
the subtotals for the windows and doors are computed and subtracted from the
wall and gable areas.

Worksheet

This concludes the section on business applications. You can probably think of
many more ways to use the VisiCalc program, and hopefully you will. This collection should get you started on implementing your own versions.

Comments

The formulas shown in Figure 2.10(b) use simple geometry to compute the
areas. The window and door areas are subtracted from the wall and gable areas.

Formulas

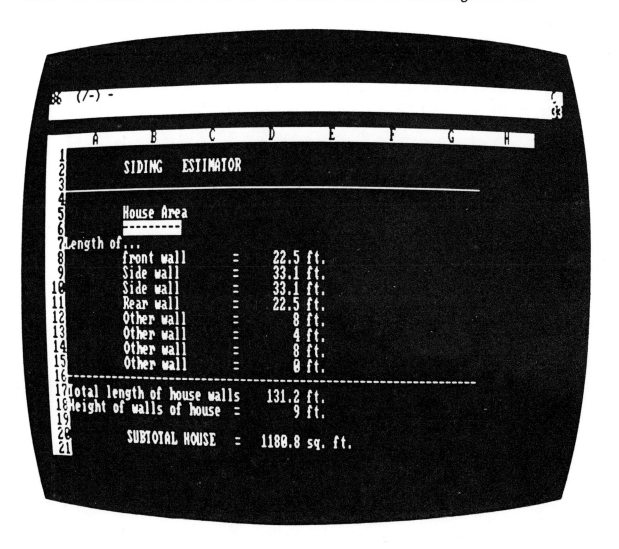

```
              SIDING   ESTIMATOR
-------------------------------------------------

             House Area
             ---------
Length of...
             front wall        =      22.5 ft.
             Side wall         =      33.1 ft.
             Side wall         =      33.1 ft.
             Rear wall         =      22.5 ft.
             Other wall        =         8 ft.
             Other wall        =         4 ft.
             Other wall        =         8 ft.
             Other wall        =         0 ft.
-------------------------------------------------
Total length of house walls       131.2 ft.
Height of walls of house  =           9 ft.

             SUBTOTAL HOUSE    =    1180.8 sq. ft.


             Gables
             ---------
Length of gables           =          5 ft.
Height of gables           =        8.5 ft.

             SUBTOTAL GABLES  =      42.5 sq. ft.


             Windows and Doors
             -----------------
Total of window areas      =        210 sq. ft.
Total of door areas        =        430 sq. ft.

             SUBTOTAL W & D   =      640 sq. ft.

Siding required = House + Gables - Windows & Doors

             SIDING TOTAL     =     583.3 sq. ft.

-------------------------------------------------
```

Figure 2.10(a). A siding estimation sheet

```
>F39:/-_                        >E36:"indows & Do
>E39:/-_                        >D36:"ables - Wind
>D39:/-_                        >C36:"House + G
>C39:/-_                        >B36:"quired =
>B39:/-_                        >A36:"Siding re
>A39:/-_                        >E34:" sq. ft.
>E38:" sq. ft.                  >D34:(D31+D32)
>D38:@SUM(D20,D27)-D34          >C34:"W & D    =
>C38:"TAL     =                 >B34:"SUBTOTAL
>B38:"SIDING TO                 >E32:" sq. ft.
>F36:"Doors                     >D32:430
```

```
>C32:"s            =          >C15:"1            =
>B32:"door area               >B15:"Other wal
>A32:"Total of                >E14:" ft.
>E31:" sq. ft.                 >D14:8
>D31:210                       >C14:"1            =
>C31:"eas         =            >B14:"Other wal
>B31:"window are               >E13:" ft.
>A31:"Total of                 >D13:4
>C30:/--                       >C13:"1            =
>B30:/--                       >B13:"Other wal
>C29:"nd Doors                 >E12:" ft.
>B29:"Windows a                >D12:8
>E27:" sq. ft.                 >C12:"1            =
>D27:(D24*D25)                 >B12:"Other wal
>C27:"GABLES  =                >E11:" ft.
>B27:"SUBTOTAL                 >D11:22.5
>E25:" ft.                     >C11:/FR"=
>D25:8.5                       >B11:"Rear wall
>C25:/FR"=                     >E10:" ft.
>B25:" gables                  >D10:33.1
>A25:"Height of                >C10:/FR"=
>E24:" ft.                     >B10:"Side wall
>D24:5                         >E9:" ft.
>C24:/FR"=                     >D9:33.1
>B24:" gables                  >C9:/FR"=
>A24:"Length of                >B9:"Side wall
>B23:/--                       >E8:" ft.
>B22:"Gables                   >D8:22.5
>E20:" sq. ft.                 >C8:"1            =
>D20:(D17*D18                  >B8:"front wal
>C20:"HOUSE   =                >B7:"...
>B20:"SUBTOTAL                 >A7:"Length of
>E18:" ft.                     >B6:/--
>D18:9                         >C5:"a
>C18:" house  =                >B5:"House Are
>B18:" walls of                >G3:/-_
>A18:"Height of                >F3:/-_
>E17:" ft.                     >E3:/-_
>D17:@SUM(D8...D15             >D3:/-_
>C17:"use walls                >C3:/-_
>B17:"gth of hous              >B3:/-_
>A17:"Total len                >A3:/-_
>G16:/--                       >C2:"ESTIMATOR
>F16:/--                       >B2:"SIDING
>E16:/--                       /W1
>D16:/--                       /GOC
>C16:/--                       /GRA
>B16:/--                       /GC9
>A16:/--                       /X>A1:>A3:/TH
>E15:" ft.                     /X>A1:>A1:
>D15:0
```

Figure 2.10(b). Formulas for a siding estimator sheet

Chapter 3
Household Applications

In this chapter we turn our attention to the computational needs of the house-husband and housewife. If home computers are the latest in "mind appliances," then the household worksheets presented in this chapter are the latest boost to mind appliances.

The first worksheet in this collection will help you balance your checkbook. CHECK is a worksheet that lets you reconcile your bank statement in the same way that your bank's computer does. In today's modern home, homeowners ought to be as well equipped as the bank that handles their money.

METRIC is a worksheet that helps you convert from those strange metric measurements into British measurements. It is inevitable that the metric system will replace the antiquated British system, but until that day arrives, we can all use some help in conversion.

CALORIES and CARBOS are essential to persons watching their weight. CALORIES tells you how much energy you expend daily. Then CARBOS tells you how many calories and carbohydrates you consume. This way you can keep the two in balance, or if you seek weight loss, you can reduce intake appropriately.

CANNING and COOKINGU are two helpful worksheets for the kitchen. One tells you how many quarts you should be able to can from a certain amount of fresh fruit. The other tells you how to increase or decrease a recipe to adjust the amount of food prepared. If you keep forgetting how many tablespoons are in a cup, then this worksheet may be the answer.

Finally, we offer two energy guides for the energy-conscious consumer. AP-PLIANC will help you compute the amount of electrical energy consumed by your household appliances. HEAT is a worksheet for computing your heating energy index.

This collection of worksheets was selected to be interesting, useful, fun, and educational. It will give you further ideas of how to use the VisiCalc program to serve you better.

3.1. CHECK: Checkbook Balancer

Purpose   Do you make mistakes when you add up your checks, do you deduct the amount of a check from the total incorrectly, or do you simply not bother to figure it all out until the bank statement arrives at the end of the month? If so, then the worksheet in Figure 3.1(a) may solve your problems. The purpose of the checkbook balancer worksheet is to provide a record and error-free calculations for your checks.

Worksheet   To use this worksheet, start with a "beginning balance" as shown at the top of the worksheet. Then enter the date and amount of each deposit and/or withdrawal (check that you write) in the column shown. The running balance will be computed for you. You can also enter a brief reminder of what the deposit or withdrawal was for.

The total value of all deposits and withdrawals is automatically computed and stored at the top of the worksheet. The "current balance" is computed by summing the total deposits and the beginning balance minus the total withdrawals.

The worksheet can be extended as suggested by the "NA" values shown in the lower right-hand corner of Figure 3.1(a). Since the VisiCalc program allows up to 255 rows per worksheet, you could possibly have a very long list of deposits and withdrawals.

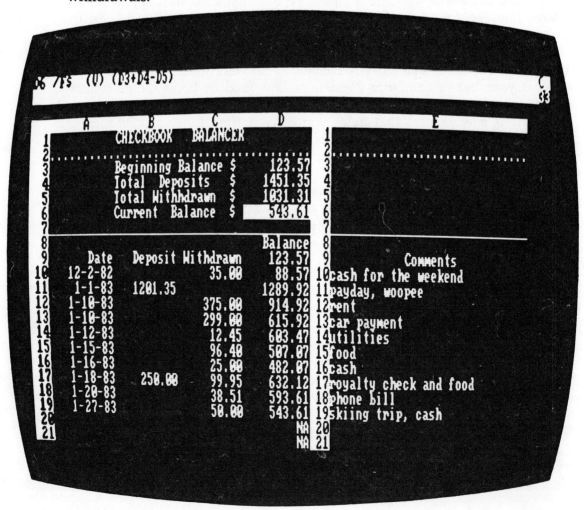

```
     CHECKBOOK   BALANCER
. . . . . . . . . . . . . . . . . . . . . . . . . . . . . . . . . . . . . . . .
     Beginning Balance $      123.57
     Total   Deposits   $     1451.35
     Total Withhdrawn   $     1031.31
     Current  Balance   $      543.61

_____
                                     Balance
     Date    Deposit Withdrawn       123.57
   12-2-82               35.00        88.57cash for t
    1-1-83   1201.35                1289.92payday, wo
    1-10-83             375.00       914.92rent
    1-10-83             299.00       615.92car paymen
    1-12-83              12.45       603.47utilities
    1-15-83              96.40       507.07food
    1-16-83              25.00       482.07cash
    1-18-83    250.00    99.95       632.12royalty ch
    1-20-83              38.51       593.61phone bill
    1-27-83              50.00       543.61skiing tri
                                        NA
                                        NA
```

Figure 3.1(a). Checkbook balancer worksheet

This is a simple application of the VisiCalc program, but you might learn something new by looking at the last seven lines at the bottom of Figure 3.1(b). What do /W1, /GOC, and /GRA mean, for example? (/WINDOW 1, /GLOBAL O C, and /GLOBAL R A). **Comments**

Figure 3.1(b) contains the formulas that you will need to reconstruct the worksheet. If you enter these manually, use /REPLICATE to cut down on typing. Notice how the formulas are adjusted relative to cells D10, D11,...etc. **Formulas**

The @IF function is used to check the cells that may contain a deposit and/or withdrawal to see if they really do. Thus, if both cells are empty (@AND), the "NA" value is stored. Otherwise, the running balance is updated, e.g., (B10+D9−C10). This in turn causes the totals to be modified. Note that the /GLOBAL O C option is set.

```
>D21:/F$@IF(@AND(B21=0,C21=0),@NA,(B21+D20-C21)
>D20:/F$@IF(@AND(B20=0,C20=0),@NA,(B20+D19-C20)
>C20:/F$
>B20:/F$
>A20:/FR
>E19:"skiing trip, cash
>D19:/F$@IF(@AND(B19=0,C19=0),@NA,(B19+D18-C19)
>C19:/F$50
>B19:/F$
>A19:/FR"1-27-83
>E18:"phone bill
>D18:/F$@IF(@AND(B18=0,C18=0),@NA,(B18+D17-C18)
>C18:/F$38.51
```

```
>B18:/F$
>A18:/FR"1-20-83
>E17:"royalty check and food
>D17:/F$@IF(@AND(B17=0,C17=0),@NA,(B17+D16-C17)
>C17:/F$99.95
>B17:/F$250
>A17:/FR"1-18-83
>E16:"cash
>D16:/F$@IF(@AND(B16=0,C16=0),@NA,(B16+D15-C16)
>C16:/F$25
>B16:/F$
>A16:/FR"1-16-83
>E15:"food
>D15:/F$@IF(@AND(B15=0,C15=0),@NA,(B15+D14-C15)
>C15:/F$96.4
>B15:/F$
>A15:/FR"1-15-83
>E14:"utilities
>D14:/F$@IF(@AND(B14=0,C14=0),@NA,(B14+D13-C14)
>C14:/F$12.45
>B14:/F$
>A14:/FR"1-12-83
>E13:"car payment
>D13:/F$@IF(@AND(B13=0,C13=0),@NA,(B13+D12-C13)
>C13:/F$299
>B13:/F$
>A13:/FR"1-10-83
>E12:"rent
>D12:/F$@IF(@AND(B12=0,C12=0),@NA,(B12+D11-C12)
>C12:/F$375
>B12:/F$
>A12:/FR"1-10-83
>E11:"payday, woopee
>D11:/F$@IF(@AND(B11=0,C11=0),@NA,(B11+D10-C11)
>C11:/F$
>B11:/F$1201.35
>A11:/FR"1-1-83
>E10:"cash for the weekend
>D10:/F$@IF(@AND(B10=0,C10=0),@NA,(B10+D9-C10)
>C10:/F$35
>B10:/F$
>A10:/FR"12-2-82
>E9:"            Comments
>D9:/FR(D3)
>C9:/FR"Withdrawn
>B9:/FR"Deposit
>A9:/FR"Date
>D8:/FR"Balance
>H7:/-_
>G7:/-_
>F7:/-_
>E7:/-_
>D7:/-_
>C7:/-_
>B7:/-_
```

```
>A7:/-_
>D6:/F$(D3+D4-D5)
>C6:"alance   $
>B6:"Current   B
>D5:/F$@SUM(C10...C21
>C5:"hdrawn   $
>B5:"Total With
>D4:/F$@SUM(B10...B21
>C4:"osits    $
>B4:"Total  Dep
>D3:/F$123.57
>C3:"Balance $
>B3:"Beginning
>H2:/-.
>G2:/-.
>F2:/-.
>E2:/-.
>D2:/-.
>C2:/-.
>B2:/-.
>A2:/-.
>C1:/FR"BALANCER
>B1:"CHECKBOOK
/W1
/GOC
/GRA
/XV43
/GC10
/X>A1:>A1:;/GC30
/X>F1:>F21:;/WS
```

Figure 3.1(b). Formulas for checkbook balancer worksheet

3.2. METRIC: Metric Conversion Table

Purpose   An "intelligent" conversion table can be constructed in VisiCalc software by storing the conversion formulas in a worksheet. This idea is illustrated in the Metric Conversion Table of Figure 3.2(a).

The purpose of this example is to show how to implement a conversion table, in general, and to give you a metric conversion table in particular. The table of Figure 3.2(a) may be useful to you when using recipes, shipping packages to another country, etc.

Worksheet   Figure 3.2(a) contains a list of commonly used measures of length, weight, and volume expressed in metric and British units. The worksheet also contains formulas for computing the number in English units given the number of metric units. This is the secret to the application of the VisiCalc program to conversion tables.

If you enter 3.5 in the first row (for centimeters), then the corresponding value in feet will be computed and displayed as shown in Figure 3.2(a). Suppose further that 10 replaces 1 in the row containing pounds and grams. The formula for grams will be used to recalculate 453.6 to get 4536.0, instead.

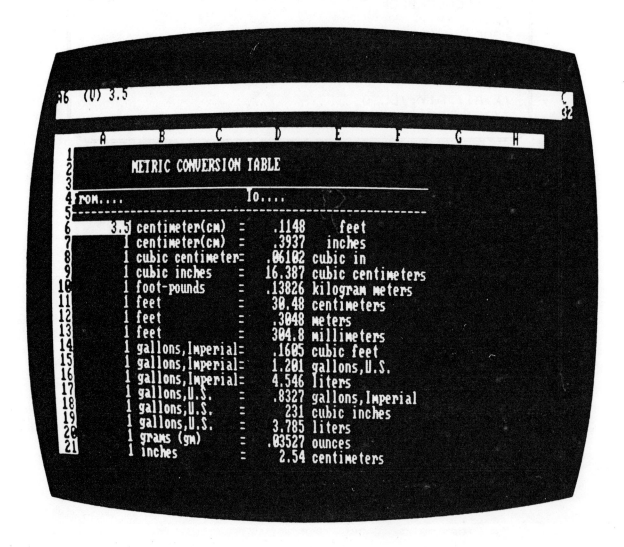

```
                 METRIC CONVERSION TABLE
----------------------------------------------------------------
From....                        To....
----------------------------------------------------------------
       3.5 centimeter(cm)    =    .1148      feet
         1 centimeter(cm)    =    .3937      inches
         1 cubic centimeter=     .06102 cubic in
         1 cubic inches      =  16.387  cubic centimeters
         1 foot-pounds       =    .13826 kilogram meters
         1 feet              =  30.48   centimeters
         1 feet              =    .3048  meters
         1 feet              = 304.8    millimeters
         1 gallons,Imperial=      .1605  cubic feet
         1 gallons,Imperial=     1.201   gallons,U.S.
         1 gallons,Imperial=     4.546   liters
         1 gallons,U.S.      =    .8327  gallons,Imperial
         1 gallons,U.S.      =   231     cubic inches
         1 gallons,U.S.      =     3.785  liters
         1 grams (gm)        =    .03527 ounces
         1 inches            =     2.54  centimeters
         1 inches            =    25.4   millimeters
         1 kilograms(kg)     =     2.205 pounds
         1 kilometers(km)    =     .6214 miles
         1 kilometers(km)    =  3280.7  feet
         1 liters(l)         =     .22   gallons,Imperial
         1 liters            =    .2642  gallons,U.S.
         1 liters            =    .03531 cubic feet
         1 liters            =   61.022  cubic inches
         1 meters(m)         =     3.281 feet
         1 meters            =    39.37  inches
         1 meters            =     1.094 yards
         1 miles(mi)         =     1.609 kilometers
         1 pounds            =   453.6   grams
         1 pounds            =    .4536  kilograms
         1 sq centimeter     =    .155   sq inches
         1 sq inches         =     6.452 sq centimeters
         1 yards             =    .9144  meters
----------------------------------------------------------------
```

Figure 3.2(a). Metric conversion table

Comments

You may want to add to this table. You can add additional columns or rows. If you add more columns, then the conversions must work for several units rather than one other unit. For example, you might convert pounds to grams and grains, all in one row of the table. If you add rows, then you might add conversions that go in the "opposite" direction. That is, you could add rows that convert British units to metric units. For example, a row could be added that converts from kilogram-meters to foot-pounds much like the grams-to-pound row.

Formulas

All formulas and labels needed to reconstruct the conversion table are shown in Figure 3.2(b). The labels can be entered to get the form shown in the worksheet. The formulas will need to be entered one at a time, however, because each conversion factor is unique. Thus, cell D34 computes 453.6*A34 to get 453.6 grams.

The column of 1s in column A can be entered quickly using /REPLICATE. Also notice that /TITLE H has been used to lock the title rows (row 1 through row 5). This prevents the title row from scrolling up and off the screen when using the lengthy table.

```
>F39:/-_                        >E31:" inches
>E39:/-_                        >D31:39.37*A31
>D39:/-_                        >C31:/FR"=
>C39:/-_                        >B31:" meters
>B39:/-_                        >A31:1
>A39:/-_                        >E30:" feet
>E38:" meters                   >D30:3.281*A30
>D38:.9144*A38                  >C30:/FR")            =
>C38:/FR"=                      >B30:" meters(m
>B38:" yards                    >A30:1
>A38:1                          >F29:"ches
>F37:"meters                    >E29:" cubic in
>E37:" sq centimete             >D29:61.022*A29
>D37:6.452*A37                  >C29:/FR"=
>C37:/FR"s         =            >B29:" liters
>B37:" sq inches                >A29:1
>A37:1                          >F28:"et
>F36:"s                         >E28:" cubic fee
>E36:" sq inche                 >D28:.03531*A28
>D36:.155*A36                   >C28:/FR"=
>C36:/FR"meter     =            >B28:" liters
>B36:" sq centi                 >A28:1
>A36:1                          >F27:"U.S.
>F35:"s                         >E27:" gallons,
>E35:" kilogram                 >D27:.2642*A27
>D35:.4536*A35                  >C27:/FR"=
>C35:/FR"=                      >B27:" liters
>B35:" pounds                   >A27:1
>A35:1                          >F26:"Imperial
>E34:" grams                    >E26:" gallons,
>D34:453.6*A34                  >D26:.22*A26
>C34:/FR"=                      >C26:")           =
>B34:" pounds                   >B26:" liters(l
>A34:1                          >A26:1
>F33:"rs                        >E25:" feet
>E33:" kilomete                 >D25:3280.7*A25
>D33:1.609*A33                  >C25:"rs(km)   =
>C33:/FR")         =            >B25:" kilometer
>B33:" miles(mi                 >A25:1
>A33:1                          >E24:" miles
>E32:" yards                    >D24:.6214*A24
>D32:1.094*A32                  >C24:"rs(km)   =
>C32:/FR"=                      >B24:" kilometer
>B32:" meters                   >A24:1
>A32:1                          >E23:" pounds
```

```
>D23:2.205*A23        >A14:1
>C23:"s(kg)     =     >F13:"ers
>B23:" kilogram       >E13:" millimet
>A23:1                >D13:304.8*A13
>F22:"ers             >C13:/FR"=
>E22:" millimet       >B13:" feet
>D22:25.4*A22         >A13:1
>C22:/FR"=            >E12:" meters
>B22:" inches         >D12:.3048*A12
>A22:1                >C12:/FR"=
>F21:"ers             >B12:" feet
>E21:" centimeter     >A12:1
>D21:2.54*A21         >F11:"ers
>C21:/FR"=            >E11:" centimeter
>B21:" inches         >D11:30.48*A11
>A21:1                >C11:/FR"=
>E20:" ounces         >B11:" feet
>D20:.03527*A20       >A11:1
>C20:"m)        =     >F10:" meters
>B20:" grams (g       >E10:" kilogram
>A20:1                >D10:.13826*A10
>E19:" liters         >C10:"nds       =
>D19:3.785*A19        >B10:" foot-pou
>C19:"U.S.      =     >A10:1
>B19:" gallons,       >F9:"ntimeters
>A19:1                >E9:" cubic cent
>F18:"ches            >D9:16.387*A9
>E18:" cubic in       >C9:"ches      =
>D18:231*A18          >B9:" cubic inch
>C18:"U.S.      =     >A9:1
>B18:" gallons,       >E8:/FR"cubic in
>A18:1                >D8:.06102*A8
>F17:"Imperial        >C8:"ntimeter=
>E17:" gallons,       >B8:" cubic centi
>D17:.8327*A17        >A8:1
>C17:"U.S.      =     >E7:/FR"inches
>B17:" gallons,       >D7:.3937*A7
>A17:1                >C7:"er(cm)   =
>E16:" liters         >B7:" centimet
>D16:4.546*A16        >A7:1
>C16:"Imperial=       >E6:/FR"feet
>B16:" gallons,       >D6:.0328*A6
>A16:1                >C6:"er(cm)   =
>F15:"U.S.            >B6:" centimete
>E15:" gallons,       >A6:3.5
>D15:1.201*A15        >F5:/--
>C15:"Imperial=       >E5:/--
>B15:" gallons,       >D5:/--
>A15:1                >C5:/--
>F14:"et              >B5:/--
>E14:" cubic feet     >A5:/--
>D14:.1605*A14        >D4:"To....
>C14:"Imperial=       >A4:"From....
>B14:" gallons,       >F3:/-_
```

```
>E3:/-_                    >B2:"METRIC CO
>D3:/-_                    /W1
>C3:/-_                    /GOC
>B3:/-_                    /GRA
>A3:/-_                    /GC9
>D2:"TABLE                 /X>A1:>A5:/TH
>C2:"NVERSION              /X>A1:>A1:
```

Figure 3.2(b). Formulas for metric conversion table

3.3. CALORIES: Personal Energy Expended Per Day

Suppose you are planning to gain or lose weight through control of your caloric intake. Before changing your eating habits it might be a good idea to find out how many calories per day you already burn. The questionnaire shown in Figure 3.3(a) can be used to compute your daily expenditure of energy.

Purpose

The purpose of the Personal Energy Expended Table shown in Figure 3.3(a) is to calculate the total number of calories used given the number of hours each activity is performed. This table is based on averages for normal humans. It should give good results for you, but remember that the metabolic rate varies with different bodies.

Figure 3.3(a) shows the results obtained by an average office worker that gets eight hours of sleep every night. The user enters the estimated time spent doing each of the activities listed in column A. The VisiCalc program uses this estimate and the calories-per-hour estimates to compute a subtotal per activity. These subtotals are summed to arrive at the grand total number of calories burned up in the 24-hour period.

Worksheet

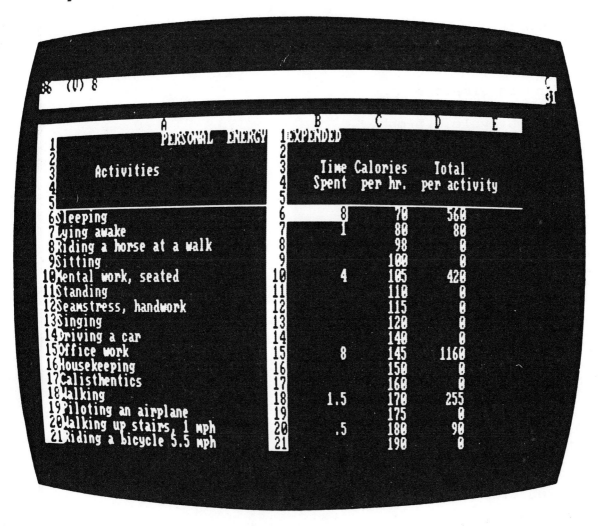

	Activities		Time Spent	Calories per hr.	Total per activity
1	PERSONAL ENERGY EXPENDED				
2					
3	Activities		Time	Calories	Total
4			Spent	per hr.	per activity
5					
6	Sleeping		8	70	560
7	Lying awake		1	80	80
8	Riding a horse at a walk			90	0
9	Sitting			100	0
10	Mental work, seated		4	105	420
11	Standing			110	0
12	Seamstress, handwork			115	0
13	Singing			120	0
14	Driving a car			140	0
15	Office work		8	145	1160
16	Housekeeping			150	0
17	Calisthentics			160	0
18	Walking		1.5	170	255
19	Piloting an airplane			175	0
20	Walking up stairs, 1 mph		.5	180	90
21	Riding a bicycle 5.5 mph			190	0

To use this worksheet, first blank-out the time estimate column. You can do this quickly by using a /BLANK command followed by a /REPLICATE command that replaces every entry in the column with a blank. Next, use the cursor to move down the "time spent" column entering the approximate number of hours you spend each day doing each activity.

The total number of hours and calories will be automatically computed and displayed at the bottom of the questionnaire. This gives you an idea of how many calories per day you need in order to maintain your present weight.

```
              PERSONAL  ENERGY  EXPENDED

         Activities           Time Calories      Total
                              Spent  per hr.   per activity
---------------------------------------------------------------
Sleeping                        8       70          560
Lying awake                     1       80           80
Riding a horse at a walk                98            0
Sitting                                100            0
Mental work, seated             4      105          420
Standing                               110            0
Seamstress, handwork                   115            0
Singing                                120            0
Driving a car                          140            0
Office work                     8      145         1160
Housekeeping                           150            0
Calisthentics                          160            0
Walking                       1.5      170          255
Piloting an airplane                   175            0
Walking up stairs, 1 mph       .5      180           90
Riding a bicycle 5.5 mph               190            0
Walking down stairs, 2 mph     .4      200           80
Bricklaying                            205            0
House painting                         210            0
Carpenter work                         230            0
Billiards                              235            0
Pitching horseshoes                    240            0
Dancing, moderate                      250            0
Swedish gymnastics                     260            0
Laundry work                           270            0
Baseball (except pitcher)              280            0
Walking, 3.5 mph                       290            0
Baseball pitcher                       390            0
Pick and shovel work                   400            0
Shoveling sand                         405            0
Swimming breastroke, 1 mph             410            0
Bicycle riding, rapidly                415            0
Swimming crawlstroke, 1 mph            420            0
Chopping wood                   .1     450           45
Body building                          460            0
Skating, 9 mph                         470            0
Sawing wood                            480            0
Skiing, 3mph                           540            0
Swimming sidestroke, 1 mph             550            0
```

```
High speed walking, 5.3 mph                580         0
Mountain climbing                          600         0
Fencing                                    630         0
Skating, 11 mph                            640         0
Rowing, 3.5 mph                            660         0
Parallel bar work                          710         0
Running, 5.7 mph                    .5     720       360
Wrestling                                  790         0
Running, 7 mph                             870         0
Rowing, 11 mph                             970         0
Football                                  1000         0
Running, 14.8 mph                         2880         0
-----------------------------------------------------------
     TOTALS          =        24 Hrs.          3050 Calories
```

Figure 3.3(a). Personal energy table

It may surprise you that over one-sixth of the energy expended by the office **Comments** worker in Figure 3.3(a) was due to sleeping. Sleeping eight hours is as much hard work as walking a mile in three hours! You may want to add other activities to the list given here. If so, don't forget to extend the formulas to include your new entries.

Also notice that the split-window option is used to display this worksheet. The activities are displayed in a left-side window with a column width set at 32 characters. The numerical columns are displayed in a right-side window with column width set to nine characters. You can see these settings at the bottom of Figure 3.3(b). The /GC32 and /GC9 codes refer to these two column widths.

The /WS option is used to synchronize the two halves of the split window screen. This means that both halves are simultaneously scrolled up and down. Use the ; command to switch back and forth between the two halves.

If you reconstruct this worksheet from the labels and formulas in Figure 3.3(b), be sure to enter the list of activities first. Set the column width /GLOBAL C 32, before you begin and do not worry about the other columns until you have entered all of the activities. Next, set the cursor on a cell in column B and enter /WINDOW V to split the screen vertically. Secondly, enter /WINDOW S to cause the two halves to be synchronized.

Now, the ; command can be used to switch between the two windows. If you are "in" the right-side window, enter the /GLOBAL C 9 command to force all cells in the right-side window to become nine characters wide. This is the only way to make the VisiCalc program hold cells of two different character widths.

Figure 3.3(b) can be used to reconstruct the personal energy questionnaire if **Formulas** you did not purchase the diskette containing the worksheet. You can use /REPLICATE to reduce your typing effort, because the formula that computes the subtotal column can be replicated into each cell of that column.

The @SUMs in cells B58 and D58 total the number of hours and calories consumed. All other entries must be entered individually.

```
>E58:" Calories                        >D41:(B41*C41)
>D58:@SUM(D6...D56                      >C41:470
>C58:" Hrs.                             >A41:"Skating, 9 mph
>B58:@SUM(B6...B56                      >D40:(B40*C40)
>A58:"        TOTALS        =           >C40:460
>D57:/--                                >A40:"Body building
>C57:/--                                >D39:(B39*C39)
>B57:/--                                >C39:450
>A57:/--                                >B39:.1
>D56:(B56*C56)                          >A39:"Chopping wood
>C56:2880                               >D38:(B38*C38)
>A56:"Running, 14.8 mph                 >C38:420
>D55:(B55*C55)                          >A38:"Swimming crawlstroke, 1 mph
>C55:1000                               >D37:(B37*C37)
>A55:"Football                          >C37:415
>D54:(B54*C54)                          >A37:"Bicycle riding, rapidly
>C54:970                                >D36:(B36*C36)
>A54:"Rowing, 11 mph                    >C36:410
>D53:(B53*C53)                          >A36:"Swimming breaststroke, 1 mph
>C53:870                                >D35:(B35*C35)
>A53:"Running, 7 mph                    >C35:405
>D52:(B52*C52)                          >A35:"Shoveling sand
>C52:790                                >D34:(B34*C34)
>A52:"Wrestling                         >C34:400
>D51:(B51*C51)                          >A34:"Pick and shovel work
>C51:720                                >D33:(B33*C33)
>B51:.5                                 >C33:390
>A51:"Running, 5.7 mph                  >A33:"Baseball pitcher
>D50:(B50*C50)                          >D32:(B32*C32)
>C50:710                                >C32:290
>A50:"Parallel bar work                 >A32:"Walking, 3.5 mph
>D49:(B49*C49)                          >D31:(B31*C31)
>C49:660                                >C31:280
>A49:"Rowing, 3.5 mph                   >A31:"Baseball (except pitcher)
>D48:(B48*C48)                          >D30:(B30*C30)
>C48:640                                >C30:270
>A48:"Skating, 11 mph                   >A30:"Laundry work
>D47:(B47*C47)                          >D29:(B29*C29)
>C47:630                                >C29:260
>A47:"Fencing                           >A29:"Swedish gymnastics
>D46:(B46*C46)                          >D28:(B28*C28)
>C46:600                                >C28:250
>A46:"Mountain climbing                 >A28:"Dancing, moderate
>D45:(B45*C45)                          >D27:(B27*C27)
>C45:580                                >C27:240
>A45:"High speed walking, 5.3 mph       >A27:"Pitching horseshoes
>D44:(B44*C44)                          >D26:(B26*C26)
>C44:550                                >C26:235
>A44:"Swimming sidestroke, 1 mph        >A26:"Billiards
>D43:(B43*C43)                          >D25:(B25*C25)
>C43:540                                >C25:230
>A43:"Skiing, 3mph                      >A25:"Carpenter work
>D42:(B42*C42)                          >D24:(B24*C24)
>C42:480                                >C24:210
>A42:"Sawing wood                       >A24:"House painting
```

```
>D23:(B23*C23)                          >D10:(B10*C10)
>C23:205                                >C10:105
>A23:"Bricklaying                       >B10:4
>D22:(B22*C22)                          >A10:"Mental work, seated
>C22:200                                >D9:(B9*C9)
>B22:.4                                 >C9:100
>A22:"Walking down stairs, 2 mph        >A9:"Sitting
>D21:(B21*C21)                          >D8:(B8*C8)
>C21:190                                >C8:98
>A21:"Riding a bicycle 5.5 mph          >A8:"Riding a horse at a walk
>D20:(B20*C20)                          >D7:(B7*C7)
>C20:180                                >C7:80
>B20:.5                                 >B7:1
>A20:"Walking up stairs, 1 mph          >A7:"Lying awake
>D19:(B19*C19)                          >D6:(B6*C6)
>C19:175                                >C6:70
>A19:"Piloting an airplane              >B6:8
>D18:(B18*C18)                          >A6:"Sleeping
>C18:170                                >E5:/-_
>B18:1.5                                >D5:/-_
>A18:"Walking                           >C5:/-_
>D17:(B17*C17)                          >B5:/FR/-_
>C17:160                                >A5:/-_
>A17:"Calisthentics                     >E4:"ivity
>D16:(B16*C16)                          >D4:/FR"per act
>C16:150                                >C4:/FR"per hr.
>A16:"Housekeeping                      >B4:/FR"Spent
>D15:(B15*C15)                          >D3:/FR"Total
>C15:145                                >C3:/FR"Calories
>B15:8                                  >B3:/FR"Time
>A15:"Office work                       >A3:/FL"         Activities
>D14:(B14*C14)                          >B1:"EXPENDED
>C14:140                                >A1:/FR"PERSONAL  ENERGY
>A14:"Driving a car                     /W1
>D13:(B13*C13)                          /GOC
>C13:120                                /GRA
>A13:"Singing                           /XV35
>D12:(B12*C12)                          /GC32
>C12:115                                /X>A1:>A5:/TH
>A12:"Seamstress, handwork              /X>A1:>A1:;/GC9
>D11:(B11*C11)                          /X>A1:>A5:/TH
>C11:110                                /X>B1:>B1:;/WS
>A11:"Standing
```

Figure 3.3(b). Formulas for personal energy table

3.4. CARBOS: Daily Intake of Carbohydrates and Calories

Purpose
The previous worksheet helps you find out how many calories of energy you consume in a day. This worksheet helps you compute the total number of calories you eat. The purpose of the Calorie Counting Chart of Figure 3.4(a) is to tally the number of calories and carbohydrates eaten in a meal.

Worksheet
The chart of Figure 3.4(a) is actually a questionnaire. To use it all you have to do is enter numbers as shown in the column labeled "QTY CONSUMED." For example, if you eat 6 oz. of ground beef, then enter 1.5 in the appropriate cell.

If you /BLANK and /REPLICATE the "QTY CONSUMED" column to start, then you can enter the desired amounts into each cell as you move the VisiCalc cursor down the chart.

The total number of calories and carbohydrates will be displayed in the last row of the chart. In the example of Figure 3.4(a), the totals of 1742.45 and 174.6 were obtained for a meal of apples, artichokes, avocados, lima beans, ground beef, wholewheat bread, a carrot, celery, oatmeal, cheddar cheese, chocolate drink, whole milk, orange juice, and one baked potato.

	A	B	C	D	E	F
1	CALORIE & CARBOHYDRATE COMPUTER					
2						
3	Item	Qty	Calories	Calories	Carbos	Carbos
4	serving size	Consumed	serving	consumed	serving	consumed
5	--------	--------				
6	Apples					
7	fresh, average size	1	66	66	16.9	16.9
8	baked, 2T brown sugar		184	0	51.3	0
9	Apricots			0		0
10	fresh, 3 medium		55	0	13	0
11	canned in water, 1 C		76	0	19.8	0
12	Artichoke heart,5 canned	.5	40	20	8	4
13	Asparagus, 6 boiled		19	0	6	0
14	Avocado, 1/2 medium	.75	185	138.75	6	4.5
15	Bacon, fried 2 strips		98	0	.2	0
16	Bananas, fresh 1 medium		87	0	35	0
17	Beans			0		0
18	pork, 1/2 C canned		197	0	27	0
19	green, 1/2 C canned		21	0	3	0
20	lima, 1/2 C canned	.35	82	28.7	15	5.25
21	pinto, 1/2 C dry		349	0	63.7	0

```
┌─────────────────────────────────────────────────────────────────┐
```

CALORIE & CARBOHYDRATE COMPUTER

Item serving size	Qty Consumed	Calories serving	Calories consumed	Carbos serving	Carbos consumed
Apples					
fresh, average size	1	66	66	16.9	16.9
baked, 2T brown sugar		184	0	51.3	0
Apricots			0		0
fresh, 3 medium		55	0	13	0
canned in water, 1 C		76	0	19.8	0
Artichoke heart,5 canned	.5	40	20	8	4
Asparagus, 6 boiled		19	0	6	0
Avocado, 1/2 medium	.75	185	138.75	6	4.5
Bacon, fried 2 strips		98	0	.2	0
Bananas, fresh 1 medium		87	0	35	0
Beans			0		0
pork, 1/2 C canned		197	0	27	0
green, 1/2 C canned		21	0	3	0
lima, 1/2 C canned	.35	82	28.7	15	5.25
pinto, 1/2 C dry		349	0	63.7	0
Beef			0		0
ground, 4 oz (lean)	1.5	250	375	0	0
ground, 4 oz (regular)		326	0	0	0
stew, 4 oz canned		91	0	0	0
roast, 4 oz canned		255	0	0	0
vegetable soup 4 oz		90	0	0	0
Berries, 1/2 C, fresh		42	0	10.6	0
Bread			0		0
wholewheat, 1 slice	2	56	112	11.3	22.6
white, 1 slice		58	0	11.9	0
Carrot, 1 medium	1	21	21	5.1	5.1
Celery, 1 stalk	.5	6	3	1.5	.75
Cereals			0		0
all-bran, 1 C		192	0	42.5	0
cornflakes, 1 C		79	0	21	0
cream-wheat, 1C cooked		133	0	26.8	0
oatmeal, 1C cooked	1	130	130	26	26
Wheaties, 1C		108	0	23	0
Cheese			0		0
American, 1 oz		105	0	.6	0
cheddar, 1 oz	3	111	333	.6	1.8
cottage, creamed 1 oz		30	0	.6	0
swiss, 1 oz		95	0	.5	0
Velveeta, 1 oz		84	0	3	0
Chicken, fried 11 oz		435	0	6.2	0
Chocolate drink, 3 tsp	1	84	84	27.9	27.9
Eggs, fried 1 large		81	0	.4	0
Flour			0		0
corn, 1 C		405	0	84.6	0
wheat, 1 C		400	0	83.7	0
white, 1 C		449	0	83.7	0
Frankfurter, 1 average		151	0	1	0
Grape juice, 8 oz		134	0	31	0
Ice cream cone 1 sugar		215	0	15.2	0

Ice milk, 1/3 pt.	135	0	29.2	0
Macaroni-cheese, 4 oz	108	0	44	0
Milk		0		0
whole 3.5%, 8 oz 1	159	159	11.8	11.8
skim, 8 oz	89	0	13	0
Muffin, 1 English	140	0	17.5	0
Noodles, egg, cooked 1C	200	0	37	0
Oil, cooking 1 T	128	0	0	0
Orange juice, 8 oz 1	117	117	27	27
Pancake, 4" diameter	71	0	12.9	0
Peanut butter, 1 T	100	0	3.4	0
Popcorn, 1 c	54	0	11	0
Potatoes		0		0
baked, 1 medium 1	155	155	21	21
Frenchfried, 10 pcs	156	0	20	0
sweet, 1 medium	155	0	36	0
Rice		0		0
brown, 1 C	200	0	43	0
white, 1 C	185	0	44	0
Tuna, canned 4 oz	327	0	0	0
Turkey, roasted 4 oz	215	0	0	0
Yogurt, plain 1 C	123	0	11.7	0
TOTALS =		1742.45		174.6

Figure 3.4(a). Calorie counting chart

Comments   The worksheet in this example is rather long and yet it does not contain nearly as many foods as you usually eat. Therefore you will probably want to add to the list. Remember, the VisiCalc program will only hold 255 rows. If you run out of space, then perhaps you will have to divide the chart into food groups. For example, you can build one chart for meats only, another chart for dairy products, etc. This way you can increase the size of the chart without overflowing the VisiCalc worksheet. Each of the charts will be stored on diskette until you need them.

Formulas   The formulas in Figure 3.4(b) can be used to reconstruct the chart. The /REPLICATE command can be used to replicate the formulas needed to compute the subtotals in the calorie and carbohydrate columns. Otherwise, the labels and formulas must be entered one at a time.

    The worksheet is split into vertical halves using the /WINDOW V and /WINDOW S commands. The list of foods is stored in 24 character columns, while the other window is stored in nine character columns. For a detailed explanation of how to split the screen in this fashion, see the comments in the previous section on CALORIES.

```
>F80:/-_                    >A80:/-_
>E80:/-_                    >F79:@SUM(F6...F77
>D80:/-_                    >D79:@SUM(D6...D77
>C80:/-_                    >A79:"        TOTALS =
>B80:/-_                    >F78:/--
```

```
>E78:/--                          >C67:54
>D78:/--                          >A67:"Popcorn, 1 c
>C78:/--                          >F66:(B66*E66)
>B78:/--                          >E66:3.4
>A78:/--                          >D66:(B66*C66)
>F77:(B77*E77)                    >C66:100
>E77:11.7                         >A66:"Peanut butter, 1 T
>D77:(B77*C77)                    >F65:(B65*E65)
>C77:123                          >E65:12.9
>A77:"Yogurt, plain 1 C           >D65:(B65*C65)
>F76:(B76*E76)                    >C65:71
>E76:0                            >A65:"Pancake, 4" diameter
>D76:(B76*C76)                    >F64:(B64*E64)
>C76:215                          >E64:27
>A76:"Turkey, roasted 4 oz        >D64:(B64*C64)
>F75:(B75*E75)                    >C64:117
>E75:0                            >B64:1
>D75:(B75*C75)                    >A64:"Orange juice, 8 oz
>C75:327                          >F63:(B63*E63)
>A75:"Tuna, canned 4 oz           >E63:0
>F74:(B74*E74)                    >D63:(B63*C63)
>E74:44                           >C63:128
>D74:(B74*C74)                    >A63:"Oil, cooking 1 T
>C74:185                          >F62:(B62*E62)
>A74:"  white, 1 C                >E62:37
>F73:(B73*E73)                    >D62:(B62*C62)
>E73:43                           >C62:200
>D73:(B73*C73)                    >A62:"Noodles, egg, cooked 1C
>C73:200                          >F61:(B61*E61)
>A73:"  brown, 1 C                >E61:17.5
>F72:(B72*E72)                    >D61:(B61*C61)
>D72:(B72*C72)                    >C61:140
>A72:"Rice                        >A61:"Muffin, 1 English
>F71:(B71*E71)                    >F60:(B60*E60)
>E71:36                           >E60:13
>D71:(B71*C71)                    >D60:(B60*C60)
>C71:155                          >C60:89
>A71:"  sweet, 1 medium           >A60:"  skim, 8 oz
>F70:(B70*E70)                    >F59:(B59*E59)
>E70:20                           >E59:11.8
>D70:(B70*C70)                    >D59:(B59*C59)
>C70:156                          >C59:159
>A70:"  Frenchfried, 10 pcs       >B59:1
>F69:(B69*E69)                    >A59:"  whole 3.5%, 8 oz
>E69:21                           >F58:(B58*E58)
>D69:(B69*C69)                    >D58:(B58*C58)
>C69:155                          >A58:"Milk
>B69:1                            >F57:(B57*E57)
>A69:"  baked, 1 medium           >E57:44
>F68:(B68*E68)                    >D57:(B57*C57)
>D68:(B68*C68)                    >C57:108
>A68:"Potatoes                    >A57:"Macaroni-cheese, 4 oz
>F67:(B67*E67)                    >F56:(B56*E56)
>E67:11                           >E56:29.2
>D67:(B67*C67)                    >D56:'B56*C56)
```

>C56:135
>A56:"Ice milk, 1/3 pt.
>F55:(B55*E55)
>E55:15.2
>D55:(B55*C55)
>C55:215
>A55:"Ice cream cone 1 sugar
>F54:(B54*E54)
>E54:31
>D54:(B54*C54)
>C54:134
>A54:"Grape juice, 8 oz
>F53:(B53*E53)
>E53:1
>D53:(B53*C53)
>C53:151
>A53:"Frankfurter, 1 average
>F52:(B52*E52)
>E52:83.7
>D52:(B52*C52)
>C52:449
>A52:" white, 1 C
>F51:(B51*E51)
>E51:83.7
>D51:(B51*C51)
>C51:400
>A51:" wheat, 1 C
>F50:(B50*E50)
>E50:84.6
>D50:(B50*C50)
>C50:405
>A50:" corn, 1 C
>F49:(B49*E49)
>D49:(B49*C49)
>A49:"Flour
>F48:(B48*E48)
>E48:.4
>D48:(B48*C48)
>C48:81
>A48:"Eggs, fried 1 large
>F47:(B47*E47)
>E47:27.9
>D47:(B47*C47)
>C47:84
>B47:1
>A47:"Chocolate drink, 3 tsp
>F46:(B46*E46)
>E46:6.2
>D46:(B46*C46)
>C46:435
>A46:"Chicken, fried 11 oz
>F45:(B45*E45)
>E45:3
>D45:(B45*C45)
>C45:84

>A45:" Velveeta, 1 oz
>F44:(B44*E44)
>E44:.5
>D44:(B44*C44)
>C44:95
>A44:" swiss, 1 oz
>F43:(B43*E43)
>E43:.6
>D43:(B43*C43)
>C43:30
>A43:" cottage, creamed 1 oz
>F42:(B42*E42)
>E42:.6
>D42:(B42*C42)
>C42:111
>B42:3
>A42:" cheddar, 1 oz
>F41:(B41*E41)
>E41:.6
>D41:(B41*C41)
>C41:105
>A41:" American, 1 oz
>F40:(B40*E40)
>D40:(B40*C40)
>A40:"Cheese
>F39:(B39*E39)
>E39:23
>D39:(B39*C39)
>C39:108
>A39:" Wheaties, 1C
>F38:(B38*E38)
>E38:26
>D38:(B38*C38)
>C38:130
>B38:1
>A38:" oatmeal, 1C cooked
>F37:(B37*E37)
>E37:26.8
>D37:(B37*C37)
>C37:133
>A37:" cream-wheat, 1C cooked
>F36:(B36*E36)
>E36:21
>D36:(B36*C36)
>C36:79
>A36:" cornflakes, 1 C
>F35:(B35*E35)
>E35:42.5
>D35:(B35*C35)
>C35:192
>A35:" all-bran, 1 C
>F34:(B34*E34)
>D34:(B34*C34)
>A34:"Cereals
>F33:(B33*E33)

```
>E33:1.5
>D33:(B33*C33)
>C33:6
>B33:.5
>A33:"Celery, 1 stalk
>F32:(B32*E32)
>E32:5.1
>D32:(B32*C32)
>C32:21
>B32:1
>A32:"Carrot, 1 medium
>F31:(B31*E31)
>E31:11.9
>D31:(B31*C31)
>C31:58
>A31:"  white, 1 slice
>F30:(B30*E30)
>E30:11.3
>D30:(B30*C30)
>C30:56
>B30:2
>A30:"  wholewheat, 1 slice
>F29:(B29*E29)
>D29:(B29*C29)
>A29:"Bread
>F28:(B28*E28)
>E28:10.6
>D28:(B28*C28)
>C28:42
>A28:"Berries, 1/2 C, fresh
>F27:(B27*E27)
>E27:0
>D27:(B27*C27)
>C27:90
>A27:"  vegetable soup 4 oz
>F26:(B26*E26)
>E26:0
>D26:(B26*C26)
>C26:255
>A26:"  roast, 4 oz canned
>F25:(B25*E25)
>E25:0
>D25:(B25*C25)
>C25:91
>A25:"  stew, 4 oz canned
>F24:(B24*E24)
>E24:0
>D24:(B24*C24)
>C24:326
>A24:"  ground, 4 oz(regular)
>F23:(B23*E23)
>E23:0
>D23:(B23*C23)
>C23:250
>B23:1.5
```

```
>A23:"  ground, 4 oz(lean)
>F22:(B22*E22)
>D22:(B22*C22)
>A22:"Beef
>F21:(B21*E21)
>E21:63.7
>D21:(B21*C21)
>C21:349
>A21:"  pinto, 1/2 C dry
>F20:(B20*E20)
>E20:15
>D20:(B20*C20)
>C20:82
>B20:.35
>A20:"  lima, 1/2 C canned
>F19:(B19*E19)
>E19:3
>D19:(B19*C19)
>C19:21
>A19:"  green, 1/2 C canned
>F18:(B18*E18)
>E18:27
>D18:(B18*C18)
>C18:197
>A18:"  pork, 1/2 C canned
>F17:(B17*E17)
>D17:(B17*C17)
>A17:"Beans
>F16:(B16*E16)
>E16:35
>D16:(B16*C16)
>C16:87
>A16:"Bananas, fresh 1 medium
>F15:(B15*E15)
>E15:.2
>D15:(B15*C15)
>C15:98
>A15:"Bacon, fried 2 strips
>F14:(B14*E14)
>E14:6
>D14:(B14*C14)
>C14:185
>B14:.75
>A14:"Avocado, 1/2 medium
>F13:(B13*E13)
>E13:6
>D13:(B13*C13)
>C13:19
>A13:"Asparagus, 6 boiled
>F12:(B12*E12)
>E12:8
>D12:(B12*C12)
>C12:40
>B12:.5
>A12:"Artichoke heart,5 canned
```

```
>F11:(B11*E11)                    >C5:/--
>E11:19.8                         >B5:/--
>D11:(B11*C11)                    >A5:/--
>C11:76`                          >F4:/FR"consumed
>A11:"  canned in water, 1 C      >E4:/FR"serving
>F10:(B10*E10)                    >D4:/FR"consumed
>E10:13                           >C4:/FR"serving
>D10:(B10*C10)                    >B4:/FR"Consumed
>C10:55                           >A4:"          serving size
>A10:"  fresh, 3 medium           >F3:/FR"Carbos
>F9:(B9*E9)                       >E3:/FR"Carbos
>D9:(B9*C9)                       >D3:/FR"Calories
>A9:"Apricots                     >C3:/FR"Calories
>F8:(B8*E8)                       >B3:/FR"Qty
>E8:51.3                          >A3:"            Item
>D8:(B8*C8)                       >D1:"TER
>C8:184                           >C1:"ATE COMPUT
>A8:"  baked, 2T brown sugar      >B1:"CARBOHYDRATE
>F7:(B7*E7)                       >A1:/FR"CALORIE &
>E7:16.9                          /W1
>D7:(B7*C7)                       /GOC
>C7:66                            /GRA
>B7:1                             /XV27
>A7:"  fresh, average size        /GC24
>A6:"Apples                       /X>A1:>A5:/TH
>G5:/--                           /X>A1:>A1:;/GC9
>F5:/--                           /X>A1:>A5:/TH
>E5:/--                           /X>B1:>B1:/WS
>D5:/--
```

Figure 3.4(b). Formulas for the calorie counting chart

3.5. CANNING: Canning and Freezing Yields For Fruit

Purpose

The next two worksheets in this collection will find use in the modern (computer-equipped) kitchens of the world. CANNING is used to convert bushels and crates of fresh fruit into quarts of canned or frozen food. Actually, you will do the conversion to canned or frozen food; this handy chart will merely tell you about how many quarts a bushel of fresh fruit will make.

Worksheet

The worksheet in Figure 3.5(a) contains a brief list of fruits and the most likely purchasing unit of measurement. The number of units used is supplied by the user, and the number of quarts will be computed by the VisiCalc program.

In the example of Figure 3.5(a), 11 units of fresh fruit will make either 212.5 canned quarts or 251.5 freezer quarts. The quarts consist of apricots, strawberries, grapes, peaches, pears, and plums.

To start with a fresh chart, use /BLANK and /REPLICATE to clear out the previous values in the column labeled "# Units Used." Then move down the column and enter the desired number of units purchased for canning or freezing.

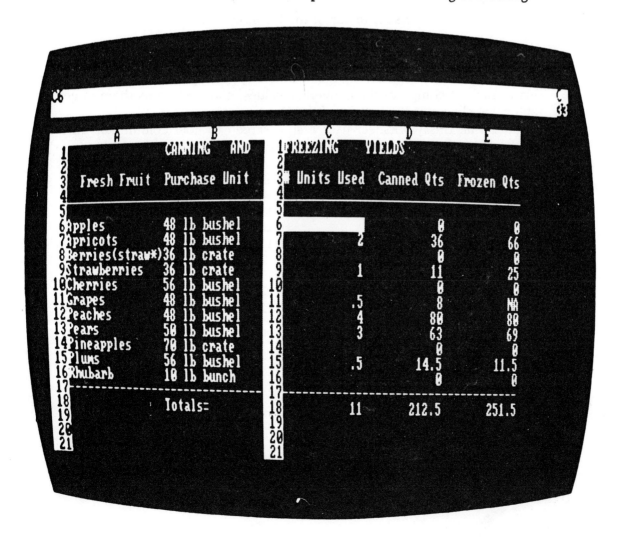

Fresh Fruit	Purchase Unit	# Units Used	Canned Qts	Frozen Qts
Apples	48 lb bushel		0	0
Apricots	48 lb bushel	2	36	66
Berries(straw*)	36 lb crate		0	0
Strawberries	36 lb crate	1	11	25
Cherries	56 lb bushel		0	0
Grapes	48 lb bushel	.5	8	NA
Peaches	48 lb bushel	4	80	80
Pears	50 lb bushel	3	63	69
Pineapples	70 lb crate		0	0
Plums	56 lb bushel	.5	14.5	11.5
Rhubarb	10 lb bunch		0	0
Totals=		11	212.5	251.5

```
          CANNING    AND   FREEZING      YIELDS

   Fresh Fruit    Purchase Unit   # Units Used   Canned Qts   Frozen Qts
   --------------------------------------------------------------------------
   Apples          48 lb bushel                        0            0
   Apricots        48 lb bushel          2            36           66
   Berries(straw*) 36 lb crate                         0            0
   Strawberries    36 lb crate           1            11           25
   Cherries        56 lb bushel                        0            0
   Grapes          48 lb bushel         .5             8           NA
   Peaches         48 lb bushel          4            80           80
   Pears           50 lb bushel          3            63           69
   Pineapples      70 lb crate                         0            0
   Plums           56 lb bushel         .5          14.5         11.5
   Rhubarb         10 lb bunch                         0            0
   --------------------------------------------------------------------------
                   Totals=              11         212.5        251.5
```

Figure 3.5(a). A canning and freezing yield chart

Comments   If you add rows, be sure to adjust the formulas to include the new additions.

Formulas   The formulas of Figure 3.5(b) are very similar to the formulas we have used in the earlier examples. Like the other conversion and questionnaire worksheets, this worksheet computes the converted values, and then sums them to get the total value shown at the bottom of the chart.

Notice that this worksheet uses a split screen to hold columns of differing widths. See the previous sections for an explanation of how this is done.

```
>E18:@SUM(E6...E16)          >B14:"70 lb crate
>D18:@SUM(D6...D16)          >A14:"Pineapples
>C18:@SUM(C6...C16)          >E13:23*C13
>B18:"Totals=                >D13:21*C13
>E17:/--                     >C13:3
>D17:/--                     >B13:"50 lb bushel
>C17:/--                     >A13:"Pears
>B17:/--                     >E12:20*C12
>A17:/--                     >D12:20*C12
>E16:7*C16                   >C12:4
>D16:9*C16                   >B12:"48 lb bushel
>B16:"10 lb bunch            >A12:"Peaches
>A16:"Rhubarb                >E11:/FR"NA
>E15:23*C15                  >D11:16*C11
>D15:29*C15                  >C11:.5
>C15:.5                      >B11:"48 lb bushel
>B15:"56 lb bushel           >A11:"Grapes
>A15:"Plums                  >E10:20*C10
>E14:32*C14                  >D10:27*C10
>D14:14*C14                  >B10:"56 lb bushel
```

```
>A10:"Cherries              >F4:/-_
>E9:25*C9                   >E4:/-_
>D9:11*C9                   >D4:/-_
>C9:1                       >C4:/-_
>B9:"36 lb crate            >B4:/-_
>A9:"Strawberries           >A4:/-_
>E8:18*C8                   >E3:/FR"Frozen Qts
>D8:16*C8                   >D3:/FR"Canned Qts
>B8:"36 lb crate            >C3:"# Units Used
>A8:"Berries(straw*)        >B3:"Purchase Unit
>E7:33*C7                   >A3:"  Fresh Fruit
>D7:18*C7                   >D1:"YIELDS
>C7:2                       >C1:"FREEZING
>B7:"48 lb bushel           >B1:"CANNING    AND
>A7:"Apricots               /W1
>E6:18*C6                   /GOC
>D6:20*C6                   /GRA
>B6:"48 lb bushel           /XV33
>A6:"Apples                 /GC15
>I4:/-_                     /X>A1:>A1:;/GC12
>H4:/-_                     /X>C1:>C1:
>G4:/-_
```

Figure 3.5(b). Formulas for canning and freezing yield chart

3.6. COOKINGU: Conversion Table For Cooks

Purpose   Have you ever become frustrated because you tried to convert a recipe from teaspoons to ounces, cups to milliliters, or quarts to liters? If so, then this worksheet may help you. The Cooking Unit Conversion Table shown in Figure 3.6(a) is used to convert cooking units.

Worksheet   The worksheet presented here is used in much the same way as the other conversion table worksheets in this collection. The only inputs to the table appear in column "QTY." This column contains the number to be converted. For example, to convert 2.5 teaspoons, enter 2.5 in the row labeled "teaspoons(T)." This number is converted to teaspoons T, tablespoons Tbl, ounces Oz, cups C, pints PTS, quarts QT, milliliters ML, and liters L.

Comments   As explained earlier in similar worksheets, the rows and columns of conversion worksheets can be extended by adding or changing what is given here. In this example, we might add more units for the purpose of extending the worksheet. Or, we might add the ability to scale up or scale down a recipe. For example, if a recipe calls for 1¾ T, how many T should you use if the recipe is to be increased by 50%?

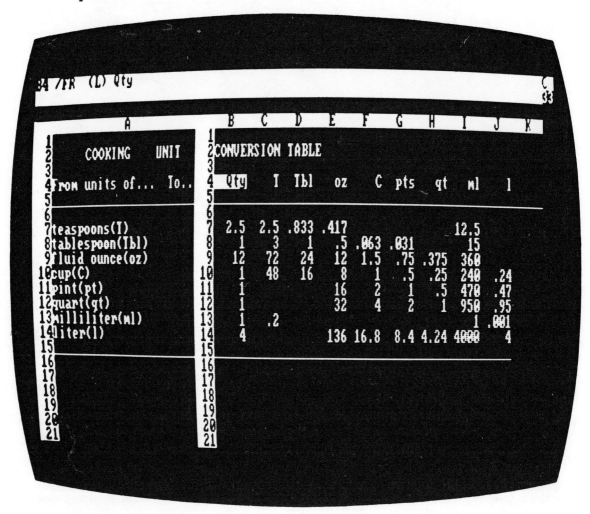

```
    COOKING    UNIT  CONVERSION  TABLE

From units of...  To..  Qty    T   Tbl   oz    C   pts   qt    ml    l
-------------------------------------------------------------------------

teaspoons(T)            2.5  2.5  .833  .417                    12.5
tablespoon(Tbl)          1    3    1    .5   .063 .031          15
fluid ounce(oz)         12   72   24    12   1.5  .75  .375    360
cup(C)                   1   48   16     8   1    .5   .25     240   .24
pint(pt)                 1               16   2    1    .5      470   .47
quart(qt)                1               32   4    2    1       950   .95
milliliter(ml)           1    .2                                 1    .001
liter(l)                 4              136  16.8 8.4  4.24    4000   4
-------------------------------------------------------------------------
```

Figure 3.6(a). Cooking unit conversion table

The formulas in Figure 3.6(b) contain the information required to convert from one unit of measurement into another. Thus if the value of "QTY" is changed, the other cells that depend on the changed value are automatically recalculated according to the conversion factors built into each formula.

Formulas

You will also notice that the worksheet is split into two vertical halves. The left-side window is used to hold up to 22 characters. This is where the labels are stored. The right-side window holds the "QTY" and conversion formulas. They are each five characters wide.

```
>J15:/-_                    >G12:2*B12
>I15:/-_                    >F12:4*B12
>H15:/-_                    >E12:32*B12
>G15:/-_                    >B12:1
>F15:/-_                    >A12:"quart(qt)
>E15:/-_                    >J11:.47*B11
>D15:/-_                    >I11:470*B11
>C15:/-_                    >H11:(B11/2)
>B15:/-_                    >G11:(B11)
>A15:/-_                    >F11:2*B11
>J14:(B14)                  >E11:16*B11
>I14:1000*B14               >B11:1
>H14:1.06*B14               >A11:"pint(pt)
>G14:2.1*B14                >J10:.24*B10
>F14:4.2*B14                >I10:240*B10
>E14:34*B14                 >H10:(B10/4)
>B14:4                      >G10:(B10/2)
>A14:"liter(1)              >F10:(B10)
>J13:(B13/1000              >E10:8*B10
>I13:(B13)                  >D10:16*B10
>C13:(B13/5)                >C10:48*B10
>B13:1                      >B10:1
>A13:"milliliter(ml)        >A10:"cup(C)
>J12:.95*B12                >I9:30*B9
>I12:950*B12                >H9:(B9/32)
>H12:(B12)                  >G9:(B9/16)
```

```
>F9:(B9/8)                    >D5:/-_
>E9:(B9)                      >C5:/-_
>D9:2*B9                      >B5:/-_
>C9:6*B9                      >A5:/-_
>B9:12                        >J4:/FR"1
>A9:"fluid ounce(oz)          >I4:/FR"ml
>I8:15*B8                     >H4:/FR"qt
>G8:(B8/32)                   >G4:/FR"pts
>F8:(B8/16)                   >F4:/FR"C
>E8:(B8/2)                    >E4:/FR"oz
>D8:(B8)                      >D4:/FR"Tbl
>C8:3*B8                      >C4:/FR"T
>B8:1                         >B4:/FR"Qty
>A8:"tablespoon(Tbl)          >A4:"From units of...   To..
>I7:5*B7                      >E2:"E
>E7:(B7/6)                    >D2:" TABL
>D7:(B7/3)                    >C2:"RSION
>C7:(B7)                      >B2:"CONVE
>B7:2.5                       >A2:"        COOKING      UNIT
>A7:"teaspoons(T)             /W1
>K5:/-_                       /GOC
>J5:/-_                       /GRA
>I5:/-_                       /XV25
>H5:/-_                       /GC22
>G5:/-_                       /X>A1:>A1:;/GC5
>F5:/-_                       /X>B1:>B1:
>E5:/-_
```

Figure 3.6(b). Formulas for cooking unit conversion table

3.7. APPLIANC: Energy Used By Electrical Appliances

Do you know where your energy dollar goes? What is the most costly electrical appliance in your house? How much would a new electric blanket add to your monthly electricity bill? These and other questions are answered by completing the Electrical Energy Consumption chart shown in Figure 3.7(a).

Purpose

The worksheet of Figure 3.7(a) consists of a list of appliances that use electrical energy, a table of power consumption estimates for each appliance, and a place for you to enter the estimated number of hours per month that you use each appliance.

Worksheet

You can /BLANK the entire column labeled "HRS USED," and enter the cost per kilowatt-hour in the upper right-hand corner of the worksheet as shown in Figure 3.7(a). Then move down the "HRS USED" column and enter the number of hours each appliance is used per month. This value will be used by the VisiCalc program to calculate the monthly cost for the power consumed by the appliance. This cost is displayed in the final column.

```
B5 (V) .1

              A                    B       C        D        E
 1     ELECTRICAL  ENERGY    CONSUMPTION  IN  THE   HOME
 2
 3
 4
 5                             Cost per kwh =$        .1
 6              Appliance      Watts  Hrs Used     $Cost
 7     ------------------------------------------------
 8   Aircondition(central)     10000      4        4.00
 9   Aircondition(window unit)  5000      8        4.00
10   Baking oven                800      10        0.80
11   Blanket, electric          150     240        3.60
12   Blender, food              250       2        0.05
13   Bottle warmer              350      20        0.70
14   Broiler, rotisserie       1500       5        0.75
15   Can opener                 175       1        0.02
16   Cleaner, vacuum            650      15        0.98
17   Clipper, hair               15       4        0.01
18   Clock                        5     720        0.36
19   Coffee maker               700      15        1.05
20   Clothes dryer-electric    7000      15       10.50
21   Clothes dryer-gas          200      15        0.30
```

After you have entered all the time estimates for your household look at the total cost in the bottom line. This is the estimate of your electrical bill. Furthermore, the resulting table tells how much each appliance is costing you.

Comments   Again, this worksheet can be modified to include other appliances, or to change the estimated power consumption of an appliance whenever an energy-efficient appliance replaces one in the list. We might also modify the worksheet to include a @MAX and @MIN function to compute the most expensive and least expensive appliances in the list. Finally, you may want to use the results of your own analysis to control the amount of electricity you are currently using.

```
ELECTRICAL  ENERGY  CONSUMPTION  IN  THE   HOME
```

Appliance	Watts	Cost per kwh =$ Hrs Used	.1 $Cost
Aircondition(central)	10000	4	4.00
Aircondition(window unit)	5000	8	4.00
Baking oven	800	10	0.80
Blanket, electric	150	240	3.60
Blender, food	250	2	0.05
Bottle warmer	350	20	0.70
Broiler, rotisserie	1500	5	0.75
Can opener	175	1	0.02
cleaner, vacuum	650	15	0.98
Clipper, hair	15	4	0.01
Clock	5	720	0.36
Coffee maker	700	15	1.05
Clothes dryer-electric	7000	15	10.50
Clothes dryer-gas	200	15	0.30
Corn popper	900	2	0.18
Dishwasher w/heat unit	1300	30	3.90
Dishwasher w/o heat unit	250	30	0.75
Dryer, hair	700	10	0.70
Fan, attic	400	100	4.00
Fan, portable	75	100	0.75
Freezer, food storage	450	150	6.75
Fry pan, skillet	1200	15	1.80
Furnace, oil	300	1	0.03
Furnace, gas	25	1	0.00
Furnace blower	425	180	7.65
Garbage disposal	500	3	0.15
Heater, radiant	1000	15	1.50
Heating, electric resist	10000		0.00
Heating pad	80	10	0.08
Iron, clothes	1100	10	1.10
Knife, carving	100	6	0.06
Light(night)	1	300	0.03
Organ, electric	75	30	0.23
Oven, microwave	400	20	0.80
Pressure cooker	1400	10	1.40
Projector, movie	500	4	0.20

```
 Projector, slide           500        1        0.05
 Radio                      200       60        1.20
 Range, electric          15000       35       52.50
 Record player               75       10        0.08
 Refrigerator,conventional  350      180        6.30
 Refrigerator,ice maker     675      180       12.15
 Refrigerator w/freezer     675      180       12.15
 Sewing machine              75       10        0.08
 Shaver                      12        8        0.01
 Sunlamp                    375        5        0.19
 Television ( B&W )         300      200        6.00
 Television ( color )       400      200        8.00
 Toaster                   1200        5        0.60
 Trash compactor            400        4        0.16
 Vacuum cleaner             500        6        0.30
 waffle iron               1200        5        0.60
 Washer, automatic          750       25        1.88
 Water heater, automatic   5000      240      120.00
 Water pump, shallow well   500       30        1.50
 ----------------------------------------------------
                              Total $ =      282.90
```

Figure 3.7(a). Energy used by appliances

Formulas

The worksheet is reconstructed from the formulas and labels shown in Figure 3.7(b). This is a "questionnaire type" of worksheet. Therefore, you can use /REPLICATE to save time when entering the formulas that compute the cost of operating an appliance for a certain number of hours each month.

The formulas compute the cost per appliance by multiplying the watt rating of a certain appliance by the number of hours it is operated. This product is then divided by 1000 to convert watts to kilowatts. For example in cell D53, the cost is computed by multiplying C53, B53, and the cost per kilowatt-hour D5. The product is divided by 1000 to convert to units of kilowatt-hours.

This is another example of a split screen worksheet. The appliances are listed in one half of the screen, and the remainder of the worksheet is listed in the right-side of the screen. At the end of the formulas in Figure 3.7(b) you can see that one side contains cells which are 25 characters wide, and the other side contains cells which are 10 characters wide.

The global format /GLOBAL F $ is used in the cells that compute formulas, and /FORMAT R, etc., in the other cells.

```
>D64:/F$@SUM(D8...D62)          >A62:"Water pump, shallow well
>C64:"Total $ =                 >D61:/F$(D5*C61*(B61/1000))
>E63:/-_                         >C61:240
>D63:/-_                         >B61:5000
>C63:/-_                         >A61:"Water heater, automatic
>B63:/-_                         >D60:/F$(D5*C60*(B60/1000))
>A63:/-_                         >C60:25
>D62:/F$(D5*C62*(B62/1000))      >B60:750
>C62:30                          >A60:"Washer, automatic
>B62:500                         >D59:/F$(D5*C59*(B59/1000))
```

>C59:5
>B59:1200
>A59:"waffle iron
>D58:/F$(D5*C58*(B58/1000))
>C58:6
>B58:500
>A58:"Vacuum cleaner
>D57:/F$(D5*C57*(B57/1000))
>C57:4
>B57:400
>A57:"Trash compactor
>D56:/F$(D5*C56*(B56/1000))
>C56:5
>B56:1200
>A56:"Toaster
>D55:/F$(D5*C55*(B55/1000))
>C55:200
>B55:400
>A55:"Television (color)
>D54:/F$(D5*C54*(B54/1000))
>C54:200
>B54:300
>A54:"Television (B&W)
>D53:/F$(D5*C53*(B53/1000))
>C53:5
>B53:375
>A53:"Sunlamp
>D52:/F$(D5*C52*(B52/1000))
>C52:8
>B52:12
>A52:"Shaver
>D51:/F$(D5*C51*(B51/1000))
>C51:10
>B51:75
>A51:"Sewing machine
>D50:/F$(D5*C50*(B50/1000))
>C50:180
>B50:675
>A50:"Refrigerator w/freezer
>D49:/F$(D5*C49*(B49/1000))
>C49:180
>B49:675
>A49:"Refrigerator,ice maker
>D48:/F$(D5*C48*(B48/1000))
>C48:180
>B48:350
>A48:"Refrigerator,conventional
>D47:/F$(D5*C47*(B47/1000))
>C47:10
>B47:75
>A47:"Record player
>D46:/F$(D5*C46*(B46/1000))
>C46:35
>B46:15000
>A46:"Range, electric

>D45:/F$(D5*C45*(B45/1000))
>C45:60
>B45:200
>A45:"Radio
>D44:/F$(D5*C44*(B44/1000))
>C44:1
>B44:500
>A44:"Projector, slide
>D43:/F$(D5*C43*(B43/1000))
>C43:4
>B43:500
>A43:"Projector, movie
>D42:/F$(D5*C42*(B42/1000))
>C42:10
>B42:1400
>A42:"Pressure cooker
>D41:/F$(D5*C41*(B41/1000))
>C41:20
>B41:400
>A41:"Oven, microwave
>D40:/F$(D5*C40*(B40/1000))
>C40:30
>B40:75
>A40:"Organ, electric
>D39:/F$(D5*C39*(B39/1000))
>C39:300
>B39:1
>A39:"Light(night)
>D38:/F$(D5*C38*(B38/1000))
>C38:6
>B38:100
>A38:"Knife, carving
>D37:/F$(D5*C37*(B37/1000))
>C37:10
>B37:1100
>A37:"Iron, clothes
>D36:/F$(D5*C36*(B36/1000))
>C36:10
>B36:80
>A36:"Heating pad
>D35:/F$(D5*C35*(B35/1000))
>B35:10000
>A35:"Heating, electric resist
>D34:/F$(D5*C34*(B34/1000))
>C34:15
>B34:1000
>A34:"Heater, radiant
>D33:/F$(D5*C33*(B33/1000))
>C33:3
>B33:500
>A33:"Garbage disposal
>D32:/F$(D5*C32*(B32/1000))
>C32:180
>B32:425
>A32:"Furnace blower

```
>D31:/F$(D5*C31*(B31/1000))
>C31:1
>B31:25
>A31:"Furnace, gas
>D30:/F$(D5*C30*(B30/1000))
>C30:1
>B30:300
>A30:"Furnace, oil
>D29:/F$(D5*C29*(B29/1000))
>C29:15
>B29:1200
>A29:"Fry pan, skillet
>D28:/F$(D5*C28*(B28/1000))
>C28:150
>B28:450
>A28:"Freezer, food storage
>D27:/F$(D5*C27*(B27/1000))
>C27:100
>B27:75
>A27:"Fan, portable
>D26:/F$(D5*C26*(B26/1000))
>C26:100
>B26:400
>A26:"Fan, attic
>D25:/F$(D5*C25*(B25/1000))
>C25:10
>B25:700
>A25:"Dryer, hair
>D24:/F$(D5*C24*(B24/1000))
>C24:30
>B24:250
>A24:"Dishwasher w/o heat unit
>D23:/F$(D5*C23*(B23/1000))
>C23:30
>B23:1300
>A23:"Dishwasher w/heat unit
>D22:/F$(D5*C22*(B22/1000))
>C22:2
>B22:900
>A22:"Corn popper
>D21:/F$(D5*C21*(B21/1000))
>C21:15
>B21:200
>A21:"Clothes dryer-gas
>D20:/F$(D5*C20*(B20/1000))
>C20:15
>B20:7000
>A20:"Clothes dryer-electric
>D19:/F$(D5*C19*(B19/1000))
>C19:15
>B19:700
>A19:"Coffee maker
>D18:/F$(D5*C18*(B18/1000))
>C18:720
>B18:5
```

```
>A18:"Clock
>D17:/F$(D5*C17*(B17/1000))
>C17:4
>B17:15
>A17:"Clipper, hair
>D16:/F$(D5*C16*(B16/1000))
>C16:15
>B16:650
>A16:"cleaner, vacuum
>D15:/F$(D5*C15*(B15/1000))
>C15:1
>B15:175
>A15:"Can opener
>D14:/F$(D5*C14*(B14/1000))
>C14:5
>B14:1500
>A14:"Broiler, rotisserie
>D13:/F$(D5*C13*(B13/1000))
>C13:20
>B13:350
>A13:"Bottle warmer
>D12:/F$(D5*C12*(B12/1000))
>C12:2
>B12:250
>A12:"Blender, food
>D11:/F$(D5*C11*(B11/1000))
>C11:240
>B11:150
>A11:"Blanket, electric
>D10:/F$(D5*C10*(B10/1000))
>C10:10
>B10:800
>A10:"Baking oven
>D9:/F$(D5*C9*(B9/1000))
>C9:8
>B9:5000
>A9:"Aircondition(window unit)
>D8:/F$(D5*C8*(B8/1000))
>C8:4
>B8:10000
>A8:"Aircondition(central)
>E7:/--
>D7:/--
>C7:/--
>B7:/--
>A7:/--
>D6:/FR" $Cost
>C6:/FR"Hrs Used
>B6:/FR"Watts
>A6:/FR"Appliance
>D5:.1
>C5:"per kwh =$
>B5:"      Cost
>E4:/-_
>D4:/-_
```

```
>C4:/-_                          /GOC
>B4:/-_                          /GRA
>A4:/-_                          /XV28
>D2:"HOME                        /GC25
>C2:"N IN THE                    /X>A1:>A7:/TH
>B2:"CONSUMPTIO                  /X>A1:>A1:;/GC10
>A2:"      ELECTRICAL  ENERGY    /X>A1:>A7:/TH
/W1                              /X>B1:>B1:/WS
```

Figure 3.7(b). Formulas for energy table

3.8. HEAT: Energy Index For Home Heating

Purpose

Do you consume more electricity to heat your home than you should? Is your house energy efficient? What is the "energy index" of your home?

The final worksheet in this collection is used to compute an energy index which tells you how efficient your home heating system is. Given the amount of electricity, natural gas, fuel oil, and LP gas used to heat your home, this worksheet computes the total number of BTUs used (*British Thermal Units* are a measure of heat). Then, given the number of "degree days," and the size of your house, this worksheet computes your energy index.

The "degree days" of a month is the measure of "coldness" or "warmness" used by energy companies to estimate how much fuel will be needed to keep a house comfortable for the month. It is obtained by estimating the number of degrees that the temperature will have to be "warmed-up" in order to keep your house warm for a certain number of days.

Worksheet

Figure 3.8(a) shows how to use this worksheet. The numbers under the column labeled "AMOUNT USED" must be entered from your heating bill. For example, if you used 3.6 CCF of natural gas during the month, then enter 3.6 as shown. This amount is converted into BTUs by the formulas stored in the worksheet.

```
                     ENERGY     INDEX    FOR              HOME  HEATING
                                                  Amount                  Amount
     Form of heating you use:                       Used                 in BTUs
     ------------------------------------------------------------------------------

     Electricity (Kwh)                                   .3                1023.9
     Natural gas ( CCF )                                3.6                360000
     Fuel oil ( Gal.)                                     O                     O
     LP Gas ( Gal.)                                       O                     O
     ..........................................................................
                                              Total BTU =                361023.9

     Degree days for month   =                          45
      BTU per Degree day     =                     8022.75
      Size of home in sq ft  =                        2100
         Energy Index        =                        3.82    Index
     --------------------------------------------------------------------------
                                    Index :
     RATINGS :
        Excellent ---->               0 - 6
        Good      ---->               7 - 9
        Fair      ---->              10 - 12
        Poor      ---->             over 13

     --------------------------------------------------------------------------
```

Figure 3.8(a). Energy index worksheet

Next, enter the number of degree days and the size of your house. The number of degree days for the month can be obtained from your heating company. You should already know the size of your house in square feet of living space.

These numbers will be used by the formulas in the worksheet to come up with an index as shown in the sample worksheet. Thus, an index of 3.82 is excellent. The legend at the bottom of the worksheet can be used to evaluate your index.

Comments   This worksheet can also be used to estimate the capacity of a new heating system. Suppose you are going to build a new house with a certain square footage and a desirable energy index in a climate where the number of degree days is known for the month of January. You then can work backwards to get the number of BTUs needed. This will help you choose the right-sized heating system.

Formulas   The formulas in Figure 3.8(b) are conversion formulas that convert the units of energy consumption that you enter into BTUs. The equation in cell C7, for example, converts Kwh of electricity into BTUs.

Next, the formulas convert the number of BTUs per degree day and the size of the house into an index. The index value is a measure of how well your house utilizes the heat.

An index rating above 13 is very poor. This may indicate poor insulation, open doors and windows, etc. If you get a poor rating from your house, perhaps you should find out where your heat is going.

```
>C25:/-_                          >A11:/-.
>B25:/-_                          >C10:95000*B10
>A25:/-_                          >B10:0
>B24:"    over 13                 >A10:"LP Gas ( Gal.)
>A24:"      Poor      --->        >C9:140000*B9
>B23:"   10 - 12                  >B9:0
>A23:"      Fair      --->        >A9:"Fuel oil ( Gal.)
>B22:"    7 - 9                   >C8:100000*B8
>A22:"      Good      --->        >B8:3.6
>B21:"    0 - 6                   >A8:"Natural gas ( CCF )
>A21:"      Excellent --->        >C7:3413*B7
>A20:"RATINGS :                   >B7:.3
>B19:"    Index :                 >A7:"Electricity (Kwh)
>C18:/-_                          >C5:/--
>B18:/-_                          >B5:/--
>A18:/-_                          >A5:/--
>C17:"   Index                    >C4:/FR"in BTUs
>B17:/F$(B15/B16)                 >B4:/FR"Used
>A17:/FR"Energy Index      =      >A4:"Form of heating you use:
>B16:2100                         >C3:/FR"Amount
>A16:" Size of home in sq ft =    >B3:/FR"Amount
>B15:/F$(C12/B14)                 >C2:"HOME HEATING
>A15:" BTU per Degree day    =    >B2:"INDEX   FOR
>B14:45                           >A2:"              ENERGY
>A14:"Degree days for month  =    /W1
>C12:@SUM(C7...C10                /GOC
>B12:/FR"Total BTU =              /GRA
>C11:/-.                          /GC24
>B11:/-.                          /X>A1:>A1:
```

Figure 3.8(b). Formulas for energy index

Chapter 4
Statistical Analysis

This chapter gives you a chance to exercise the number crunching power of the VisiCalc program. The statistical analysis worksheets presented in the following pages quickly tell you what your experimental (observed) data looks like in histogram form, whether it is correlated with hypothesized data, how well it fits a straight line, whether it fits a contingency table, and how it ranks with someone else's data. You get all of this for the price of a few equations that do such a large number of calculations that your computer becomes indispensable.

The first worksheet illustrates how the VisiCalc program can be made to print a bar chart. HISTOGRM displays the observed data as an experimentally determined frequency chart.

VARIANCE is a worksheet that compares observed data with what is expected, and statistically determines if the two sets of data are from the same statistical population. A "low" chi-squared value implies that the two sets of data are related.

If you want to know if two observations are correlated, then use the correlation analysis worksheet, CORREL. This worksheet is used to compare two sets of observations and decide if they are directly related.

If two sets of observations are related in a linear fashion, then they can be described by a straight line. Another way to look at this is as follows. Can a straight line be made to pass through a graph of the two sets of data? The formula for the "best" possible straight line is computed by this worksheet.

A contingency table is used to compare two sets of observed data that may not be described in numerical terms. Instead, we may be interested in whether observations fall into one or more categories or classifications. If we count the number of observations which fall into the categories and compare that number with the expected number, then we can use a contingency table to tell if the two sets are related. CONTINGE does this for you and calculates the chi-squared statistic as a measure of similarity between the observed and expected numbers.

Finally, the Spearman rank correlation test is used to compare two sets of rankings to see if they are correlated. The Spearman rank-correlation coefficient tells how similar the two sets of rankings are. RANK can be used to evaluate the results of independent rankings.

These worksheets can be used by anyone that must test a hypothesis. For example, if you hypothesize that a person's income increases with his education, that chickens fed with brand X feed grow bigger than those fed with brand Y, or that gasoline mileage increases as car speed decreases, then use these worksheets to prove your hypothesis.

4.1. HISTOGRM: Histogram of Observed Data

Purpose

The purpose of this worksheet is twofold: 1. to illustrate how to create bar charts with the /FORMAT * option in VisiCalc software, and 2. to use the /FORMAT * option to build a frequency chart of experimental data.

Worksheet

The sample worksheet of Figure 4.1(a) shows a column of observations (numbers) and a column of asterisks. The observations are entered as input data, and the "bar chart" of asterisks is automatically displayed.

The /FORMAT * option was used to set the format of every cell in column B to "bar chart" mode of operation. The formulas in each of these cells are evaluated and their values turned into the bar chart you see in Figure 4.1(a).

The last two numbers shown in the column of numerical observations are respectively the total and maximum values in the column. They are shown for convenience only and are not turned into bars.

The bar chart shows the relative frequency of each observation by dividing their sum into each value. Thus each bar represents the relative importance of a number in comparison with all the others.

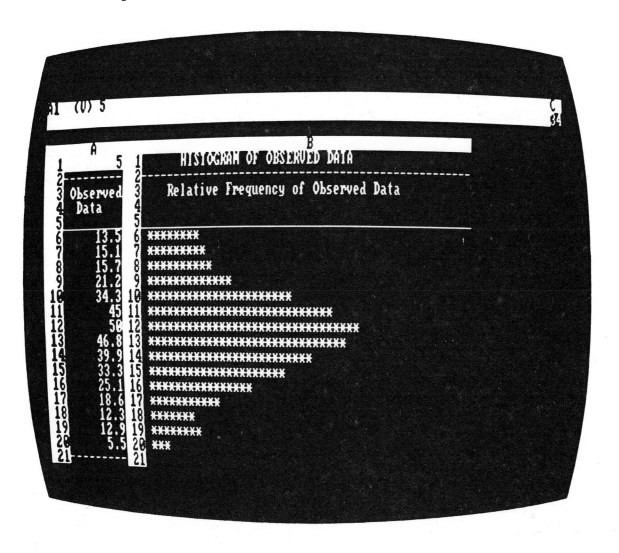

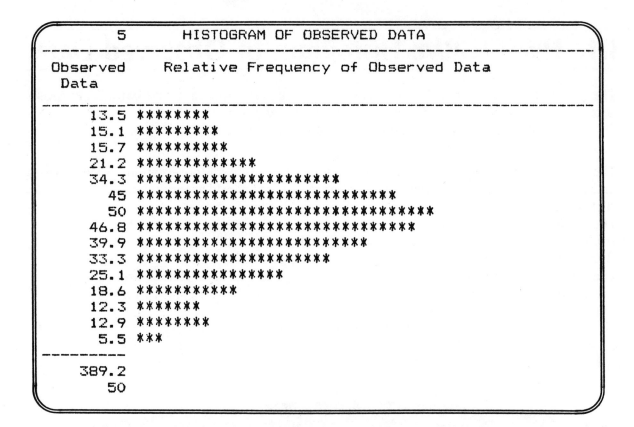

```
        5        HISTOGRAM OF OBSERVED DATA
-----------------------------------------------------------------
Observed      Relative Frequency of Observed Data
 Data
-----------------------------------------------------------------
    13.5 ********
    15.1 *********
    15.7 **********
    21.2 *************
    34.3 **********************
      45 ****************************
      50 ***********************************
    46.8 *******************************
    39.9 **************************
    33.3 *********************
    25.1 ****************
    18.6 ***********
    12.3 *******
    12.9 ********
     5.5 ***
-----------
   389.2
      50
```

Figure 4.1(a). Histogram worksheet

Comments   This example also demonstrates the importance of being able to change the order of calculations. If row-major order is used, the bar chart cells will be displayed before the sum and maximum values are known. Since the height of each bar chart depends on the sum and maximum, we must evaluate all formulas in column A before recalculating the values in column B.

Formulas   The formulas in Figure 4.1(b) can be entered manually by liberally using the /REPLICATE command. Also notice that the calculations should be performed in column-major order to ensure that the maximum and total values are computed before the bar chart is computed.

The height of each bar is guaranteed to not exceed the width of the cell containing it. The maximum value computed in cell A23 is used to scale down the value in each bar chart cell. The total or sum of all data values is also used to adjust the data into "frequency" form. Finally, notice that A1 contains an additional scale factor (5) which can be used to adjust the height of the bar chart.

The worksheet of Figure 4.1(a) is split into two vertical halves. The /WINDOW V command divides the A and B columns. In the left screen the columns are nine characters wide. In the right screen they are 50 characters wide.

```
>A23:@MAX(A6...A20
>A22:@SUM(A6...A20)
>A21:/--
>B20:/F*(A20/A22)*A23*A1
>A20:5.5
>B19:/F*(A19/A22)*A23*A1
```

```
>A19:12.9
>B18:/F*(A18/A22)*A23*A1
>A18:12.3
>B17:/F*(A17/A22)*A23*A1
>A17:18.6
>B16:/F*(A16/A22)*A23*A1
>A16:25.1
>B15:/F*(A15/A22)*A23*A1
>A15:33.3
>B14:/F*(A14/A22)*A23*A1
>A14:39.9
>B13:/F*(A13/A22)*A23*A1
>A13:46.8
>B12:/F*(A12/A22)*A23*A1
>A12:50
>B11:/F*(A11/A22)*A23*A1
>A11:45
>B10:/F*(A10/A22)*A23*A1
>A10:34.3
>B9:/F*(A9/A22)*A23*A1
>A9:21.2
>B8:/F*(A8/A22)*A23*A1
>A8:15.7
>B7:/F*(A7/A22)*A23*A1
>A7:15.1
>B6:/F*(A6/A22)*A23*A1
>A6:13.5
>G5:/-_
>F5:/-_
>E5:/-_
>D5:/-_
>C5:/-_
>B5:/-_
>A5:/-_
>A4:"  Data
>B3:"     Relative Frequency of Observed Data
>A3:/FR"Observed
>G2:/--
>F2:/--
>E2:/--
>D2:/--
>C2:/--
>B2:/--
>A2:/--
>B1:"        HISTOGRAM OF OBSERVED DATA
>A1:5
/W1
/GOC
/GRA
/XV12
/GC9
/X>A1:>A1:;/GC50
/X>B1:>B1:
```

Figure 4.1(b). Formulas for histogram worksheet

4.2. VARIANCE: Chi-squared Test

Purpose   The purpose of the worksheet shown in Figure 4.2(a) is to compute the chi-square statistic so you can use it to decide if two sets of data are drawn from the same population.

Worksheet   Suppose we use the following problem to explain the chi-square statistic. A farmer wants to know if his chickens are laying as many eggs as expected. The farmer's neighbor claims that healthy chickens lay a certain number of small, medium, large, and extra large eggs in a day's work. So the farmer takes this data as the "EXPECTED" numbers. The expected number for each size of egg is entered into the "EXPECTED NUMBER" column as shown in the worksheet.

Next, the farmer enters the actual number of eggs layed by his chickens in a day. These are the observed values that are put into the "OBSERVED NUMBER" column of the worksheet. From this point on, the VisiCalc program does the rest. The answer appears at the bottom of the worksheet as the chi-squared value.

The differences between expected and observed data values are calculated in the column labeled "DIFF." This difference is squared as shown in the next column. Then, in the last column, the squared difference is divided by the expected number of eggs. It is this last column that is summed to obtain the chi-square statistic.

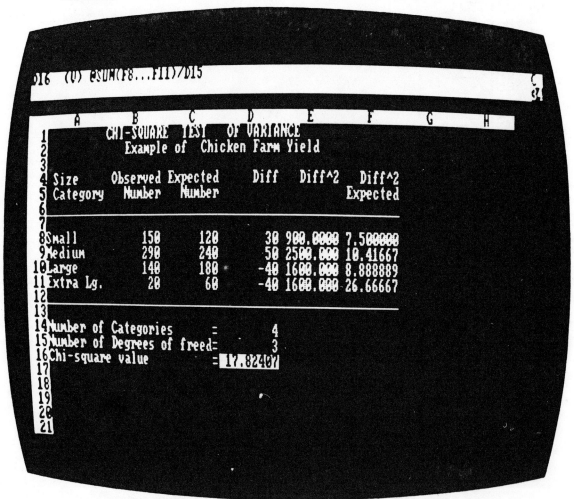

```
        CHI-SQUARE   TEST   OF VARIANCE
           Example of   Chicken Farm Yield

  Size      Observed Expected    Diff    Diff^2   Diff^2
  Category   Number   Number                      Expected

------------------------------------------------------------------

  Small        150      120        30  900.0000  7.500000
  Medium       290      240        50  2500.000  10.41667
  Large        140      180       -40  1600.000  8.888889
  Extra Lg.     20       60       -40  1600.000  26.66667

------------------------------------------------------------------

  Number of Categories      =        4
  Number of Degrees of freed=        3
  Chi-square value          = 17.82407
```

Figure 4.2(a). Chi-squared test worksheet

The result shown in Figure 4.2(a) is 17.8 for a chi-square of 3 degrees of freedom (one less than the number of observations). What does this mean? Is there a difference between the expected and the observed?

The farmer must use a chi-squared table (not shown) to decide if 17.8 is "too big" or not. Chi-squared tables are readily available in most statistics books and books of mathematical tables. If the chi-squared table is consulted for 3 degrees of freedom and a certain level of confidence, and if the chi-square number is less than what the table says it should be, then the chickens are doing their best!

Comments

The chi-squared statistic is a measure of the similarity between two sets of data. The expected set is a kind of theoretical or "perfect" result while the observed data are the actual data obtained by taking measurements or observations. Since the measurements or observations are subject to slight errors in an imperfect world, we must attempt to ignore these errors in observations by computing a statistic that is tolerant of fluctuations in the data. The chi-square table is a table of values that consider the fluctuations in the chi-squared statistic. The question is how much is a "valid" fluctuation versus a distinct difference? In statistical terms we say the difference is "significantly" different if it exceeds statistical expectations.

In the farmer example, the number of eggs laid in each size category differed by a certain amount. We had to trust in statistics to decide if the fluctuation was acceptable in statistical terms or if the difference was "significant."

Formulas

Figure 4.2(b) shows how to reconstruct the chi-squared table. This table contains as many formulas as can be entered quickly using the /REPLICATE command. For example, the three formulas in cells D8, E8, and F8 can all be replicated into the other columns of the table.

```
>D16:@SUM(F8...F11)/D15        >F8:(B8-C8)^2/C8
>C16:/FR"=                     >E8:(B8-C8)^2
>B16:"e value                  >D8:(B8-C8)
>A16:"Chi-squar                >C8:120
>D15:(D14-1)                   >B8:150
>C15:"of freed=                >A8:"Small
>B15:" Degrees                 >F6:/-_
>A15:"Number of                >E6:/-_
>D14:@COUNT(B8...B11)          >D6:/-_
>C14:"es       =               >C6:/-_
>B14:" Categorie               >B6:/-_
>A14:"Number of                >A6:/-_
>F12:/-_                       >F5:/FR"Expected
>E12:/-_                       >C5:/FR"Number
>D12:/-_                       >B5:/FR"Number
>C12:/-_                       >A5:/FR"Category
>B12:/-_                       >F4:/FR"Diff^2
>A12:/-_                       >E4:/FR"Diff^2
>F11:(B11-C11)^2/C11           >D4:/FR"Diff
>E11:(B11-C11)^2               >C4:/FR"Expected
>D11:(B11-C11)                 >B4:/FR"Observed
>C11:60                        >A4:/FL" Size
>B11:20                        >E2:" Yield
>A11:"Extra Lg.                >D2:"cken Farm
>F10:(B10-C10)^2/C10           >C2:"e of  Chic
>E10:(B10-C10)^2               >B2:"    Exampl
>D10:(B10-C10)                 >E1:"NCE
>C10:180                       >D1:" OF VARIANCE
>B10:140                       >C1:"E  TEST
>A10:"Large                    >B1:"CHI-SQUAR
>F9:(B9-C9)^2/C9               /W1
>E9:(B9-C9)^2                  /GOC
>D9:(B9-C9)                    /GRA
>C9:240                        /GC9
>B9:290                        /X>A1:>A1:
>A9:"Medium
```

Figure 4.2(b). Formulas for chi-squared test

4.3. CORREL: Correlation Coefficient

The purpose of this worksheet is to compute the correlation coefficient and use it to determine if two sets of data are related to one another. If they are directly related, the correlation coefficient will approach one. If one set of data decreases while the other increases the coefficient will approach minus one; if they are not related, it will approach zero.

Purpose

Suppose the worksheet in Figure 4.3(a) is used to decide if annual income increases with years of formal education. The first column contains the set of observations for years of schooling. The second column contains the observations for the annual income corresponding to the value of years of schooling. For example, the first entry was obtained from a head-of-household who attended school for 10 years and made $16,000 last year.

Worksheet

The object of the example is to decide if the income levels correlate with the educational levels. The "CORRELATION R" coefficient shown at the bottom of the worksheet is "near" +1, so we might conclude that income and education are correlated.

The "FISHER Z TRANSFORM" is another measure of correlation that some statisticians use. It has been included here for convenience. Similarly, the "Sigma-f" statistic may be preferred.

A	B	C	D	E	F	G	H
CORRELATION		**ANALYSIS**					
	Example of Education vs. Income						

Schooling	Income	x^2	y^2	x*y			
x yrs	$y 1000s						
10	16	100	256	160			
7	14	49	196	98			
12	17	144	289	204			
12	18	144	324	216			
9	20	81	400	180			
16	17	256	289	272			
12	20	144	400	240			
18	25	324	625	450			
8	15	64	225	120			
12	16	144	256	192			
14	21	196	441	294			
16	23	256	529	368			
TOTALS FOR N=		12 SAMPLES					

```
         CORRELATION          ANALYSIS
         Example of Education vs. Income
---------------------------------------------------
Schooling      Income      x^2        y^2        x*y
  x yrs      $y 1000s
---------------------------------------------------

          10          16       100        256        160
           7          14        49        196         98
          12          17       144        289        204
          12          18       144        324        216
           9          20        81        400        180
          16          17       256        289        272
          12          20       144        400        240
          18          25       324        625        450
           8          15        64        225        120
          12          16       144        256        192
          14          21       196        441        294
          16          23       256        529        368
---------------------------------------------------
   TOTALS FOR N=            12 SAMPLES
       146         222      1902       4230       2794
CORRELATION   R =    .7480323
FISHER Z TRANSFORM  .9684788=Z-f
                    .1111111=Sigma-f
```

Figure 4.3(a). Correlation analysis worksheet

Comments   This worksheet is commonly used to decide if there is a linear relationship between the Xs and Ys. The Xs represent the set of observations that you might think of as being plotted along the x-axis of a graph. The Ys can be plotted along the vertical y-axis of the same graph. The pair (X,Y) defines a point in the graph. In the next example, you will learn how to draw the best straight line through these points. When this is done, the correlation coefficient is exactly the same as the slope of the straight line.

Formulas   The correlation coefficient is computed from the following formula:

$$R = (@SUM(X - @AVERAGE(X))*@SUM(Y - @AVERAGE(Y)))/D$$
$$D = @SQRT((@SUM(X - @AVERAGE(X)) \wedge 2)*(@SUM(Y - @AVERAGE(Y)) \wedge 2)$$

This formula is implemented in parts as indicated in the worksheet and as shown in Figure 4.3(b).

The second, third, and fourth columns of the worksheet are used to compute the intermediate values needed by the formula. These values are used in a "short-cut" formula to get the coefficient R.

```
>D25: "=Sigma-f
>C25: (1/(C21-3))
>D24: "=Z-f
>C24: (1.1513)*@LOG10((1+C23)/(1-C23))
>B24: "TRANSFORM
>A24: "FISHER Z
```

```
>C23: ((E22-(A22*B22/C21)/(@SQRT((C22-(A22^2/C21))*(D22-(B22^2/C21)))))
>B23: "ON   R =
>A23: "CORRELATIO
>E22: @SUM(E8...E19)
>D22: @SUM(D8...D19)
>C22: @SUM(C8...C19)
>B22: @SUM(B8...B19)
>A22: @SUM(A8...A19)
>D21: " SAMPLES
>C21: 12
>B21: " FOR N=
>A21: /FR"TOTALS
>F20: /-_
>E20: /-_
>D20: /-_
>C20: /-_
>B20: /-_
>A20: /-_
>E19: (A19*B19)
>D19: (B19*B19)
>C19: (A19*A19)
>B19: 23
>A19: 16
>E18: (A18*B18)
>D18: (B18*B18)
>C18: (A18*A18)
>B18: 21
>A18: 14
>E17: (A17*B17)
>D17: (B17*B17)
>C17: (A17*A17)
>B17: 16
>A17: 12
>E16: (A16*B16)
>D16: (B16*B16)
>C16: (A16*A16)
>B16: 15
>A16: 8
>E15: (A15*B15)
>D15: (B15*B15)
>C15: (A15*A15)
>B15: 25
>A15: 18
>E14: (A14*B14)
>D14: (B14*B14)
>C14: (A14*A14)
>B14: 20
>A14: 12
>E13: (A13*B13)
>D13: (B13*B13)
>C13: (A13*A13)
>B13: 17
>A13: 16
>E12: (A12*B12)
>D12: (B12*B12)
>C12: (A12*A12)
```

```
>B12:20
>A12:9
>E11:(A11*B11)
>D11:(B11*B11)
>C11:(A11*A11)
>B11:18
>A11:12
>E10:(A10*B10)
>D10:(B10*B10)
>C10:(A10*A10)
>B10:17
>A10:12
>E9:(A9*B9)
>D9:(B9*B9)
>C9:(A9*A9)
>B9:14
>A9:7
>E8:(A8*B8)
>D8:(B8*B8)
>C8:(A8*A8)
>B8:16
>A8:10
>F6:/-_
>E6:/-_
>D6:/-_
>C6:/-_
>B6:/-_
>A6:/-_
>B5:" $y 1000s
>A5:"   x yrs
>E4:/FR"x*y
>D4:/FR"y^2
>C4:/FR"x^2
>B4:/FR"Income
>A4:"Schooling
>F3:/--
>E3:/--
>D3:/--
>C3:/--
>B3:/--
>A3:/--
>E2:" Income
>D2:"ation vs.
>C2:"e of Educat
>B2:"   Example
>D1:"ANALYSIS
>C1:"ON
>B1:"CORRELATIO
/W1
/GOC
/GRA
/GC9
/X>A1:>A1:
```

Figure 4.3(b). Formulas for correlation analysis

4.4. REGRESS: Linear Regression Coefficients

The previous example showed how to statistically decide if two sets of data are correlated. If they are, and if they are linearly related, then you can fit a straight line to the plot of one set versus the other set. That is the purpose of this example.

Purpose

The same example of education versus income will be used to show you how to obtain a straight line that fits the data. In fact, the straight line will fit the data as "closely as possible." That is, the line will pass through the plot of Y versus X in such a manner that the differences between the line and the plot are minimized.

The worksheet in Figure 4.4(a) takes the first two columns as input just as in the previous example. Column one is the observed number of years of schooling, and column two is the observed amount of income. The calculations necessary for the other columns are automatically performed by the VisiCalc program.

Worksheet

The results are shown at the bottom of the worksheet. The slope and intercept of the straight line are calculated. Thus the formula for the straight line that best fits the data is given.

$$\text{LINE} = 0.74*X + 9.49$$

Notice that the slope and correlation coefficient are identical.

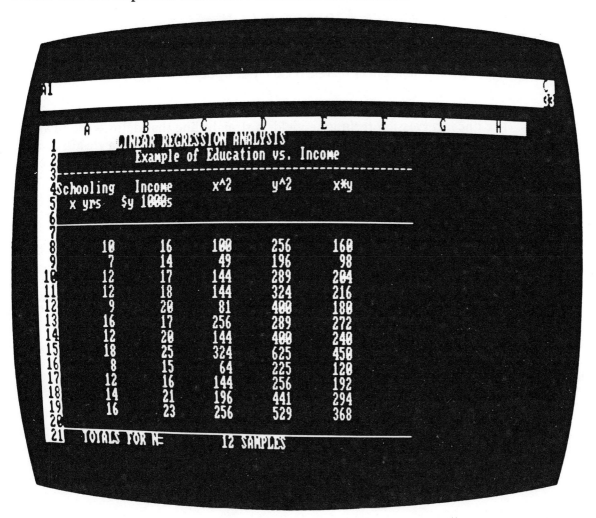

Schooling x yrs	Income $y 1000s	x^2	y^2	x*y
10	16	100	256	160
7	14	49	196	98
12	17	144	289	204
12	18	144	324	216
9	20	81	400	180
16	17	256	289	272
12	20	144	400	240
18	25	324	625	450
8	15	64	225	120
12	16	144	256	192
14	21	196	441	294
16	23	256	529	368

LINEAR REGRESSION ANALYSIS
Example of Education vs. Income

TOTALS FOR N=   12 SAMPLES

```
                    LINEAR REGRESSION ANALYSIS
                    Example of Education vs. Income
      ------------------------------------------------------------
      Schooling     Income        x^2         y^2         x*y
        x yrs      $y 1000s
      ------------------------------------------------------------

            10          16         100         256         160
             7          14          49         196          98
            12          17         144         289         204
            12          18         144         324         216
             9          20          81         400         180
            16          17         256         289         272
            12          20         144         400         240
            18          25         324         625         450
             8          15          64         225         120
            12          16         144         256         192
            14          21         196         441         294
            16          23         256         529         368
      ------------------------------------------------------------
        TOTALS FOR N=              12 SAMPLES
            146         222        1902        4230        2794
      SLOPE          B=  .7400530
      INTERCEPT      A=  9.496021
            LINE     =  .7400530 * x + (  9.496021 )
```

Figure 4.4(a). Linear regression analysis worksheet

Comments   The linear regression technique yields a straight line that defines the relationship between two sets of data. Recall, however, that all of the data we are dealing
with here is subject to statistical error in measurement. Thus, we will not get an
exact fit. To be scientifically correct we must subject the slope and intercept of
the straight line to tests of hypothesis. This is beyond the scope of this presenta-
tion, however, and will not be discussed. What we can discuss, though, is the use
of this technique.

   If you have two sets of observations that you believe are linearly related, then
use this worksheet to fit a straight line to the pairs of observations. If the line is a
good fit, then the slope "correlates" one set with another. Furthermore, you can
use the slope and intercept as inputs to a formal test of hypothesis to prove your
point.

Formulas   Figure 4.4(b) contains the formulas needed to reconstruct the worksheet. You
can use the /REPLICATE command to fill in most of the formulas given the patterns shown in cells C8, D8, and E8, for example. The formulas for computing
the slope and intercept are shown in cells C23 and C24. These formulas minimize
the "chi-squared" difference between the observed and straight line points in the
graph of Y versus X.

```
>F25:"  )
>E25:(C24)
>D25:"  *  x  +  (
>C25:(C23)
>B25:/FR"=
>A25:"         LINE
>C24:(B22/C21)-(C23*(A22/C21))
>B24:"          A=
>A24:"INTERCEPT B=
>C23:((E22-((A22*B22)/C21))/(C22-(A22^2/C21)))
>B23:"          B=
>A23:"SLOPE
>E22:@SUM(E8...E19)
>D22:@SUM(D8...D19)
>C22:@SUM(C8...C19)
>B22:@SUM(B8...B19)
>A22:@SUM(A8...A19)
>D21:"  SAMPLES
>C21:12
>B21:"  FOR N=
>A21:/FR"TOTALS
>F20:/-_
>E20:/-_
>D20:/-_
>C20:/-_
>B20:/-_
>A20:/-_
>E19:(A19*B19)
>D19:(B19*B19)
>C19:(A19*A19)
>B19:23
>A19:16
>E18:(A18*B18)
>D18:(B18*B18)
>C18:(A18*A18)
>B18:21
>A18:14
>E17:(A17*B17)
>D17:(B17*B17)
>C17:(A17*A17)
>B17:16
>A17:12
>E16:(A16*B16)
>D16:(B16*B16)
>C16:(A16*A16)
>B16:15
>A16:8
>E15:(A15*B15)
>D15:(B15*B15)
>C15:(A15*A15)
>B15:25
>A15:18
>E14:(A14*B14)
```

```
>D14: (B14*B14)
>C14: (A14*A14)
>B14: 20
>A14: 12
>E13: (A13*B13)
>D13: (B13*B13)
>C13: (A13*A13)
>B13: 17
>A13: 16
>E12: (A12*B12)
>D12: (B12*B12)
>C12: (A12*A12)
>B12: 20
>A12: 9
>E11: (A11*B11)
>D11: (B11*B11)
>C11: (A11*A11)
>B11: 18
>A11: 12
>E10: (A10*B10)
>D10: (B10*B10)
>C10: (A10*A10)
>B10: 17
>A10: 12
>E9: (A9*B9)
>D9: (B9*B9)
>C9: (A9*A9)
>B9: 14
>A9: 7
>E8: (A8*B8)
>D8: (B8*B8)
>C8: (A8*A8)
>B8: 16
>A8: 10
>F6: /-_
>E6: /-_
>D6: /-_
>C6: /-_
>B6: /-_
>A6: /-_
>B5: "  $y 1000s
>A5: "   x yrs
>E4: /FR"x*y
>D4: /FR"y^2
>C4: /FR"x^2
>B4: /FR"Income
>A4: "Schooling
>F3: /--
>E3: /--
>D3: /--
>C3: /--
>B3: /--
>A3: /--
>E2: " Income
```

```
>D2:"ation vs.
>C2:"e of Educat
>B2:"    Example
>D1:"ANALYSIS
>C1:"GRESSION
>B1:"LINEAR RE
/W1
/GOC
/GRA
/GC9
/X>A1:>A1:
```

Figure 4.4(b). Formulas for linear regression

4.5. CONTINGE: Contingency Table

Purpose
In an experimental situation it may be very difficult to quantify your observations beyond merely counting. The counts can be classified into one or more *categories* or *levels* as statisticians call them. If the counts are compared with the expected number in each category, then a chi-squared statistic can be used to tell if the counts are from the same population. If so, then you can say the experimental counts are the "same" as the expected counts. This approach is called *contingency analysis*, and the table used to do the calculations is called a *contingency table*. Figure 4.5(a) shows a worksheet that holds a contingency table.

The purpose of this example is to show you how to build a contingency table that can be used to see if a set of observations fall into certain categories "as they should" in order for some hypothesis to be true.

Worksheet
The worksheet in Figure 4.5(a) illustrates the idea of a contingency table. Suppose we want to know if the frequency of eye color and hair color combinations in people follow the expected pattern shown in Figure 4.5(a). For example, in the

```
C23    (V) @SUM(C22...F22)/E23                                        C
                                                                      83

        A          B          C          D          E          F
 4                          Criterion            #2
 5                          Hair color
 6                      Blond      Brown        Black        Red
 7              ----------------------------------------------------
 8           Blue(obs)      60         40         60         40
 9           Blue(exp)      32        100         32         36
10    #1     ----------------------------------------------------
11 Criterion Brown(obs)     10        160         10         20
12 Eye Color Brown(exp)     32        100         32         36
13           ----------------------------------------------------
14           Hazel(obs)     10         50         10         30
15           Hazel(exp)     16         50         16         18
16           ----------------------------------------------------
17
18           TOTALS (obs)   80        250         80         90
19           TOTALS (exp)   80        250         80         90
20    --------------------------------------------------------------
21
22      Chi-Square = 41.87499994 71.99999994 41.87499994 15.55555555
23      Sum Chi-Sq = 28.55092589  Degrees  =            6
24      --------------------------------------------------------------
```

```
                              CONTINGENCY TABLE
                          Example of Hair and Eye Color
----------------------------------------------------------------------------
                                 Criterion      #2
                                 Hair color
                              Blond       Brown        Black        Red
          ------------------------------------------------------------------
          Blue(obs)            60          40           60           40
          Blue(exp)            32         100           32           36
  #1      ------------------------------------------------------------------
Criterion Brown(obs)           10         160           10           20
Eye Color Brown(exp)           32         100           32           36
          ------------------------------------------------------------------
          Hazel(obs)           10          50           10           30
          Hazel(exp)           16          50           16           18
          ------------------------------------------------------------------

          TOTALS  (obs)        80         250           80           90
          TOTALS  (exp)        80         250           80           90
----------------------------------------------------------------------------
          Chi-Square = 41.87499994 71.99999994 41.87499994 15.55555555
          Sum Chi-Sq = 28.55092589 Degrees   =          6
          -------------------
```

Figure 4.5(a). Contingency table analysis

first row the frequency of occurance of eye-hair color combinations in a group of 500 people is

$$Blue\text{-}blond = 60$$
$$Blue\text{-}brown = 40$$
$$Blue\text{-}black = 60$$
$$Blue\text{-}red = 40$$

These observations are to be compared with the expected numbers shown in the same row as 32, 100, 32, and 35, respectively. The question is, are these numbers "significantly" different from the expected counts?

The table of Figure 4.5(a) is used by entering the observed counts for each pair of eye-hair colors. These counts are summed and then used in the formula for computing the chi-squared value shown at the bottom of the worksheet. This value is used to test your hypothesis of whether the observed and expected values are sufficiently correlated to be considered the same.

Comments

The chi-squared value obtained here has $(r-1)*(c-1)$ degrees of freedom, where r, c are the number of rows, columns, respectively. This fact is needed along with the level of confidence before you can use the chi-squared table to decide if the observed counts are similar to the expected counts.

If you want to modify this table to work with other applications simply erase (/BLANK) the labels and counts shown here and substitute your own. You can also expand the number of rows and columns to make the table bigger, but remember to adjust the formulas to include all the counts.

Formulas The expected count for each pair is computed as follows:

$$\text{Expected} = (\text{Row total count}) * (\text{Column total count})/N$$
$$\text{where } N = \text{total number of observations}$$

This value is computed for every pair of counts in the contingency table.

The chi-squared value is computed by summing the difference squared in each pair:

$$((\text{Observed} - \text{Expected}) \wedge 2)/\text{Expected}$$

This is summed as shown in the formulas of Figure 4.5(b).

You can quickly reconstruct the worksheet from the formulas in Figure 4.5(b) by abundant use of the REPLICATE command.

```
>C24: /--
>E23: (@COUNT(C9,C12,C14)-1)*(@COUNT(C8...F8)-1)
>D23:" Degrees  =
>C23:@SUM(C22...F22)/E23
>B23:"Sum Chi-Sq =
>F22:@SUM((F8-F9)^2/F9,(F11-F12)^2/F12,(F14-F15)^2/F15)
>E22:@SUM((E8-E9)^2/E9,(E11-E12)^2/E12,(E14-E15)^2/E15)
>D22:@SUM((D8-D9)^2/D9,(D11-D12)^2/D12,(D14-D15)^2/D15)
>C22:@SUM((C8-C9)^2/C9,(C11-C12)^2/C12,(C14-C15)^2/C15)
>B22:"Chi-Square =
>F20:/-_
>E20:/-_
>D20:/-_
>C20:/-_
>B20:/-_
>A20:/-_
>F19:@SUM(F9,F12,F15)
>E19:@SUM(E9,E12,E15)
>D19:@SUM(D9,D12,D15)
>C19:@SUM(C9,C12,C15)
>B19:"TOTALS (exp)
>F18:@SUM(F8,F11,F14)
>E18:@SUM(E8,E11,E14)
>D18:@SUM(D8,D11,D14)
>C18:@SUM(C8,C11,C14)
>B18:"TOTALS (obs)
>F16:/--
>E16:/--
>D16:/--
>C16:/--
>B16:/--
>F15:(@SUM(C14,D14,E14,F14)*F18)/@SUM(C18,D18,E18,F18)
>E15:(@SUM(C14,D14,E14,F14)*E18)/@SUM(C18,D18,E18,F18)
>D15:(@SUM(C14,D14,E14,F14)*D18)/@SUM(C18,D18,E18,F18)
>C15:(@SUM(C14,D14,E14,F14)*C18)/@SUM(C18,D18,E18,F18)
>B15:"Hazel (exp)
>F14:30
>E14:10
>D14:50
>C14:10
```

```
>B14:"Hazel(obs)
>F13:/--
>E13:/--
>D13:/--
>C13:/--
>B13:/--
>F12:(@SUM(C11,D11,E11,F11)*F18)/@SUM(C18,D18,E18,F18)
>E12:(@SUM(C11,D11,E11,F11)*E18)/@SUM(C18,D18,E18,F18)
>D12:(@SUM(C11,D11,E11,F11)*D18)/@SUM(C18,D18,E18,F18)
>C12:(@SUM(C11,D11,E11,F11)*C18)/@SUM(C18,D18,E18,F18)
>B12:"Brown(exp)
>A12:"Eye Color
>F11:20
>E11:10
>D11:160
>C11:10
>B11:"Brown(obs)
>A11:"Criterion
>F10:/--
>E10:/--
>D10:/--
>C10:/--
>B10:/--
>A10:"   #1
>F9:(@SUM(C8,D8,E8,F8)*F18)/@SUM(C18,D18,E18,F18)
>E9:(@SUM(C8,D8,E8,F8)*E18)/@SUM(C18,D18,E18,F18)
>D9:(@SUM(C8,D8,E8,F8)*D18)/@SUM(C18,D18,E18,F18)
>C9:(@SUM(C8,D8,E8,F8)*C18)/@SUM(C18,D18,E18,F18)
>B9:"Blue(exp)
>F8:40
>E8:60
>D8:40
>C8:60
>B8:"Blue(obs)
>I7:/--
>H7:/--
>F7:/--
>E7:/--
>D7:/--
>C7:/--
>B7:/--
>F6:/FR"Red
>E6:/FR"Black
>D6:/FR"Brown
>C6:/FR"Blond
>D5:"Hair color
>E4:"   #2
>D4:"Criterion
>H3:/-_
>F3:/-_
>E3:/-_
>D3:/-_
>C3:/-_
>B3:/-_
>A3:/-_
```

```
>E2:"Color
>D2:"air and Eye
>C2:"Example of Hair
>D1:"TABLE
>C1:"CONTINGENCY
/W1
/GOC
/GRA
/GC12
/X>A1:>A1:
```

Figure 4.5(b). Formulas for contingency table analysis

4.6. RANK: Spearman Rank Correlation Test

The Spearman rank correlation test is used to decide if two sets of ranks are similar. Suppose two people are asked to evaluate job applicants by assigning a number (rank) to each of nine applicants; see Figure 4.6(a). The two evaluators are called Person A and Person B, and the applicants are numbered from 1 to 9.

The purpose of this rank correlation test is to find out if there is any agreement between two sets of orderings. If the evaluators grade something on a scale from 1 to 10, for example, and if they report similar grades for the same observations, then we say their grades are similar. Otherwise the grades are not correlated. Just as in the correlation coefficient worksheet, the rank correlation coefficient will vary between −1 and +1.

Purpose

The worksheet in Figure 4.6(a) shows how to compare two rankings reported by Persons A and B. Each person evaluates a job applicant and assigns a number to the applicant. If the number is 1, this means the evaluator has chosen the applicant as first choice.

The ranks reported by A and B are entered in the second and third columns as shown. These ranks are then compared with one another by computing the chi-squared statistic shown at the bottom of the page. This number is used in the formula for rank correlation to get the number shown.

Worksheet

SPEARMAN RANK CORRELATION
Example of Job Applicant Ratings

Applicant #	Rank by Person A	Rank by Person B	Difference Squared
1	4	2	4
2	3	4	1
3	7	6	1
4	2	1	1
5	9	9	0
6	8	8	0
7	1	3	4
8	5	7	4
9	6	5	1

9   Chi-Square = 16
SPEARMAN RANK-CORRELATION COEFF = .8666666662

```
              SPEARMAN  RANK  CORRELATION
              Example of Job Applicant Ratings

   Applicant #         Rank by       Rank by   Difference
                      Person A      Person B     Squared
   ----------------------------------------------------------
              1           4             2           4
              2           3             4           1
              3           7             6           1
              4           2             1           1
              5           9             9           0
              6           8             8           0
              7           1             3           4
              8           5             7           4
              9           6             5           1
   ----------------------------------------------------------
              9                    Chi-Square =          16
   SPEARMAN  RANK-CORRELATION COEFF   = .8666666662
```

Figure 4.6(a). Rank correlation table

In Figure 4.6(a), the correlation coefficient 0.867 is considered to be a high correlation. A perfect score would have been + 1. If the rankings were indirectly correlated then the score would have been − 1. Finally, if the score is close to zero, we say the two rankings are not correlated.

Comments   This worksheet can be used in any situation where scores or rankings are being compared. For instance, two judges can compare their evaluations of witnesses to decide if their evaluations are similar or completely different.

Formulas   The formula for rank correlation is given below.

$$R = 1 - (6*CHI/(n \wedge 2 - 1))$$
Where CHI = (sum of the difference squared)/N
and N = number of observations (number applicants)

Figure 4.6(b) can be used to reconstruct the worksheet in Figure 4.6(a). The formulas can be entered rapidly by using the /REPLICATE command to replicate the difference calculations.

The correlation coefficient is calculated in cell D18. Notice that it depends upon the constant stored in cell A17. This is equal to nine, the number of applicants. If you extend this worksheet to more or fewer applicants, then this constant must also be changed.

```
>D18:1-((6*D17)/(A17*(A17^2-1)))    >D16:/--
>C18:"ON COEFF    =                 >C16:/--
>B18:"NK-CORRELATI                  >B16:/--
>A18:"SPEARMAN  RA                  >A16:/--
>D17:@SUM(D7...D15)                 >D15:(B15-C15)^2
>C17:"Chi-Square =                  >C15:5
>A17:@COUNT(A7...A15)               >B15:6
```

```
>A15:9                           >A8:2
>D14:(B14-C14)^2                 >D7:(B7-C7)^2
>C14:7                           >C7:2
>B14:5                           >B7:4
>A14:8                           >A7:1
>D13:(B13-C13)^2                 >D6:/--
>C13:3                           >C6:/--
>B13:1                           >B6:/--
>A13:7                           >A6:/--
>D12:(B12-C12)^2                 >D5:/FR"Squared
>C12:8                           >C5:/FR"Person  B
>B12:8                           >B5:/FR"Person  A
>A12:6                           >D4:/FR"Difference
>D11:(B11-C11)^2                 >C4:/FR"Rank by
>C11:9                           >B4:/FR"Rank by
>B11:9                           >A4:"Applicant #
>A11:5                           >D2:" Ratings
>D10:(B10-C10)^2                 >C2:"ob Applicant
>C10:1                           >B2:"Example of J
>B10:2                           >D1:"ION
>A10:4                           >C1:"NK  CORRELAT
>D9:(B9-C9)^2                    >B1:"SPEARMAN  RA
>C9:6                            /W1
>B9:7                            /GOC
>A9:3                            /GRA
>D8:(B8-C8)^2                    /GC12
>C8:4                            /X>A9:>A29:
>B8:3
```

Figure 4.6(b). Formulas for rank correlation table

Chapter 5
What-if Models

The ability to modify VisiCalc worksheets and see immediately the consequences of these modifications is one of the major advantages, and most popular features, of the VisiCalc program. Changing a number in one cell may lead to a recalculation in another cell, for example. The recalculation can be done automatically and the result displayed immediately. This feature makes it possible to explore a number of questions that you may have concerning the interaction of cells and cell values. These questions are called *"what-ifs,"* because they are the kind of questions that begin with "what if I did the following," or "what if this number is changed."

In the final chapter of this collection of worksheets we look at some typical applications of the VisiCalc program that lead to a lot of "what-ifs." These worksheets are sometimes called models because they represent real world systems. A VisiCalc model is a mathematical representation of a system of interacting cells. The system being modeled can be almost anything from a factory to a financial transaction.

This collection includes five models. The first two are financial models that can be readily expanded into a model of your personal wealth. PAYMENTS is a model of installment payments, and total finance charges. What if the interest rate changes by one per cent?

SAVINGS is a worksheet that lets you explore the impact of various interest rates on your savings account. What if you move your savings to another bank that pays one-tenth of a percent more on savings accounts?

The third worksheet is a model of a small business. The business used as an example is that of a building contractor. SPECHOUS is a model of the financial interconnections involved in building a "spec" house as the general contractors call it. What if the house takes three months to sell instead of two months? How much profit is there in the sale if it costs 20% for the construction loan?

PILOT is a worksheet for navigating. If you own a sailboat or airplane, this worksheet will be a winner. The worksheet computes the direction that you should go in order to get from point A to point B at a certain speed. What if the prevailing winds change? Then the new bearings can be instantly recalculated.

The final worksheet is a bonus model. ECON is a model of the national economy. It uses values for the amount of money spent by the government, investors, taxes, etc., to come up with an estimate of inflation rate and national wealth. What if the government spends less next year? What causes inflation to go up? How can inflation be decreased? This bonus model will intrigue you for hours.

5.1. PAYMENTS: Installment Payments

The purpose of this example is to explore the impact of interest rates and length of repayment period on monthly payments and total interest charges on installment payments.

Purpose

The example of Figure 5.1(a) illustrates the basic worksheet. If you borrow $60,000 at 16% interest rate for 29 years then the monthly payments will be $808.05. The inputs to this worksheet are the amount borrowed, the interest rate, and the term of the loan. If any one of these inputs is changed, the results will also be changed. Thus, you can ask, "What if the interest rate changes to 15%?" Another question might be, "How much money will I save on interest if I repay the loan in 25 years?"

Worksheet

The inputs can be changed to see the impact on the answers. The /GLOBAL R A option must be enabled to get automatic recalculation. In addition, the /GLOBAL O R option must be on to cause row-major recalculation.

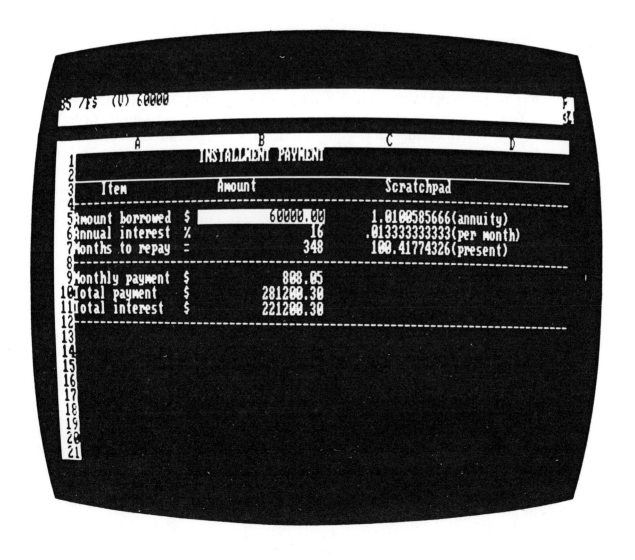

```
                    INSTALLMENT PAYMENT
-------------------------------------------------------------------
      Item               Amount              Scratchpad
-------------------------------------------------------------------
Amount borrowed    $           60000.00      1.0100585666(annuity)
Annual interest    %                 16      .013333333333(per month)
Months to repay    =                348      100.41774326(present)
-------------------------------------------------------------------
Monthly payment    $             808.05
Total payment      $          281200.30
Total interest     $          221200.30
-------------------------------------------------------------------
```

Figure 5.1(a). Installment payment worksheet

Comments   The circuitous dependence illustrated in this worksheet occurs often in the VisiCalc program. Sometimes you can avoid it by changing the order of recalculation. Other times the error persists no matter what order you use for the recalculations. In this case, you must recalculate the whole worksheet, repeatedly, until the dependence "dies out." This will be indicated by no further changes in the values after the recalculation.

Formulas   Figure 5.1(b) contains the formulas needed to reconstruct the worksheet. Notice the /FORMAT $ settings and the column widths (see /GC19).

You might notice the order of recalculation in this worksheet. Even with automatic recalculation in row-major order, the ! recalculation command should be used because of the "circuitous" calculations that are part of this worksheet. See cell C5 as an example. The value of cell C5 depends on the value of cell C7. But the value of cell C7 will not be updated until after the value calculated in C5. This circular dependence will cause the values in the worksheet to "get out of synch." You can correct for this by causing an additional recalculation to take place.

```
>D12:"-------------------
>C12:"-------------------
>B12:"-------------------
>A12:"-------------------
>B11:/F$(B10-B5)
>A11:"Total interest     $
>B10:/F$(B9*B7)
>A10:"Total payment      $
>B9:/F$(C6*C5*B5)
>A9:"Monthly payment    $
>D8:"-------------------
>C8:"-------------------
>B8:"-------------------
>A8:"-------------------
>D7:"(present)
>C7:(C6+1)^B7
```

```
>B7:/FI348
>A7:"Months to repay   =
>D6:"(per month)
>C6:+B6/1200
>B6:/FG16
>A6:"Annual interest   %
>D5:"(annuity)
>C5:+C7/(C7-1)
>B5:/F$60000
>A5:"Amount borrowed   $
>D4:"--------------------
>C4:"--------------------
>B4:"--------------------
>A4:"--------------------
>C3:/FR"Scratchpad
>B3:"   Amount
>A3:/FL"      Item
>D2:/-_
>C2:/-_
>B2:/-_
>A2:/-_
>B1:"INSTALLMENT PAYMENT
/W1
/GOR
/GRA
/GC19
/X>A1:>A1:
```

Figure 5.1(b). Formulas for installment payments

5.2. SAVINGS: Interest On Savings Account

Purpose   The purpose of this simple worksheet is to explore the impact of compounding interest rate on the growth of your savings account.

Worksheet   The worksheet shown in Figure 5.2(a) is an example of a savings account worksheet. If you enter the original amount, number of times per month the interest is compounded (added back into the account), and the interest rate, the worksheet will compute the amount of savings that accrues at maturity.

What if the compounding rate doubles, or the interest rate changes? Suppose the length of time to maturity is changed. What happens?

Comments   This simple worksheet can be extended as follows. Suppose you begin a monthly payroll deduction plan where a certain amount of money is deducted from your paycheck and put into a savings account. The question is, "How much money will accumulate in Y years at R percentage interest rate?"

The payroll deduction worksheet can be modified to compute the retirement fund that can be accumulated by purchasing IRA (Individual Retirement Account) certificates.

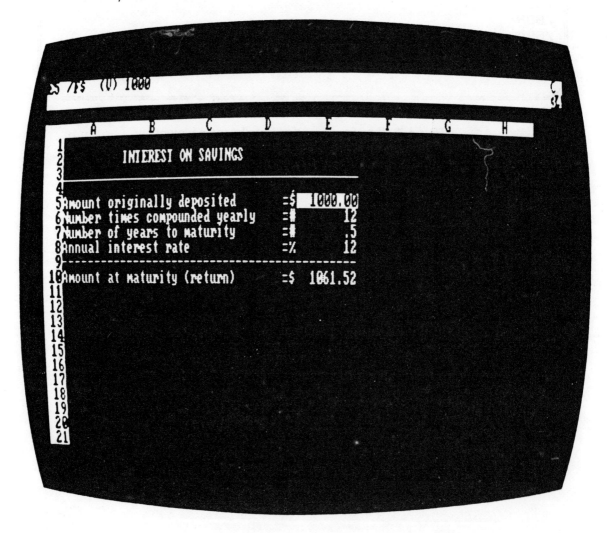

```
          INTEREST ON SAVINGS
 ---------------------------------------------

 Amount originally deposited      =$   1000.00
 Number times compounded yearly   =#        12
 Number of years to maturity      =#        .5
 Annual interest rate             =%        12
 ---------------------------------------------
 Amount at maturity (return)      =$   1061.52
```

Figure 5.2(a). Interest on savings worksheet

Figure 5.2(a) contains the formulas needed to reconstruct the worksheet. This **Formulas** worksheet contains only one formula of any significance, shown in cell E10. This is the formula for computing the amount at maturity. Since it depends on the values stored in cells E5, E8, E6, and E7, any changes in these cells will be reflected in the value recalculated by this formula.

```
>E10:/F$(E5*((1+(E8/(100*E6)))^(E6*E7))    >C6:"unded year
>D10:/FR"=$                                >B6:"mes compo
>C10:" (return)                            >A6:"Number tim
>B10:" maturity                            >E5:/F$1000
>A10:"Amount at                            >D5:/FR"=$
>E9:/--                                    >C5:"deposited
>D9:/--                                    >B5:"iginally
>C9:/--                                    >A5:"Amount or
>B9:/--                                    >E3:/-_
>A9:/--                                    >D3:/-_
>E8:12                                     >C3:/-_
>D8:/FR"=%                                 >B3:/-_
>C8:"te                                    >A3:/-_
>B8:"terest ra                             >D2:"S
>A8:"Annual in                             >C2:"ON SAVING
>E7:.5                                     >B2:"INTEREST
>D7:/FR"=#                                 /W1
>C7:" maturity                             /GOC
>B7:" years to                             /GRA
>A7:"Number of                             /GC9
>E6:12                                     /X>A1:>A1:
>D6:"rly      =#
```

Figure 5.2(b). Formulas for interest on payments worksheet

5.3. SPECHOUS: Builders Financial Model

Purpose   Many small businesses need to know the financial risks involved in making various decisions. This is called *"risk analysis."* In a small firm, though, you want to know how much it will cost if a certain event occurs.

Furthermore, a business needs to know what the actual costs are for doing business. Hidden costs must be revealed so that accurate estimates are made and the company ends up with a profit. It will do a company no good at all to sell a lot of product if a profit is not made on each unit.

A general contractor who speculates by building a house without a buyer needs a risk analysis model as much as any small business. Therefore, the example in this section explores a financial model of a spec house project.

The purpose of the worksheet in Figure 5.3(a) is to explore the impact of construction, interest rate, and length of time to build and sell the house at a builder's profit.

Worksheet   Figure 5.3(a) contains a split-screen worksheet that takes inputs for the cost to build a house and adds the costs associated with the construction loan, time to build, time to sell, real estate fees, and lot purchase to come up with a sale price. If the builder is successful with the plan, then the profit is as shown in the last row of the worksheet.

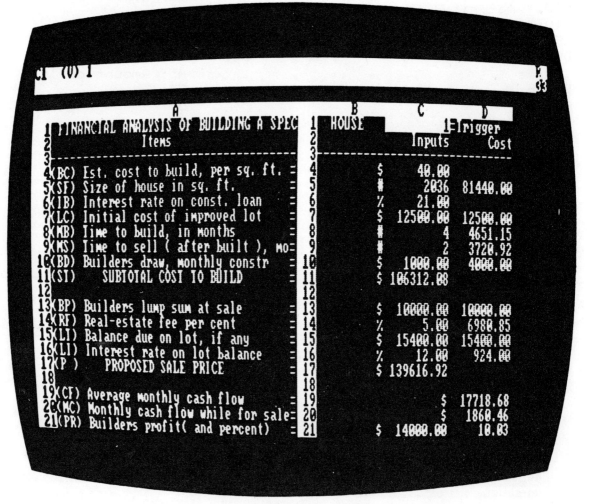

```
/‾FINANCIAL ANALYSIS OF BUILDING A SPEC HOUSE        1=Trigger
          Items                               Inputs        Cost
---------------------------------------------------------------
(BC) Est. cost to build, per sq. ft. =       $      40.00
(SF) Size of house in sq. ft.        =       #       2036   81440.00
(IB) Interest rate on const. loan    =       %      21.00
(LC) Initial cost of improved lot    =       $   12500.00   12500.00
(MB) Time to build, in months        =       #          4    4651.15
(MS) Time to sell ( after built ), mo=       #          2    3720.92
(BD) Builders draw, monthly constr   =       $    1000.00    4000.00
(ST)     SUBTOTAL COST TO BUILD      =       $  106312.08

(BP) Builders lump sum at sale       =       $   10000.00   10000.00
(RF) Real-estate fee per cent        =       %       5.00    6980.85
(LT) Balance due on lot, if any      =       $   15400.00   15400.00
(LI) Interest rate on lot balance    =       %      12.00     924.00
(P )     PROPOSED SALE PRICE         =       $  139616.92

(CF) Average monthly cash flow       =                 $   17718.68
(MC) Monthly cash flow while for sale=                 $    1860.46
(PR) Builders profit( and percent)   =       $   14000.00      10.03
```

Figure 5.3(a). Spec house model

But what if the house doesn't sell right away? If it takes 2 months to sell the house, the builder must add $3,720.92 to the cost to build and sell the house. What if it takes 4 months to sell the house? How many months can the builder hold on to the house and still make a profit? These and other questions can be explored with this model.

This model is quite complete. It tells a builder what the financial risk might be for a new project. The builder must decide if the house can be sold for the proposed sale price. If the house does not sell, then the builder must decide when it is time to lower the price and sell at a lower profit. If this model is used to its fullest extent, then the builder can determine his potential loss before it happens and possibly avoid it.

Comments

Figure 5.3(b) contains the information needed to reconstruct the worksheet. Note that the screen is split into left and right halves. The columns in the left window are 41 characters long, and the columns in the right window are 10 characters long. The two halves of the screen are synchronized.

Formulas

The formulas compute simple interest on the borrowed construction loan. Each month the interest is computed on only the amount loaned. The amount loaned is assumed to be uniformly spread out over the building period. That is, the total is divided evenly by the number of months to complete construction.

There is a circular dependency in this worksheet just like the one we saw earlier. The real estate fee will be calculated as a percentage of the sale price, but the sale price is the sum of all other costs including the real estate fee. So, you will have to press the ! recalculation key several times in order to force the oscillation between these calculations to die out. This is the method of successive approximation.

```
>D21:/F$100*(C21/C17)
>C21:/F$+D10+C13
>B21:/FR"$
>A21:"(PR) Builders profit( and percent)   =
>D20:/F$(C6*C11)/1200
>C20:/FR"$
>B20:/FR
>A20:"(MC) Monthly cash flow while for sale= $
>D19:/F$(C11)/(C8+C9)
>C19:/FR"$
>B19:/FR
>A19:"(CF) Average monthly cash flow       = $
>D18:/F$
>C18:/F$
>B18:/FR
>D17:/F$
>C17:/F$(100*(C11+D13+D15+D16))/(100-C14)
>B17:/FR"$
>A17:"(P )      PROPOSED SALE PRICE        = $
>D16:/F$(C15*C16/1200)*(C8+C9)
>C16:/F$12
>B16:/FR"%
>A16:"(LI) Interest rate on lot balance    =
>D15:/F$+C15
>C15:/F$15400
>B15:/FR"$
>A15:"(LT) Balance due on lot, if any      = $
>D14:/F$(C14*C17)/100
>C14:/F$5
>B14:/FR"%
>A14:"(RF) Real-estate fee per cent        = %
>D13:/F$(C13)
>C13:/F$10000
>B13:/FR"$
>A13:"(BP) Builders lump sum at sale       = $
>D12:/F$
>C12:/F$
>B12:/FR
>D11:/F$
>C11:/F$@SUM(D5...D10
>B11:/FR"$
>A11:"(ST)     SUBTOTAL COST TO BUILD      = $
>D10:/F$(C10*C8)
>C10:/F$1000
>B10:/FR"$
>A10:"(BD) Builders draw, monthly constr   = $
>D9:/F$@IF(C1=0,C9*C6*C5/1200,(C9*C6*C11)/1200)
>C9:/FI2
>B9:/FR"#
>A9:"(MS) Time to sell ( after built ), mo= #
>D8:/F$@IF(C1=0,C8*C6*D5/1200,((C8+1)*C11*C6)/2400)
>C8:/FI4
>B8:/FR"#
>A8:"(MB) Time to build, in months         = #
```

```
>D7:/F$+C7
>C7:/F$12500
>B7:/FR"$
>A7:"(LC) Initial cost of improved lot   = $
>D6:/F$
>C6:/F$21
>B6:/FR"%
>A6:"(IB) Interest rate on const. loan    = %
>D5:/F$(C4*C5)
>C5:/FI2036
>B5:/FR"#
>A5:"(SF) Size of house in sq. ft.        = #
>D4:/F$
>C4:/F$40
>B4:/FR"$
>A4:"(BC) Est. cost to build, per sq. ft. = $
>D3:/--
>C3:/--
>B3:/--
>A3:/--
>D2:/FR"Cost
>C2:/FR"Inputs
>A2:"              Items
>D1:"=Trigger
>C1:1
>B1:/FL"  HOUSE
>A1:/FR" FINANCIAL ANALYSIS OF BUILDING A SPEC
/W1
/GOR
/GRA
/XV41
/GC38
/X>A1:>A1:;/GC10
/X>B1:>B1:/WS
```

Figure 5.3(b). Formulas for spec house model

5.4. PILOT: Flyer's Navigation Model

Purpose   Suppose you are a pilot of an airplane or boat and you want to know the correct bearing given your airspeed or the prevailing wind speed and direction. This in itself is a good problem in trigonometry, but now suppose the wind shifts to a different direction. Now, in what direction do you fly?

The worksheet in Figure 5.4(a) contains a model of the navigator's problem. Given the distance, cruising speed, direction of destination, wind speed, and wind direction, calculate the bearing and speed that you must fly or sail. Also, how long will it take?

Worksheet   Suppose you are going to fly your private airplane 400 nautical miles toward a city that is directly west of your origin. West is 270 degrees on the compass, so you travel 270 degrees from north. Your airplane is able to travel at 250 knots airspeed.

The weather report says the winds are blowing at 45 knots out of the southwest (210 degrees) at the elevation you want to fly. The problem that you must solve is to compute your bearing (direction of flight) and to compute how long it will take for you to fly to your destination. The worksheet of Figure 5.4(a) does this for you. The answers are displayed in the last three rows of the worksheet.

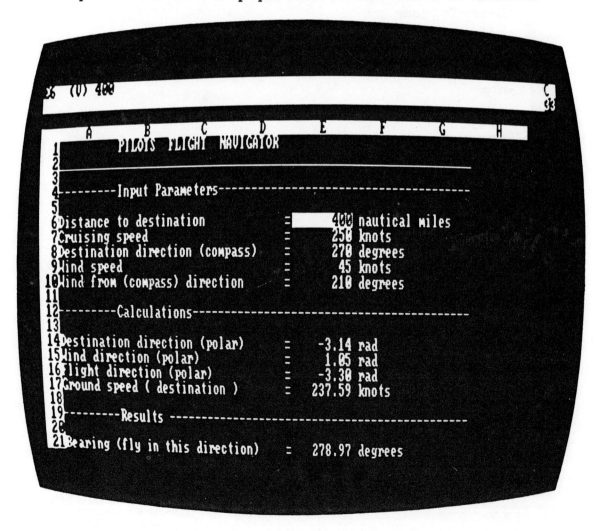

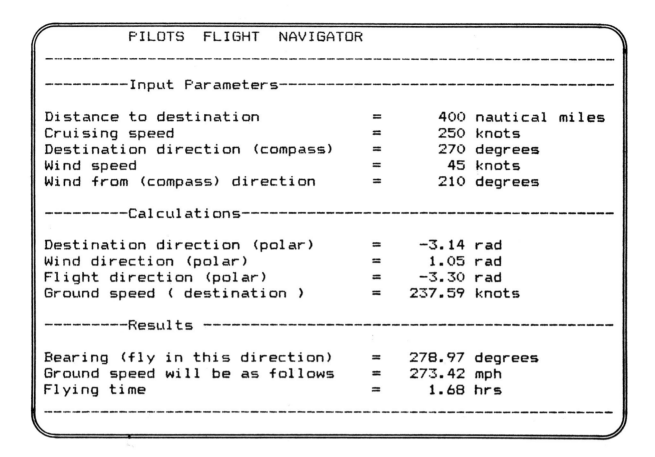

```
              PILOTS  FLIGHT  NAVIGATOR
-----------------------------------------------------------------

-----------Input Parameters--------------------------------------

Distance to destination          =         400 nautical miles
Cruising speed                   =         250 knots
Destination direction (compass)  =         270 degrees
Wind speed                       =          45 knots
Wind from (compass) direction    =         210 degrees

-----------Calculations------------------------------------------

Destination direction (polar)    =       -3.14 rad
Wind direction (polar)           =        1.05 rad
Flight direction (polar)         =       -3.30 rad
Ground speed ( destination )     =      237.59 knots

-----------Results ----------------------------------------------

Bearing (fly in this direction)  =      278.97 degrees
Ground speed will be as follows  =      273.42 mph
Flying time                      =        1.68 hrs

-----------------------------------------------------------------
```

Figure 5.4(a). Worksheet for navigators

Obviously this worksheet can compute navigational directions much faster **Comments** than any human. If the computer is taken along with you on your airplane, then you can ask "what-if" questions in real time. For example, what if you get half way there and the wind shifts to a different direction and speed. All you have to do is enter the new information into the worksheet and out comes the new bearing and estimated time to complete the trip.

How the formulas in Figure 5.4(b) were obtained is a long story. The calcula- **Formulas** tions are complicated by two facts. First, the VisiCalc trig functions like @SIN and @COS (sine and cosine) require arguments in radians instead of degrees. There are 2 * PI radians in 360 degrees, so the calculations must convert between radians and degrees. Secondly, the angles obtained from a compass are 90 degrees off from the angles used in trig to compute the sides of a triangle. Furthermore, the compass measures angles in a clockwise direction, while the trig functions use counterclockwise directions.

The trigonometric calculations in cells E16 and E17 are the most difficult formulas to derive. They were obtained by converting the angles from compass settings to radians in polar coordinates, and then using some pretty sophisticated trigonometry.

The results shown in Figure 5.4(a) include the ground speed in both knots and miles per hour. The conversion table for this conversion is included in METRIC. We have simply used it here.

```
>G24:/-_
>F24:/-_
>E24:/-_
>D24:/-_
>C24:/-_
>B24:/-_
>A24:/-_
>F23:" hrs
>E23:/F$(E6/E17)
>D23:/FR"=
>B23:"me
>A23:"Flying ti
>F22:" mph
>E22:/F$1.1508*E17
>D22:"lows      =
>C22:"be as foll
>B22:"eed will
>A22:"Ground sp
>F21:" degrees
>E21:/F$90-(180*E16/@PI)
>D21:"ion)     =
>C21:"is directio
>B21:"fly in this
>A21:"Bearing (
>G19:/--
>F19:/--
>E19:/--
>D19:/--
>C19:/--
>B19:"Results ---
>A19:/--
>F17:" knots
>E17:/F$@SQRT((E7*E7)+(E9*E9)+(2*E7*E9*@COS(E16-E15))
>D17:/FR")      =
>C17:"tination
>B17:"eed ( destination
>A17:"Ground sp
>F16:" rad
>E16:/F$(E14+(@ASIN((E9/E7)*@SIN(E14+E15))))
>D16:/FR"=
>C16:"polar)
>B16:"rection (p
>A16:"Flight dir
>F15:" rad
>E15:/F$((270-E10)*@PI/180)
>D15:/FR"=
>C15:"lar)
>B15:"ction (pol
>A15:"Wind dire
>F14:" rad
>E14:/F$(@PI*(90-E8))/180
>D14:"r)          =
>C14:"ion (polar)
>B14:"on direct
```

```
>A14:"Destinatio
>G12:/--
>F12:/--
>E12:/--
>D12:/--
>C12:"ons------
>B12:"Calculatio
>A12:/--
>F10:" degrees
>E10:210
>D10:"on        =
>C10:") directi
>B10:" (compass
>A10:"Wind from
>F9:" knots
>E9:45
>D9:/FR"=
>C9:/FR
>B9:"d
>A9:"Wind speed
>F8:" degrees
>E8:270
>D8:"ass)      =
>C8:"ion (compass)
>B8:"on direct
>A8:"Destinatio
>F7:" knots
>E7:250
>D7:/FR"=
>C7:/FR
>B7:"speed
>A7:"Cruising
>G6:" miles
>F6:" nautical
>E6:400
>D6:/FR"=
>C6:"ation
>B6:"to destina
>A6:"Distance
>G4:/--
>F4:/--
>E4:/--
>D4:/--
>C4:"ameters--
>B4:"Input Par
>A4:/--
>G2:/-_
>F2:/-_
>E2:/-_
>D2:/-_
>C2:/-_
>B2:/-_
>A2:/-_
>D1:"VIGATOR
```

```
>C1:"LIGHT  NA
>B1:"PILOTS  F
/W1
/GOC
/GRA
/GC9
/X>A1:>A1:
```

Figure 5.4(b). Formulas for navigation worksheet

5.5. ECON: Macro-economic Model of the National Economy (Bonus)

Purpose

The purpose of this bonus worksheet is to explore the cause and effect of money flow in the national economy. This model is called a "macro" model because it represents the broad view of money flow rather than the intricate details of individual transactions that might affect the economy (like war, famine, failure of a large corporation).

Worksheet

Figure 5.5(a) shows a worksheet divided into two parts. The top half contains the input parameters that constitute the starting values and constants of the economy. The lower half contains a trigger that is used to reset the calculations and the results of the calculations.

Suppose the initial and constant value of government spending is set at 1000 as shown in Figure 5.5(a). Set the constant tax rate at 20%, cost of living due to consumables at $75 billion, consumer spending rate at 80%, starting investment capital at $50 billion, investment rate at 10%, and the initial inflation rate at 5%. These inputs are shown in the sample worksheet in Figure 5.5(a).

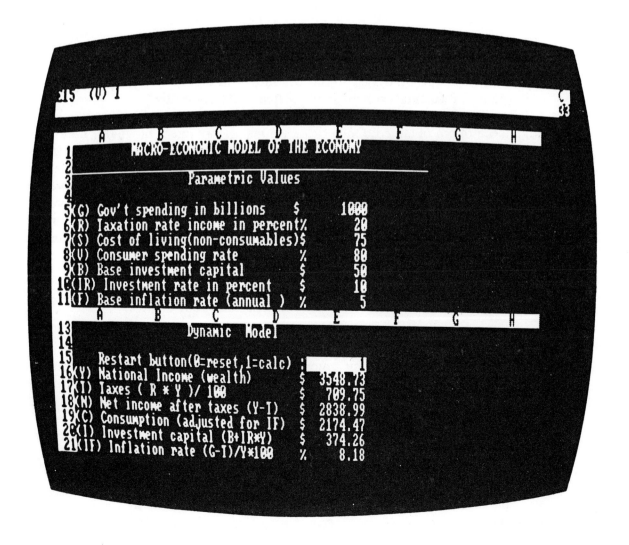

```
   ╭─────────────────────────────────────────────────────────╮
   │           MACRO-ECONOMIC MODEL OF THE ECONOMY            │
   │  ─────────────────────────────────────────────────────   │
   │                   Parametric Values                      │
   │                                                          │
   │  (G)  Gov't spending in billions      $       1000       │
   │  (R)  Taxation rate income in percent%         20        │
   │  (S)  Cost of living(non-consumables)$         75        │
   │  (V)  Consumer spending rate          %         80       │
   │  (B)  Base investment capital         $         50       │
   │  (IR) Investment rate in percent      $         10       │
   │  (F)  Base inflation rate (annual )   %          5       │
   │  ─────────────────────────────────────────────────────   │
   │                    Dynamic   Model                       │
   │                                                          │
   │       Restart button(0=reset,1=calc) :           0       │
   │  (Y)  National Income (wealth)        $     1000.00      │
   │  (T)  Taxes ( R * Y )/ 100            $      200.00      │
   │  (N)  Net income after taxes (Y-T)    $      800.00      │
   │  (C)  Consumption (adjusted for IF)   $      684.52      │
   │  (I)  Investment capital (B+IR*Y)     $      142.86      │
   │  (IF) Inflation rate (G-T)/Y*100      %        5.00      │
   ╰─────────────────────────────────────────────────────────╯
```

Figure 5.5(a). Model of the economy: Initial values

The trigger is set to zero (see Restart button). This causes the initial values from the upper half of the worksheet to be used as starting values in the lower half of the worksheet. Set the trigger to one, as shown in Figure 5.5(b), and the model will begin to recalculate a new stable plateau of money flow.

You must press ! to recalculate many times before the calculated values in Figure 5.5(b) are obtained. Once these values are obtained, however, they will persist until one or more of the parameters in the upper half is changed. In Figure 5.5(b), the measure of wealth is shown as the National Income. This plateau is reached after many recalculations. Notice that the taxes are less than the government spending (709.75 versus 1000). This leads to inflation because the government must print extra money to pay its bills. The inflation rate has gone up to 8.18% as a result of the "policy" set up by the initial values of the parameters.

What if the government spending was cut to 709 billion? Would this lead to lower inflation? The answer to this question will surprise you. To get it, enter 709 in place of 1000 for government spending, and then press ! repeatedly until the calculations stabilize. When they do, you will have your answer.

Comments   As mentioned above, this model is based on a number of assumptions. If you want to try other relationships among the variables then replace the formulas here with your own. The model is an adaptation of one of the oldest and simplest macro-economic models around. It can be found in almost any introductory book on macro-economic theory.

Hopefully this example will give you ideas for your own model building. The recalculation command must almost always be used as we have used it here to cause *iteration* of the model. Each iteration brings the model closer to a stable state. If you implement a model that cannot be iterated to a stable state, then your model is not reliable. In this case, you should find out why the instability exists and remove it.

```
           MACRO-ECONOMIC MODEL OF THE ECONOMY
---------------------------------------------------------
                    Parametric Values

    (G) Gov't spending in billions     $      1000
    (R) Taxation rate income in percent%        20
    (S) Cost of living(non-consumables)$        75
    (V) Consumer spending rate         %        80
    (B) Base investment capital        $        50
    (IR) Investment rate in percent    $        10
    (F) Base inflation rate (annual )  %         5
---------------------------------------------------------
                    Dynamic   Model

        Restart button(0=reset,1=calc) :         1
    (Y) National Income (wealth)       $   3548.73
    (T) Taxes ( R * Y )/ 100           $    709.75
    (N) Net income after taxes (Y-T)   $   2838.98
    (C) Consumption (adjusted for IF)  $   2174.47
    (I) Investment capital (B+IR*Y)    $    374.26
    (IF) Inflation rate (G-T)/Y*100    %      8.18
```

Figure 5.5(b). Model of the economy: Final values

The formulas for this model are shown in Figure 5.5(c). They are based on some assumptions about the way money flows in the national economy. If you disagree with these assumptions, then you can change the formulas as desired.

The interrelationship among the values in the model are shown in the rows of the worksheet. These formulas have been implemented accordingly, except for the @IF functions that have been used to detect the trigger. If the trigger is zero then the initial values of the model are used instead.

Formulas

```
>E21:/F$@IF(E15=0,E11,@IF(E17>E5,0,100*(E5-E17)/E16))
>D21:/FR"*100      %
>C21:"e (G-T)/Y
>B21:"ation rat
>A21:"(IF) Infl
>E20:/F$(E9+((E10/100)*E16)/(1+(E21/100)))
>D20:/FR"R*Y)      $
>C20:"ital (B+IR
>B20:"tment cap
>A20:"(I) Inves
>E19:/F$(E7+(E18/(1+(E21/100))*(E8/100)))
>D19:/FR"or IF)   $
>C19:"djusted f
>B19:"mption (adj
>A19:"(C) Consumption
>E18:/F$(E16-E17)
>D18:"(Y-T)      $
>C18:"er taxes
>B18:"ncome aft
>A18:"(N) Net i
```

```
>E17:/F$(E6*E16)/100
>D17:/FR"$
>C17:")/ 100
>B17:" ( R * Y )
>A17:"(T) Taxes
>E16:/F$@IF(E15=0,E5,(E5+E19+E20))
>D16:")           $
>C16:"e (wealth
>B16:"nal Incom
>A16:"(Y) National
>E15:1
>D15:"1=calc) :
>C15:"(0=reset,
>B15:"rt button "(
>A15:"     Restart
>D13:"Model
>C13:"Dynamic
>F12:/--
>E12:/--
>D12:/--
>C12:/--
>B12:/--
>A12:/--
>E11:/FG5
>D11:"nual )  %
>C11:" rate (an
>B11:"inflation
>A11:"(F) Base in
>E10:/FG10
>D10:"cent      $
>C10:"te in per
>B10:"stment rate
>A10:"(IR) Inves
>E9:/FG50
>D9:/FR"$
>C9:"t capital
>B9:"investmen
>A9:"(B) Base
>E8:/FG80
>D8:/FR"%
>C8:"ing rate
>B8:"mer spending
>A8:"(V) Consumer sp
>E7:/FG75
>D7:"umables)$
>C7:"(non-cons
>B7:"of living
>A7:"(S) Cost of living
>E6:/FG20
>D6:" percent%
>C6:"income in
>B6:"ion rate on
>A6:"(R) Taxat
>E5:/FG1000
```

```
>D5:"ons      $
>C5:" in billion
>B5:" spending
>A5:"(G) Gov't
>D3:"c Values
>C3:"Parametri
>F2:/-_
>E2:/-_
>D2:/-_
>C2:/-_
>B2:/-_
>A2:/-_
>E1:" ECONOMY
>D1:"EL OF THE
>C1:"NOMIC MODEL
>B1:"MACRO-ECO
/W1
/GOC
/GRA
/XH11
/GC9
/X>A1:>A1:;/GC9
/X>A15:>E23:;
```

Figure 5.5(c). Formulas for ECON

Appendix A
VisiCalc Commands

/B   BLANK. Erase the contents from a cell.

/C   CLEAR. Erase the entire worksheet

/D   DELETE. Delete the row (or column) pointed at by the cursor. All formulas are adjusted for the deleted row.

/E   EDIT. Edit the cell pointed at by the cursor. The arrow keys are used to move over the edit line.

/F   FORMAT. Format a single cell. D, G, I, L, R, $, *.

/G   GLOBAL. Set global options. C, F, O, R.

/I   INSERT. Insert a row or column.

/M   MOVE. Move a row or column to another row or column.

/P   PRINT. Output to the printer.

/R   REPLICATE. Duplicate a cell, row, or column into another cell, row, or column.

/S   STORE. Store the worksheet on disk or print it.

/T   TITLE. Lock rows or columns as titles.

/V   VERSION. Lists the version number of the VisiCalc program.

/W   WINDOW. Split the screen into two windows.

Appendix B
VisiCalc Functions

@ABS(v)	Absolute value of v
@AVERAGE(list)	Average of list
@COUNT(list)	Count the number of numbers in the list
@EXP(v)	e raised to v power
@INT(v)	Integer part of v
@Ln(v)	Natural logarithm of v
@LOG10(v)	Base 10 logarithm of v
@MAX(list)	Maximum value in the list
@MIN(list)	Minimum value in the list
@NPV(dr, range)	Net present value at discount rate, dr
@SQRT(v)	Square root of v
@SUM(list)	Sum of the numbers in list

Trigonometric Functions

@ACOS(v)	Arccosine of v radians
@ASIN(v)	Arcsine of v radians
@ATAN(v)	Arctangent of v radians
@COS(v)	Cosine of v radians
@SIN(v)	Sine of v radians
@TAN(v)	Tangent of v radians

Search Functions

@CHOOSE(v, list)	Search list for v and if found return the value v. If not found, return NA
@LOOKUP(v, list)	Search list for v and if found, return the value that is adjacent to v

Functions Without Arguments

@ERROR	Returns ERROR to all cells referencing this
@FALSE	Returns FALSE
@NA	Returns NA
@PI	Returns 3.1415926536
@TRUE	Returns TRUE

Logic Functions

@AND(list)	Returns TRUE if all values in list are TRUE
@IF(test, v1, v2)	Returns v1 if test is TRUE, otherwise returns v2
@ISERROR(v)	Returns TRUE if v is ERROR, returns FALSE Otherwise
@ISNA(v)	Returns TRUE if v is NA, returns FALSE otherwise.
@NOT(v)	Returns TRUE if v is FALSE, returns FALSE otherwise
@OR(list)	Returns FALSE unless one or more values in list are TRUE

Index

Ted Lewis is currently an Associate Professor of Computer Science at Oregon State University in Corvallis, Oregon. Dr. Lewis has over 20 years of experience in computing, beginning with the vacuum tube minicomputers, and more recently working with personal computers in education and business. With ten previous books to his credit and countless papers and magazine articles, veteran writer Lewis adds *32 VisiCalc®Worksheets* to his literary merit.

Software
for
32 VisiCalc® Worksheets

Here are all the worksheets from this book on disk, ready to use on your Apple II® or IBM PC®. Developed to save you the time of typing them in yourself, the disk gives you a variety of ways to take advantage of your VisiCalc program.

The **32 VisiCalc Worksheets** are available on a 5¼″ disk for the IBM PC or the Apple II Computer at $19.95 for each disk. If you are interested in using the 32 VisiCalc disk in another microcomputer, simply fill out the information needed below.

Yes, please send me the software for **32 VisiCalc Worksheets** in the format(s) indicated at $19.95 each, plus $1.00 each for shipping and handling.

_____ disk for Apple II (0021-1004a)
_____ disk for IBM PC (0021-1003a)

_____ I would be interested if this program was offered on the
_____ computer, _____ disk size. Please let me know if it becomes available.

_____ Check/Money Order enclosed for $ _____.
_____ Visa   _____ MasterCard

Acct. No. _____ Expires _____

Name _____

Address _____

City _____ State _____ Zip _____

Signature _____

Mail To: **TAB BOOKS Inc.**
Blue Ridge Summit, PA 17214

Orders outside U.S. must be prepaid with international money orders in U.S. dollars.